Mr. Wodehouse's idyllic world can never stale. He will continue to release future generations from captivity that may be more irksome than our own. He has made a world for us to live in and delight in.

—Evelyn Waugh

He who has not met Wodehouse has not lived a full life.

—*San Francisco Chronicle*

Cover illustration by Henry Raleigh, from "Right Ho Jeeves," originally appearing in The Saturday Evening Post *in 1934. Gussie Fink-Nottle is emerging from under the bed as Bertie and Jeeves look on.*

About the author

When he is minding his own business, Daniel Garrison teaches classical literature at Northwestern University in Evanston, Illinois.

WHO'S WHO
IN
WODEHOUSE
DANIEL H. GARRISON

Revised Edition

INTERNATIONAL POLYGONICS, LTD.
New York

Revised edition 1989, published by arrangement with Peter Lang Publishing, Inc.

Library of Congress Card Catalog No. 91-70594
ISBN 1-55882-087-6

First paperback edition published August 1991
Printed in the United States of America
10 9 8 7 6 5 4 3 2 1

I hate stories without names.
—James Corcoran in
"A Bit of Luck For Mabel" (1925)

I am not very well up in the Peerage.
I seldom read it except to get a laugh out of the names.
—Frederick Altamont Cornwallis Twistleton,
fifth Earl of Ickenham
in *Uncle Fred in the Springtime* (1939)

CONTENTS

PREFACE

Since the death of P.G. Wodehouse in 1975, the canon of his published novels and collected stories has become well enough fixed for Wodehouse lovers to expect a comprehensive guide to his characters. So great was the enthusiasm of his earlier chroniclers that the first character lists, David Jasen's Index to Characters in his *Bibliography and Reader's Guide to the First Editions of P.G. Wodehouse* (Archon Books, 1970) and Geoffrey Jaggard's two concordances, *Wooster's World* (Macdonald, 1967) and *Blandings the Blest* (Macdonald, 1968), were outrun by The Master's continued profligacy in the invention of characters.

Besides bringing the tally up to date, the present book should be serviceable by virtue of its attention to characters only. It does not aspire to be a concordance, nor have I tried to include every personage mentioned in Wodehouse. The main business here is with characters who actually enter Wodehouse's stage and speak lines. A few others have found their way in: butlers, manservants, parlormaids, and other persons in domestic service are generally exempted from the requirement that they appear onstage and speak lines, as are a few other characters with interesting names or exploits. Besides these there are two moustaches, a bath sponge, a pig, assorted cats and dogs, and a beverage, chiefly because their omission seemed to do less than full justice to the joyful irrationality of Wodehouse's human world.

PREFACE

My treatment of characters falls somewhere between that of Jasen, who simply identifies them, and Jaggard, who editorializes (though with no small judgement and wit). This prosopography, in the tradition of the lists of Roman magistrates with which classical historians occupy themselves, is poker-faced and factual. When a character is described as looking like a parrot that has been drawn through a hedge backwards, it is because Wodehouse himself provided that information. In order to make my account of Wodehouse characters as authoritative as possible, I have with the kind permission of the Wodehouse estate used the author's own language wherever feasible, omitting quotation marks. Consequently, much of the language and all of the invention herein is Wodehouse's, not mine.

The lists of titles and collections at the end of this book will serve as an elementary Wodehouse bibliography; more deeply afflicted Wodehouse fans should consult the revised and enlarged 1986 edition of David A. Jasen's *Bibliography and Reader's Guide to the First Editions of P.G. Wodehouse,* published in London by Greenhill Books. Those who must know all will have the pleasure of consulting James H. Heineman's comprehensive bibliography (all editions worldwide, including translations), *P.G. Wodehouse. A Comprehensive Bibliography and Checklist,* published in the U.K. by James H. Heineman and St. Paul's Bibliographies, and in the U.S. by Omni Graphics.

No one who has made as many embarrassing slips as I have in various stages of assembling this list can claim to be a meticulous worker. By any reasonable reckoning, there are over 2100 characters in Wodehouse, half again as many as in Dickens and more than double the number in Shakespeare. More than 300 of these—about one in seven—reappear in at least one other Wodehouse title, making a truly accurate and comprehensive account risky business, even for a pious drudge. In spite of my best efforts, there are certain to be mistakes in this book. There would be many more, had I not had the broad shoulders of David Jasen's bibliography and Geoffrey Jaggard's concordances to stand on. Norman Murphy's *In Search of Blandings* added biographical background to that provided earlier by Jasen's *P.G. Wodehouse. A Portrait of a Master,* Frances Donaldson's *P.G. Wodehouse,* and the Wodehouse centenary volume edited by James H. Heineman and Donald R. Bensen. For their personal help, I would like to thank Charles E. Gould, Jr. and James H. Heineman for their frequent encouragement and aid. Heineman deserves additional thanks for supplying the illustrations. Richard Usborne took the trouble to read the entire text with great care before it was committed to print; his extraordinary knowledge of Wodehouse, together with his command of English usage, saved me from publicly disgracing myself more times than I care to think about. For making the special Wodehouse collection at Northwestern available, I am grateful to Russell Maylone, and to Marjorie Carpenter for getting me copies of Wodehouse books not at Northwestern.

Since publishing the first edition of this book, I have added characters from the three novels and forty-eight stories which so far have not been reprinted since their first appearance. This supplementary canon of Wodehouse fiction is based on Eileen Mc-Ilvaine's *P.G. Wodehouse in Periodicals,* a 1985 bibliography now included in James Heineman's *P.G. Wodehouse. A Comprehensive Bibliography and Checklist.* My Appendix IV lists those items. For photocopies of these pieces, I am chiefly indebted to Len Lawson and (once again) to Marjorie Carpenter, now retired from the Interlibrary Loan Department at the Northwestern University Library. Charles Gould, whose business it is to *sell* rare editions of Wodehouse rather than give out free copies, filled in several critical gaps with photocopies of early school stories. Phil Ayers, Richard Usborne, James Heineman, Bill and Nancy Horn, Pauline Blanc, and James B. Meriwether have also rendered valuable assistance. The inspiration for this enlarged second edition came during a meeting of the Wodehouse Society in San Francisco on the very day the first edition was officially published in the U.S.: *sic volvere Parcas.* Special thanks are therefore due to the San Francisco chapter of the Society, and to many members nationwide who encouraged me to proceed.

It is customary at this point in a preface to thank the little woman who typed all seven drafts of the manuscript, but I am happy to report that technology has relegated the tiresome chore to a congeries of computer hardware and software. I would therefore like to address my gratitude to Greg Ney of Software First, a literary scholar in his own right, who helped me find and showed me how to use the equipment with which this book was prepared.

Lacking as I do the usual people to blame for whatever may have gone wrong in my book, I wish nevertheless to point an accusing finger at Jeanne Tubman, who brought me my first Wodehouse when I lay ill, at Terry Connors, who sent the book (a well-thumbed copy of *The Most of P.G. Wodehouse*), and at Charles Tubman, an unindicted co-conspirator. To them, as the *primum mobile*, I dedicate this book, spots and all.

Northwestern University
Evanston, Illinois
June, 1989

How to use this book

In order to keep the bulk of this volume within reasonable limits, I have reduced the titles of Wodehouse's novels and stories to a four-character code. All stories are represented by a two-letter abbreviation preceded by the year of first publication: "Uncle Fred Flits By," which first appeared in 1935, is thus abbreviated as 35UF. All novels are similarly represented, but in reverse order, with the year of first publication following the title: *Uncle Dynamite*, first published in 1948, is abbreviated as UD48. This is tiresome but necessary. To unravel the mystery of the codes, there is a key beginning on page 233 arranged by year. As an additional mercy, there is an alphabetical list of titles (pp. 249-66) which have been appended to Wodehouse fiction over the years by editors on both sides of the Atlantic, and a chronological list of Wodehouse collections in English to date (pp. 267-74).

ILLUSTRATIONS

WHO'S WHO IN WODEHOUSE

Alice or Toots, Lady **Abbott**, sister of Sam Bulpitt in SM37, wife of Sir Buckstone and mother of Jane. A large, blonde, calm woman, formerly a New York chorus girl.

Sir Buckstone **Abbott**, Bart., master of Walsingford Hall, Berks., where he takes in paying guests in SM37. Father of Jane and author of *My Sporting Life*, published at his own expense.

Imogen or Jane **Abbott**, daughter of Sir Buckstone, a small, slim, pretty girl of twenty with fair hair, cornflower-blue eyes and a boyish jauntiness of carriage. Owner of a Widgeon Seven two-seater. Engaged to Adrian Peake in SM37, courted by Joe Vanringham.

George **Abercrombie**, suitor of Lord Emsworth's niece Jane in 36CW; belongs to one of the oldest families in Devonshire, but opposed by Lady Constance because of his lack of a fortune. Formerly land-agent on an estate in Devonshire; appointed land-agent to the Threepwood estates.

Arnold **Abney**, M.A., headmaster of Sanstead House in 13EC and LN13; tall, suave, benevolent, with an Oxford manner, a high forehead, thin white hands, a cooing intonation, and a general air of hushed importance, as of one in constant communication with the Great. In MO71 Bertie Wooster erroneously names him as headmaster of his own school.

Isadore **Abrahams**, founder-proprietor of a dancing resort named The Flower Garden, employer of Sally Nicholas in AS22.

Adair, captain of cricket and football at Sedleigh and head of Downing's house in MK09. Broad shoulders, wiry, light hair, almost white; square jaw, very bright blue eyes, an excellent all-around athlete completely devoted to Sedleigh.

J. Sheringham **Adair**: see Chimp Twist.

Adams is head steward of the Senior Conservative Club in SN15. Remembers everybody, has earned a substantial reputation as a humorist in his circle by his imitations of certain members of his club.

Adamson of Dawson's house, St Austin's, abnormally wealthy boy in PH02 who loses £2 in the robbery of the Pavilion.

Dr. **Adamson**, College doctor at St Austin's in 02WM and 03MC, lives in Stapleton, one mile from school.

Sir Jasper **Addleton**, O.B.E., fat, bald, goggle-eyed financier whom Lord Brangbolton wants his daughter Millicent to marry in 31SW.

Adolf, German door-boy at Harrow House in 09OS.

Bertie Wooster's Aunt **Agatha**: see Agatha Wooster.

Sir **Agravaine** ye Dolorous of ye Table Round: 5' 4", flaccid of muscle, with pale, mild eyes, snub nose, receding chin, and protruding upper teeth. Resembles a nervous rabbit. Goes to aid of Yvonne, daughter of Earl Dorm of the Hills in 12SA.

Albert[1], a red-headed town boy from Wrykyn, leader of the ruffians supporting Pedder's candidacy for mayor in WF07.

Albert[2], page-boy at Belpher Castle in DD19.

Georgiana, Lady **Alcester**, Marchioness of Alcester, one of Lord Emsworth's ten sisters, mother of Gertrude; Freddie's aunt in 28CG. Lives on Upper Brook Street, Hyde Park with four Pekes, two Poms, a Yorkshire terrier, five Sealyhams, a Borzoi, and an Airedale; her long association with the species has made her a sort of honorary dog herself. Refuses to buy Donaldson's Dog Joy from Freddie until converted in 31GG. Dislikes Gertrude's suitor Beefy Bingham until she discovers he is the heir of a bachelor uncle high up in the shipping business.

Gertrude **Alcester**, 23, daughter of Lady Georgiana, niece of Lord Emsworth in 28CG. In love with Beefy Bingham, to whom she remains engaged after a brief infatuation with Orlo Watkins in 31GG.

The King of **Aldebaran** discovers the pleasures of work in 03IK.

His Majesty King **Alejandro XIII**, exiled King of Paranoya in MM14, a genial-looking man of middle age, comfortably stout about the middle and a little stout as to the forehead. A Magdalen man, dislikes life in Paranoya, prefers life of an exile in England.

Alexander, fat female cat belonging to a fat American woman at the Hotel Jules Priaulx in 12MC.

Alfred, James' fellow footman at Blandings Castle in SN15 and subsequent Blandings novels.

Allardyce is a member of the Football Committee in GB04; a cricketer for Wrykyn in 05LP, he succeeds Trevor as captain of football at Wrykyn in WF07.

Allenby, a prefect in the Science Sixth of Wrykyn in MK09.

Wilfred **Allsop**, pint-size and fragile and rather like the poet Shelley in appearance, composer and piano player; cousin of Veronica Wedge, nephew of Lord Emsworth, in love with Monica Simmons in BG65.

Ambrose ye monk, author of the tale of Sir Agravaine, 12SA.

Monsieur **Anatole**, Dahlia Travers' French cook in 29SA, RH34, CW38, JF54, HR60, MO71, and AA74, suffers from bouts of *mal au foie*. A Provençal, he cooks for Bingo & Mrs. Little in 25CR, where he is hired away by Aunt Dahlia with Jeeves' help. Prior to his tenure with the Littles, he was with an American family for two years in Nice, where he learned his first English from their chauffeur, a Mulloney from Brooklyn.

"Blinky" **Anderson** is Freddie Bingham's employer at the East Side Delmonico's in 13JW.

J.G. **Anderson**, owner of the Hotel Washington in Bessemer, Ohio and the Lakeside Inn near Skeewassett, Maine; sometime employer of Barmy Fotheringay-Phipps in BW52.

Angela[1], a pretty girl with fair hair and blue eyes, is Lord Emsworth's twenty-one year-old niece who wants to marry James Belford in 27PH. She is the daughter of a deceased Jane, one of Lord Emsworth's ten sisters. Not to be confused with Angela[2], Aunt Dahlia's daughter, she may be the sister of Wilfred Allsop, though her surname is nowhere given.

Angela[2], Dahlia Wooster Travers' daughter: her surname is never given, but see Angela Travers.

Mr. **Anstruther**, a rather moth-eaten septuagenarian, old friend of Aunt Dahlia's father, prone to nervousness, becomes the wettest man in Worcestershire in 29JL when hit by a bucket of water thrown by Aunt Agatha's loathly son Thos.

Harold "Beefy" **Anstruther**, in love with Hilda Gudgeon in MS49, was Bertie Wooster's partner at Rackets for Oxford.

Monsieur Anatole

Mrs. James **Anthony**, née Dorothy (Dolly) Venables, is Richard Venables' sister in 01AF.

Mary **Anthony**, married to Bobbie Cardew in 11AT, hospital nurse who plays ragtime on the piano. About 5' 6", with a ton and a half of red-gold hair, grey eyes, and one of those determined chins.

Mr. **Appleby** sets Linton 150 lines of Virgil in 05CL. Wrykyn master and amateur gardener in 04HT, GB04, and MK09.

Professor **Appleby**, self-styled authority on Eugenics, manager of Horace French in BC24; a large and benevolent-looking man in a senatorial frock-coat, looks like a minor prophet.

Horace **Appleby**, bald and butlerine head of the Appleby gang in DB68, a stout man who looks like a Roman emperor. Lives in Restharrow, Croxley Road, Valley Fields, London S.E. 21. Woos Ada Cootes.

Augustus **Arbutt**, George Lattaker's uncle and trustee of the estate which he inherits from his Aunt Emily in 12RR.

Mr. **Archer-Cleeve**, a young man with carefully-parted fair hair and the expression of a strayed sheep, one of a deputation of four gamblers to John Maude, Prince of Mervo, in PB12.

Tommy **Armstrong**, freckled and red-haired friend of Jimmy Stewart in LS08, shares a study with him at Marleigh School. Captain of the School football eleven, reputedly the most reckless boy ever at the school. His cousin is J. de V. Patterne.

Ascobaruch, King Merolchazzar's half-brother in 21CG; a sinister, disappointed man with mean eyes and a crafty smile.

Colonel **Ashby**, great friend of Pringle's father in PU03; lives at Biddlehampton.

B. Henderson **Asher**, author of the "Moments of Mirth" page of *Peaceful Moments* in PA12 and of *Cosy Moments* in PJ15: has a face like a walnut.

Ebenezer **Attwater**, lawyer to Berry Conway's rich aunt in BM31.

J.B. **Attwater**, proprietor of the Goose & Gander in Walsingford Parva in SM37. Formerly butler to Sir Buckstone Abbott; has a son named Cyril and a niece from London who works as his barmaid.

Roland Moresby **Attwater**, essayist and literary critic; educated at Harrow, becomes engaged to Lucy Moresby in 24SS, still engaged in 25AG.

Mrs. **Attwell** is the matron at Sanstead House in 13EC.

Sir **Aubrey** Something, Bart., member of the Coldstream Guards, Ukridge's rival for the love of Mabel in 25BL.

Jefferson **Auguste**, Comte d'Escrignon, only son of Nicolas (below) and Loretta Ann Potter of Ridgeville, Connecticut in FL56; a writer living on the Rue Jacob, Paris. A striking-looking man with a humorous mouth, quick brown eyes, strong chin, and a scar on his cheek acquired when he fought with the Maquis. Tall, dark, and wiry, falls in love with Terry Trent.

Nicolas Jules St Xavier **Auguste**, Marquis de Maufrigneuse et Valerie-Moberanne, "Old Nick" in FL56, twice-divorced father of Jefferson Auguste, Comte d'Escrignon. His first wife was a rich American woman, Loretta Ann Potter, who bore him his only son; second was Hermione Pegler, aunt of Chester and Mavis Todd. Employed for some time in the troisième bureau of the Ministry de Dons et Legs, escapes via Roville-sur-mer and Belgium to Florida, where he marries a cook and migrates to New York, where he takes employment as headwaiter at The Mazarin.

Augustus[1], cat in the Prenderby household in 34GB.

Augustus[2], large black lethargic cat at Brinkley Court who resents being woken suddenly in HR60, MO71.

B

Henry **Babcock**, messenger arrested in connection with a bond-robbery in 21SE/IA21.

J.S.M. (Jack) **Babington** of Dacre's, St Austin's, goes to a play illegally with his cousin in 01AU. Plays with the school fifteen in 02HP; Still at Dacre's in 03HP and 03HS.

Izzy **Baerman**, M.C. at Geisenheimer's in 15AG.

Bagshaw is butler for the R.P. Littles in 37BP.

Bagshot[1], Sir Rackstraw Cammarleigh's butler in 35CM, has heard eighty-six repetitions of Sir Rackstraw's story of old George Bates and the rhino.

Bagshot[2], Reginald Mulliner's postman in 52BB.

Berkeley or Boko **Bagshott**, father of Samuel Galahad Bagshott, owned a whacking big house in Sussex near Petworth. One of the brightest brains in the old Pelican Club, he got his annual medical checkup each year without cost by pretending to be about to insure his life for £100,000. Fondly remembered by his friend Galahad Threepwood in HW33, FM47, BG65.

Samuel Galahad **Bagshott**, named after jockey Sam Bowles and turf expert Galahad Threepwood, son of Boko Bagshott. Writer of articles and stories, address 4 Halsey Chambers, Halsey Court (Mayfair), London W. 1. Large and chunky with a cauliflower ear, a Drone, in love with Sandy Callender in BG65.

Ellabelle **Bagster**, barber shop cashier at the Hotel Cosmopolis in 20GF, shares a little uptown flat with May Gleason.

Rev. Cuthbert "Bill" **Bailey** was at Harrow and boxed three years for Oxford, where he was a friend of Pongo Twistleton. A man of rugged, homely features and burly shoulders, curate at Bottleton East, engaged in SS61 to Myra Schoonmaker against the will of Lady Constance. Takes on the alias of Cuthbert Meriwether on a visit to Blandings.

"Gentleman" **Bailey**, broken-down Old Boy from Eton or Harrow, now a tramp living with Jack Roach as guests of Jerry Moore, whom he advises in his courtship of Jane Tuxton in 10BA.

Rupert **Bailey**, co-judge of a long hole golf match in 21LH.

Baker is Jimmy Silver's fag at Blackburn's, Eckleton in HK05.

George Albert **Balmer**, 24, employed as a clerk by the Planet Insurance Company, lives with his uncle Robert as a paying guest; inherits £1000 in 12TM.

Ma **Balsam**, stout motherly figure who looks after Jeff Miller at Halsey Chambers, Mayfair, in MB42; she is John Halliday's landlady at the same address in PB69.

Mr. **Banks** is a mathematics master at Wrykyn in GB04.

J. Cuthbert **Banks**, winner of the French Open, winner of Vladimir Brusiloff's undying admiration and Adeline Smethurst's hand in 21UC.

J.G. **Banks**, veterinary surgeon to the Empress of Blandings in PB69.

Jno. **Banks**, hairdresser-barber in Market Blandings in LP23.

Jno. Henderson **Banks**, Evangeline Pembury's literary agent in 30BS.

Myrtle **Banks**, successfully courted by William Mulliner in 27SW.

Rosie M. **Banks**, famous female novelist, described in 22BL as a tallish girl with sort of soft, soulful brown eyes, a nice figure, and rather decent hands. Marries Bingo Little at a registrar's in Holborn in 22BL/IJ23 while working as a waitress in the Senior Liberal Club collecting material for *Mervyn Keene, Clubman*. Wife of Bingo Little in 25CR, 30JO, 37AW, 37BP, 39SB, 39ER, 40WS, 54LA, JF54, 65BB, 65SS; author of some of the most pronounced and widely read tripe ever put on the market. Favorite author of one of Jeeves' aunts, who owns almost a complete set, and of Mortimer Little in 21JS; of Mabel Potter in BA73, and of thousands more. Among her heartthrob fiction for the masses are novels in which marriage with young persons of an inferior social status is held up as both feasible and admirable, e.g. *Only a Factory Girl*, *All for Love*, *A Red, Red Summer Rose*, *The Courtship of Lord Strathmorlick*, *The Woman Who Braved All*, and *Madcap Myrtle*. Other Banks titles include *By Honour Bound* and *'Twas Once in May*. Bingo Little persuades Bertie Wooster to pretend that Rosie Banks is his own *nom de plume* in 21JS/IJ23. In 25CR she has written a human interest piece for *Milady's Boudoir* entitled "How I Keep the Love of My Husband-Baby," describing Bingo as "half god, half prattling, mischievous child." Owns as many as six Pekes at a time, to which she is very devoted. Strongly disapproves of Bingo's gambling, and keeps him short of pocket money to prevent same, but is frequently out of town visiting her mother, who lives in Bognor Regis. She is a lifelong friend of Julia Purkiss, wife of Bingo's employer at *Wee*

Tots. Cf. the real Jane Emmeline Banks, author of *A Stirring Revelation of a Young Girl's Soul* (letter to W. Townend, 4/27/29).

Bannister[1] plays wing on the St Austin's fifteen in 03MC.

Bannister[2] (=prec.?), formerly of the Postage Department in the New Asiatic Bank in PC10.

Ann **Bannister**, small, brisk, energetic newspaper girl, governess-companion-nursemaid to Joey Cooley, later press agent to April June. Formerly engaged to Reggie Havershot; fiancée of Eggy Mannering in LG36.

Bailey **Bannister**, son and junior partner of financier John Bannister in WH14, brother of Ruth. About 27, faultlessly dressed, marries Sybil Wilbur.

Bill **Bannister**, nephew of Sir Hugo Drake in DS32, has a big place at Woolam Chersey, Hampshire.

Hailey **Bannister**, a successful Wall Street broker, was a rather pompous and dictatorial husband to Sybil Bannister prior to the action of 15PW.

John **Bannister**, millionaire New York financier, senior partner in Bannister & Son in WH14. Father of Bailey and Ruth Bannister.

Ruth **Bannister**, daughter of John Bannister and niece of Lora Porter, marries Kirk Winfield in WH14 and bears him William Bannister Winfield, the White Hope. Extraordinarily beautiful, full of Aunt Lora's ideas about eugenics and germs.

Sybil **Bannister**, devoted wife of Hailey Bannister in 15PW, is a small and fluffy disciple of Mrs. Lora Delane Porter.

Ellen **Barker**, wife of Horace, cooks for Freddie Rooke in LW20.

Horace **Barker** is valet to Freddie Rooke in LW20. Husband of Ellen, Rooke's cook.

Robert **Barker** is Angus McAllister's second-in-command in the management of the Blandings gardens in 24CP.

Old **Barley**, landlord of the White Boar at Lower Borlock in MK09; wag of the village cricket team.

Barlitt, vicar's son at Crofton, a silent and spectacled graduate of Sedleigh, has won a Balliol scholarship in MK09.

Barlow is butler to the Headmaster at Sedleigh in MK09.

Mrs. Barlow, housekeeper for Mrs. Steptoe at Claines Hall in QS40.

John Edwin Barlow, eldest son of George Albamont Barlow of The Mote, Shrewsbury, is one of two brothers who pitch for the Weary Willies in 06AB. A fast bowler, he only just missed his Blue at Cambridge in the previous summer.

Barmy **Barminster**, nephew and dependent of Andrew Galloway in 57WT, employer of Wilson, in love with Mabel Parker. Cf. Rollo Finch in 11AS.

Barrett of Philpott's house, St Austin's, member of the school fifteen in 02HP, where he dislocates a collar-bone. Shares a study with Reade in PH02. A keen naturalist, discovers stolen cups in a hollow tree in the Dingle on Venner's estate during a hunt for birds' eggs. Still in Philpott's in 03HS.

M. Barry, studymate of M'Todd at Seymour's, Wrykyn, in GB04, 05AB, WF07.

George Barstead, former messenger in the New Asiatic Bank in PC10.

Aubrey Barstowe, pestilential suitor of Elsa Keith in 10GA. Author of a volume of poetry called *The Soul's Eclipse*.

Barter, Julia Ukridge's butler in 25BD, 31UH, 55TC. Cf. Baxter in 26LB.

Bartholemew, Stiffy Byng's Aberdeen terrier at Totleigh Towers in CW38 (where he spills Constable Oates off his bicycle) and SU63 (where he terrorizes Pop Bassett): "There is no breed of dog quicker to take offense." — Bertie Wooster in SU63.

Bartlett, a muscular ex-soldier, is the Marleigh school porter in LS08.

Alexander Bartlett, contender in Choirboys' Hundred Yards Handicap in 22PT/IJ23.

Augustus Bartlett, friend of Sally Nicholas in AS22, employed in an intensely subordinate position in the Wall Street firm of Kahn, Morris & Brown.

John Barton, big, broad-shouldered suitor to Aline Ellison in 10LM, owns a bulldog named Reuben.

Reginald Bartling, friend of Jimmy Crocker in PJ17.

Maj. Wilfred "Plug" **Basham** was a member of the old Pelican

Club and an unruly associate of Galahad Threepwood in the
'90's; once knocked out Stinker Pyke with a side of beef. By
HW33 he is a Major. See under Puffy Benger.

Bashford[1] is the porter of the block of flats where Sue Brown
lives in FP29.

Bashford[2] is a porter at the Drones in FP29.

Fred **Basset**, real estate agent, member of Bachelors Anonymous in BA73.

Alexander **Bassett** is the Oldest Member's informant on the
summer medal competition in 36AG.

Amelia **Bassett**, addicted to mystery plays and novels, wooed
by Cyril Mulliner in 32SS. Daughter of Lady Wingham
Bassett.

Captain **Bassett**, friend of the Henderson family in 12MC and
suitor of Marion Henderson.

Lady Wingham **Bassett**, the well-known big-game hunter and
explorer, Amelia's mother in 32SS. A formidable female
variety of the Wallace Beery type, uses a tortoise-shell
lorgnette and smokes cigars. Wants her daughter to marry
Lester Mapledurham.

Madeline **Bassett**, daughter of Sir Watkyn in RH34, CW38,
MS49, SU63, MO71. A soppy girl with a soupy, treacly voice
and a tinkling, silvery laugh, she holds the view that the stars
are God's daisy chain. Undeniably an eyeful: slim, svelte, and
bountifully equipped with golden hair and all the fixings, but
has a subtle air of being on the point of talking baby talk.
Her favorite reading is Winnie the Pooh and the works of
Rosie M. Banks. Close friend of Aunt Dahlia's daughter
Angela Travers. Threatens to marry Bertie Wooster and try
to make him happy whenever her marriage plans go sour;
agrees to marry Spode in CW38, SU63, and MO71; serially
engaged to both Bertie and Gussie in RH34, to Gussie (her
ideal mate, in Bertie's view) in MS49. Lives at The Larches,
Wimbledon Common.

Sir Mortimer **Bassett**, master of Barkley Towers and father of
Amelia in 32SS.

Sir Watkyn **Bassett**, C.B.E., father of Madeline, master of
Totleigh Towers, Totleigh-in-the-Wold. A justice of the peace

Madeline Basset

in CW38, where he is engaged to Spode's aunt, a Mrs. Wintergreen, widow of the late Col. H.H. Wintergreen, of Pont Street. A small man, patriarch of the Gloucestershire Totleigh Towers gang, which includes daughter Madeline, Roderick Spode (Lord Sidcup), and niece Stiffy Byng in JF54 and SU63. Sir Watkyn and Tom Travers are rival collectors of what are known as objets d'art, such as the silver cow-creamer which is the bone of contention in CW38; he also would like to hire away the Travers' French chef Anatole. While a magistrate in the Bosher St. police court, he fined Bertie Wooster five quid for stealing a policeman's helmet on Boat Race Night, a mere lighthearted peccadillo. Bertie thinks that Pop Bassett's inherited fortune was actually accumulated from fines pocketed while he was a magistrate.

Sir Alexander **Bassinger**, Bart., master of Bludleigh Court, Lesser Bludleigh, Goresby-on-the-Ouse, Bedfordshire, head of a hunting clan in 29UB.

Aubrey **Bassinger**, son of Sir Alexander, uses Trefusis as a surname when he writes Pastels in Prose for London's higher-browed weeklies, engaged to Charlotte Mulliner in 29UB.

Sir Herbert **Bassinger**, Bart., a red-faced horsey-looking man with a walrus moustache and two chins, in IW31 was Lord Droitwich's guardian during his minority. Husband of Lady Lydia Bassinger. Host at a ball in the Hotel Mazarin in BM31, expels Berry Conway. Made about ten million in the clove market.

Lady Lydia **Bassinger**, Lord Droitwich's aunt in IW31 and BM31, sister of his father John. A woman of early middle age, lives at Langley End with Sir Herbert, Lord Droitwich, and Freddie Chalk-Marshall.

P.P. **Bassinger**, gambling trustee of George Mulliner's estate in 67GA.

Reginald **Bassinger**, hunting brother of Aubrey in 29UB.

Wilfred **Bassinger**, juvenile brother of Aubrey in 29UB, hunts sparrows with an air gun.

Cyril **Bassington-Bassington**, fish-faced chump billeted on Bertie Wooster by Aunt Agatha in 18JC/IJ23; has a falling-out with

Blumenfeld prior to the action of 29JD.

Bastable, Rupert Bingley's butler in MO71; beefy, pompous, and chilly. Bertie Wooster compares him to Jeeves' uncle Charlie Silversmith.

Major-General Sir Aylmer **Bastable**, Freddie Fitch-Fitch's gouty uncle and trustee, social snob staying at Podagra Lodge, Droitgate Lodge in 37RD.

Sir Raymond "Beefy" **Bastable**, 52, half-brother to Lady Ickenham and brother of Phoebe Wisdom, who keeps house for him in CT58; a stout, florid man who played rugby for Oxford thirty years ago, now an eminent barrister, Queen's Counsel and member of the Demosthenes club across the street from the Drones. Writes a novel *Cocktail Time* under the pseudonym Richard Blunt.

Sherman **Bastable**, tutor to Horace French in BC24.

Bates, hall-porter at the Drones in UF39 and CT58.

Old **Bates** is the porter at Wrykyn in 04JE, the school sergeant in MK09.

Anastatia **Bates**, William Bates' younger sister in 25PR, recent semifinalist in the Ladies' Open Championship: one of those small, rose-leaf girls with big blue eyes to whom good men instinctively want to give a stroke a hole and on whom bad men automatically prey. Golf instructor to her nephew Braid Vardon Bates and to Rodney Spelvin, whom she purifies. In 49RR she is Anastatia Spelvin, one-time Ladies' Champion, and mother of a young son named Timothy.

Bill **Bates**, pseud. Alan Beverley, the man upstairs in 10MU. A millionaire from Glasgow, takes up residence in a Chelsea apartment above Annette Brougham, and paints.

Braid Vardon **Bates**, son of William Bates and Jane Packard Bates in 24JG, 25PR (where he is four and taking golf lessons from his aunt Anastatia), and 49RR, where he is nine and training for the Children's Cup. In appearance a miniature edition of William, in soul and temperament a combination of the Dead End Kid and an army mule; freckled, hard-boiled.

Claude **Bates**: see Winnington-Bates.

Esmond **Bates**, Old Stinker, Wilfred Wickham's little friend in

28PA.

Rev. James **Bates**, nephew of Old Heppenstall in 22SH/IJ23, assistant-master at Eton acting as locum tenens for Mr. Spettigue, rector of Gandle-by-the-Hill, starter in Great Sermon Handicap. Engaged to Lady Cynthia Wickham-mersley.

Jane **Bates**, wife of William Bates in 49RR, mother of Braid Vardon Bates. See Jane Packard.

Stiffy **Bates**, pal of Galahad Threepwood from the old Pelican days, laid up in a nursing home with a broken leg in SB77.

William **Bates**, lymphatic golfer in a trio of golfing stories (24RF, 24JG, 25PR), resembles a motor-lorry in physique, as a rule shares that vehicle's placid and unruffled outlook on life. Lives mainly on chops and beer, weighs 14 stone 6. Attached to Jane Packard in 24RF, where he wins her hand; in 24JG he and Jane are married with a son, Braid Vardon Bates; in 25PR they are seven years married and Braid Vardon, now four, is receiving golf instruction from William's sister Anastatia. By 49RR, in which his son Braid is nine, years of incessant golf in all weathers have converted his cheeks into a substance resembling red leather.

William **Batkins**, in love with Ellen Saunders in 08LG, bowled for Sir Edward Cave's place against Much Middlefold. A Sussex man, bowls for the Players against the Gentlemen.

Baumgartner or Baumgarten, friend of William Tell in WT04, saved from the pursuing soldiers of the Swiss Governor when Tell rowed him across a stormy lake.

Baxter or Barter, Julia Ukridge's butler at The Cedars in 26LB.

Herbert or Bertie **Baxter**, brother of Blatherwick's wife in 09OS, one of Nature's touchers.

Prudence **Baxter**, daughter of Lord Wickhammersly's head gardener, ruled winner in Girls' Egg and Spoon Race in 22PT/IJ23.

Rupert J. The Efficient **Baxter**, bespectacled secretary to Lord Emsworth in SN15, where his employer (later to change his views) describes him as "invaluable, positively invaluable." Sacked in LP23, reappears in FP29, notorious for throwing flowerpots as a result of an episode in LP23. Next appears

The Efficient Baxter

in 36CW, where Lady Constance persuades him to interrupt a motor-bicycle tour of England to become tutor to Lord Bosham's son George, whose air gun eventually causes his evacuation. Employed by Alaric, Duke of Dunstable, in UF39. Thickset and handicapped by that vaguely grubby appearance which is presented by swarthy young men of bad complexion; staring through his spectacles, he often gives people the impression of possessing an eye that could pierce six inches of harveyised steel and stick out the other side. During his tenure at Blandings the domestic staff live in a perpetual state of smouldering discontent under his rule. During an interval between jobs at Blandings, employed as sec'y to the Chicago millionaire Horace Jevons; has also been in the employ of Sir Ralph Dillingsworth, a Yorkshire baronet.

Bayliss, butler and social advisor to Mr. & Mrs. Bingley Crocker in PJ17.

Sir Edward **Bayliss**, O.B.E. of Deeping Hall, Market Deeping, Sussex, a bird deeply immersed in the jute industry in 28UO. Brother of Col. Philip Bayliss. A great admirer of Julia Ukridge's novels.

Mortimer **Bayliss**, J.J. Bunyan's picture curator in SF57. A tall, thin, sardonic man who looks like a Mephistopheles with ulcers. Supercilious manner, cackling laughter; member of the Mausoleum Club. Famous art critic in PB69, where he has wrongly certified the authenticity of a forged nude attributed to Claude Robichaux.

Myrtle **Bayliss**, Sir Edward's daughter, courted by S.F. Ukridge in 28UO.

Colonel Philip **Bayliss** of Pondicherry, Market Deeping, Sir Edward's brother in 28UO. A long, lean, Anglo-Indian-looking individual, rather like a vulture with a white moustache.

Baynes is a strong member of Beckford's first eleven in PU03.

Peter **Baynes**, narrator of 05BI, is the slow bowler of the Heath Hall team; in love with Ella Heath. His father is the local curate.

Sebastian **Beach**, formerly an under-footman, then a footman,

Beach the butler

is the Butler at Blandings Castle in SN15, LP23, 27PH, 28CG, FP29, 31GG, HW33, 36CW, UF39, FM47, PW52, SS61, BG65, 66SW, PB69, SB77; a slightly hypochondriac, portly man of sixteen stone with large spectacles and heavy eyebrows, his waistcoat swells like the sails of a racing yacht. Forty years before BG65 he came in second in a choirboys' bicycle race. Invests all his actions with something of the impressiveness of a high priest conducting an intricate service at some romantic altar. Has buttled at Blandings 18 or 19 years. An occasional reader of historical fiction, prefers Rex Stout and Agatha Christie. Has a niece named Maudie Stubbs (q.v.), his brother's daughter.

Beale, a junior member of Henry's house at St. Austin's, blacks Pillingshot's eye in response to the first edition of *The Rapier* in 11PP.

Mr. **Beale,** a retired army man, red-headed keeper of the house at Combe Regis, Dorsetshire, where S.F. Ukridge installs his chicken farm in LC06.

Mrs. **Beale,** Ukridge's landlady in 25BL.

J. (for James or Jimmy) Hamilton **Beamish,** author of the famous Beamish Booklets on self-improvement in SB27. Lives in the Sheridan Apartment House near Washington Square. In the early thirties, in love with May Stubbs (Madame Eulalie).

Joe **Beamish,** retired burglar in the flock of the Rev. Anselm Mulliner in 37AG.

Luella **Beamish,** only daughter of J. Throgmorton Beamish of New York, fiancée of Lord Bridgenorth in IW31.

Rosalie **Beamish,** one of the extra girls in Perfecto-Zizzbaum's *Black Africa*, engaged to Montrose Mulliner in 32MB.

Victor **Beamish,** commercial artist in 23UA.

Elsie **Bean,** a small, sturdy girl of resolute appearance with blue eyes and turned-up nose, housemaid at Ashenden Manor in UD48. A native of Bottleton East, London; has a brother Bert, in jail for sloshing a slop on the napper with a blunt instrument.

Roland **Bean,** former office-boy to Robert Ferguson, a walking edition of *Stepping-Stones to Success, Millionaires Who Have*

Never Smoked, and *Young Man, Get Up Early*; the miasma of 10MM.

Catherine **Beaumont**: see Grace Grant.

Georgiana, Lady **Beazley-Beazley**, relict of the late Sir Cuthbert Beazley-Beazley, Bart., of Wittleford-cum-Bagsley-on-sea, aunt of Eustace Mulliner in 32OH and owner of a cat named Francis.

The Rev James **Beckett**, headmaster of Beckford College in PU03.

Augustus **Beckford**, Lord Mountry's younger brother in LN13, student at Sanstead House and Ogden Ford's freckled friend in 13EC and LN13. His mother lives in Eaton Square, London.

Myrtle **Beenstock**, relict of the late J.G. Beenstock, aunt of Bingo Little in 65BB; as stout a woman as ever paled at the sight of a diet sheet. In 65SS she marries Sir Hercules Foliot-Foljambe in Naples during a cruise.

Florence **Beezley**, a student at Girton and a friend of MacArthur's sister, the dragon of 02BD. Intensely learned, takes a morbid delight in dissecting the Babe's ignorance. Prattles about Tennyson and Browning; engaged to Mr. Dacre.

James Bartholomew **Belford**, son of Old Belford the parson, worked on a farm in Nebraska where he learned the art of hog-calling from Fred Patzel, hog-calling champion of the Western States. Angela's fiancé in 27PH.

William Egerton Bamfylde Ossingham **Belfry**, ninth Earl of Towcester (pron. Toaster) or Rowcester in RJ53, master of a dilapidated 147-room Towcester Abbey in Southmolton-shire. Brother of Moke Carmoyle. Was a Commando in WWII. A Drone and far from a mental giant, but extremely good-looking. Tries to make money as a Silver Ring Bookie named Honest Patch Perkins with the assistance of Jeeves. Engaged to Jill Wyvern.

Mrs. **Bell**, about 4' 6", is Ashe Marson's landlady at 7A Arundell St. in SN15.

Bellamy is Lady Hermione Wedge's maid in FM47.

Mr. **Bellamy**, retiring vicar at Hockley-cum-Meston in SU63, succeeded by Stinker Pinker.

Max **Bellamy**, attorney for J.B. Hoke in BM31.

Cora **Bellinger**, an upstanding light-heavyweight of some thirty summers, with a commanding eye and a square chin. Takes singing lessons. Engaged to Tuppy Glossop in 29JS, but cannot tolerate failure in a man.

John **Belpher**: see Lord Marshmoreton.

Lord **Belpher**: see Percy Wilbraham Marsh.

Richard **Belsey**, valet of Stanley Briggs in NG07.

Bellwood shares Study Sixteen with Davies at Donaldson's house, Wrykyn, in 04RS. Like Davies, he is a slacker who shelters behind a doctor's certificate and enjoys tormenting Dixon.

Joe **Bender**, 28, proprietor of the Bender Gallery in PB69, knew John Halliday at Oxford. Wears tortoise-shell-rimmed glasses.

Anne **Benedick**, niece of Lord Uffenham in MB42, secretary-companion to Clarissa Cork. Slim, 23, boyish-looking, alert. Privately educated, grandfather was a big-game hunter. Engaged at first to Lionel Green, reluctantly falls in love with Jeff Miller.

Jane **Benedick**, niece of Lord Uffenham in SF57, daughter of his sister Beatrice. Sent to America during the war and lived with a family whose summer residence was in Meadowhampton, L.I. Cooks for her uncle George. Engaged to Stanhope Twine, courted by Bill Hollister. Her sister Anne is married to Jeff Miller.

Benger is a day-boy at Wrykyn in 11EA.

Puffy **Benger**, remembered in Galahad Threepwood's memoirs in FP29 and HW33 as Gally Stale's accomplice in the theft of old Wivenhoe's pig in '95 at Hammers Easton; the pig was coated with phosphorus and left at Plug Basham's bedside at 2 AM to take him out of himself when he had been brooding on something for several days. Then they beat the gong and the experience gave Plug Basham all the fresh interests he could do with. Had a niece named Myrtle who he claimed could play Chopin's Funeral March in 48 seconds. Remembered by Gally in BG65 as a member of the old Pelican Club in the '90's, a keen golfer who got irretrievably hooked into marriage because in a careless moment he allowed a girl to lure him into reading "Pale Hands I Loved Beside the Shalimar" to her. Now the father of a son with adenoids and two daughters with braces on their teeth.

Scrubby **Benger,** a new headmaster in 31VP, was at school with J.G. Smethurst.

Cecil **Benham,** director of *Sacrifice* in BW52; well stricken in years and very dignified.

George **Benham,** playwright, a grave young man whose spectacles give him the look of a mournful owl; an artistically straggling mop of black hair sweeps down over his brow. Friend of Archie Moffam, has trouble with actress Vera Silverton in 20RH/IA21.

Miss **Benjafield,** barmaid at the Feathers in 13EC.

J. Rufus **Bennett** of Bennett, Mandelbaum & Co., a rich fat American who rents Windles from Eustace Hignett in TM22; father of Wilhelmina, partner of Henry Mortimer in the rental of Windles.

Katie **Bennett** runs a second-hand bookshop inherited from her father on 6th Ave. near Washington Square in 15CH. Courted by Ted Brady of the Glencoe Athletic Club.

Matthew **Bennett,** Katie's grandfather in 15CH, believes he is the King of England.

Wilhelmina "Billie" **Bennett,** title character of TM22, daughter of J. Rufus, red-haired girl wooed by Eustace Hignett, Bream Mortimer, and Sam Marloe.

Jeff G. "Bingo" **Bennison,** son of the late swindler Arthur Bennison, was at Wrykyn with Claude Duff. An artist employed by Daphne Winkworth teaching drawing at her girls' school near Eastbourne; in love with Vicky Underwood in SB77. Galahad gets him a job under the pseudonym Smith painting a portrait of the Empress of Blandings.

Benson is a name erroneously given to Aunt Agatha's butler Purvis in some versions of 26JI.

James **Benson** organizes Blenkinsop's benefit at Jephson's house, Beckford College, in 04BB.

Benstead, New York valet of the late eccentric George Stoker in TY34.

Luella **Benstead**, movie actress in 32MB.

Owen **Bentley**, son of the rector of a village in Shropshire. Onetime actor, placed by his uncle Henry in the London & Suburban Bank. In love with Audrey Sheppherd in 11PO.

John **Benyon**, alias Johnson, bearded former New Yorker resident in Algiers since robbing the New Asiatic Bank of $100,000 and jumping bail during his trial; a brother baseball fan in 14OT.

Berkeley, Evans' dorm-mate, is interrogated in 10PD.

Raoul De **Bertini**, "Bertie," a French boy at Wrykyn in GB04; shares a study with Drummond.

Bessemer is Ronnie Fish's man in MN28.

Mrs. **Bessemer** is Lord Blicester's cook in 36MT.

Clifton **Bessemer**, first husband of Rosalinda Banks Spottsworth (RJ53).

Smallwood **Bessemer** is marrying Celia Todd at the beginning of 48TH.

George **Bevan**, American composer for *Follow the Girl* in DD19. About 27, tall and well knit, educated at Lawrenceville and Harvard. In love with Lady Maud Marsh.

Mr. Joe **Bevan**, former Light Weight World Boxing Champion, former Shakespearean repertory actor, now trains boxers at the Blue Boar Inn near Wrykyn. A short, sturdy man given to quoting Shakespeare, trains R.D. Sheen in WF07.

Alan **Beverley** (10MU): see Bill Bates.

Bewstridge is Jeremiah Briggs' butler in 27CD.

Horace **Bewstridge** (handicap 24) loves Vera Witherby in 48EX. Employed by R.P. Crumbles, refuses to play Customer's Golf against Sir George Copstone. In 50FC it is revealed that he once spanked his wife's mother on the 18th green when she interfered with his putting.

Otis **Bewstridge**, heir to the Bewstridge Potato Chips millions, cited in BA73 as a beneficiary of Bachelors Anonymous, who prevented him from marrying his fourth show girl.

John **Bickersdyke**, schoolmate of Psmith's father, now short, stout manager of New Asiatic Bank, elected to parliament in PC10, where he hires Mike Jackson and Psmith.

Francis "Bicky" **Bickersteth**, New York friend of Bertie

Wooster who was at Oxford with him, famed for his imitations of a bull-terrier chasing a cat up a tree. Receives
monthly remittances from his uncle the Duke of Chiswick in
17JH; wants to start a chicken farm. Son of Rollo Bickersteth of the Coldstream Guards.

Boko **Bickerton**, bishop to the Rev. Stanley Brandon in 26MB,
a large, burly bishop.

Conky **Biddle**, a handsome but not very bright young man who
depends on his uncle Everard, Lord Plumpton, courts
Clarissa Binstead in 51HT.

Dinah **Biddle**, secretary to Arnold Pinckney in 66LF, successfully courted by Joe Cardinal.

Gus or Looney **Biddle**, a left-hander, pitches for the New York
Giants and has trouble with his girl friend in 20FA/IA21.

Angela **Biddlecombe** is courted by Slingsby Purvis and Lancelot
Mulliner in 27CD.

The Earl of **Biddlecombe**, Angela's Grecian-beaked father in
27CD, ekes out a living selling gadgets, remedies, subscriptions, and men's accessories.

Biffen is the ground-man at St Austin's in 01AF, PH02.

Amanda **Biffen**, courted by Reginald Mulliner in 52BB.

Charles Edward "Biffy" **Biffen**, absent-minded only son of the
late E.C. Biffen of 11, Penslow Square, Mayfair, has recently
inherited a country place in Herefordshire in 24RA; "com-
pared to Biffy I'm one of the great thinkers of all time"
—Bertie Wooster. Engaged to Honoria Glossop, then to
Jeeves' niece Mabel.

Sir George J. (or C.J.) "Fruity" **Biffen**, now Admiral Biffen, is
an old Pelican Club friend of Galahad Threepwood in FM47,
where the large false beard he wears to escape the notice of
creditors is borrowed for Bill Lister. In PW52 has been
renting a house called Sunnybrae on the Shrewsbury Road
in Shropshire.

L. Lancelot **Biffen**, editor of *Town Gossip* in SB27.

Fruity **Biffin** is an old friend of Freddie Threepwood in FM47
who never stirred abroad without a disguise.

Capt. Billy **Biffing**, one of Annabell Sprockett-Sprockett's seven
suitors in 34FW.

Biggleswade, butler to Lord Prenderby in 34GB.

Biggs is chauffeur to Nesta Ford Pett in PJ17.

Mr. **Biggs**, secretary of the Warner's Stores Social & Outing Club in 23US.

Pvt. **Biggs** of the 18th Tarantulas is a Boy Scout in SW09 and 15MI; in the latter he is Solly Quhayne's office boy and junior clerk.

Ernest **Biggs**, landlord at the Angler's Rest in 33JO.

Gladys **Biggs**, the Mayor's daughter, seen and loved by Clarence Mulliner in 27RB.

Harry **Biggs** is Billy Simpson's rival for the love of Joan Romney's maid Saunders in 05WP; plays football.

Jno. Horatio **Biggs**, O.B.E., Mayor of Tooting East in 27RB.

Bill is Eugene Warden's fox terrier in 12RE.

Thomas **Billing**, a student at George Tanner's private school in 14CI, has his air gun confiscated (cf. George Threepwood in 36CW).

Emma **Billson**, niece of Augustus Keggs in SF57, acts under the name of Elaine Dawn. Daughter of Flossie Keggs and Wilberforce Billson; a breathtaking brunette of the Cleopatra type engaged to Roscoe Bunyan.

Flossie Keggs **Billson**, mother of Emma Billson, sister of Augustus Keggs, wife of Wilberforce Billson in SF57. See Flossie Burns and Flossie Dalrymple.

Wilberforce **Billson**, "Battling Billson," onetime trimmer on the tramp steamer Hyacinth, enormous red-headed public house brawler discovered by S.F. Ukridge and unsuccessfully managed as a boxer from Bermondsey in 23DB, 23RB, 23EB and 35CB. A peerless scrapper with muscles like iron bands, but of the very maximum boneheadedness. In love with Flossie Burns in 23DB and in 23RB, where he wins £30 for defeating Alf Todd. Falls under influence of revivalist Evan Jones in 23EB and takes up crusade against drink and boxing. Back in the ring in 35CB, he makes short work of One-Round Peebles, after which he marries Flossie (her family name here is Dalrymple) and goes into the jellied eel line in Whitechapel. Permanently retired from boxing in SF57, he runs a pub near Shoreditch, and persuades Roscoe

Bunyan to carry out his plan to marry his daughter Emma.

Mrs. Amelia **Bingham**, hospital nurse at St. Swithin's and neighbor to Jane Priestley in BA73, owns a dog named Percy who torments Miss Priestley's cats. A comfortable widow with a tendency to plumpness, she radiates an atmosphere of cosiness which transforms bachelor Ephraim Trout.

Freddie **Bingham**, a young man of large, independent means left to him by a maternal aunt, is engaged to Margaret Bivatt in 13JW. Square and bullet-headed, his nose shows signs of his amateur boxing career and his teeth signs of his college football career. Hair is the color of butter. Earns $100 by staying five rounds against Sam Proctor under the pseud. Jimmy Smith the Santa Barbara Whirlwind.

Ralph **Bingham**, rival of Otis Jukes in golf and love in 21LH. Name changed to Rollo in the U.S. edition.

Rev. Rupert "Beefy" **Bingham**, Oxford schoolmate of Freddy Threepwood, Tuppy Glossop, and Bertie Wooster, was a Blood and Trial Eights man. Nephew and heir of a shipping magnate. Colossal frame, ingenuous face about the color of the inside of a salmon. East End parson running a boys' club at the East End in 27JS, where he organizes clean, bright entertainments at the Oddfellows' Hall in Bermondsey East. Wants to marry Gertrude Alcester in 28CG, where Lord Emsworth makes him vicar of Much Matchingham to spite Sir Gregory Parsloe-Parsloe. Engaged to Gertrude in 31GG, where he wins back her love by breaking up a dogfight between his dog Bottles and Lady Alcester's Airedale.

Tod **Bingham**, middleweight boxing champion in 23DB, beaten up by Battling Billson prior to their scheduled bout at the Shoreditch Empire.

Elsa **Bingley**, secretary to John Shoesmith in IB61.

Gladys **Bingley**, sweet singer of Garbidge Mews, Fulham, fiancée of Lancelot Mulliner in 32SW and 32CC.

Lancelot **Bingley**, rising young artist of the Ultramodern school engaged to Gladys Wetherby in 67GC.

Little Johnny **Bingley**, midget child actor in his forties, Idol of American Motherhood, star of "Baby Boy" in 33NO.

Marcella **Bingley**, a weather-beaten golfer in 20RS with bobbed hair and the wrists of a welterweight pugilist.

Rupert **Bingley**, formerly the butler-valet Brinkley (q.v.), man of property in MO71; smallish and now plump, a Gawd-help-us character with a familiar manner (he addresses Jeeves as "Reggie"), lives at 5 Ormond Crescent, Market Snodsbury, on an inheritance. Erstwhile employers include Bertie Wooster, L.P. Runkle and Ginger Winship. His political views, far to the left in his butler days, are now conservative. Steals the Junior Ganymede club book to blackmail Ginger Winship.

J. Arthur "Grandpop" **Binns**, leading contender in the Lawn Tennis Championship at Wambledon in 29PW, proprietor of the Sea View Hotel. In his early 70s, he plays in his Sunday trousers and a stiff shirt. Serves underhand.

Porky **Binns** is pinched by Constable Keating in 10MI.

Professor **Binstead**, a small man of middle age with tortoise-shell-rimmed glasses, dabbles in science, phrenology, and antiques in 20MH and 20DF/IA21.

Clarence **Binstead**, a soberly-dressed man, rather good-looking in a seedy way, bailiff for Duff & Trotter, wine merchants, Algy Martin's creditors in PP67. One-time actor and under-study to Henry Paradene, now a drinker.

Clarissa **Binstead**, American millionaire's daughter who agrees to marry Conky Biddle in 51HT.

Herbert **Binstead** is the young, slim, and sprightly butler at Matchingham Hall in PW52, SS61.

Patricia **Binstead** is secretary and fiancée of Cyril Grooly in 65ST.

Dr. **Bird** is the physician at Market Blandings in SN15.

J. Wilmot **Birdsey**, formerly of East 73rd St. but now living in London, a small, stout, red-faced little man who loves baseball with a love passing the love of women. Father of Mae Elinor, father-in-law of Hugo Percy de Wynter Fram-linghame in 14OT.

Joe **Bishop**, son of the late Herpina the Snake Queen, Leila Yorke's estranged husband in IB61. A small-time actor with a weak face, lives with his mother.

Godfrey Edward Winstanley Brent, Lord **Biskerton**, "the

Biscuit", son and heir of the sixth Earl of Hoddesdon in BM31, a young man with red hair and the preliminary scenario for a moustache. Heir to Edgeling Court, Sussex; engaged to Ann Moon, falls in love with Kitchie Valentine. A Drone and old school friend of Berry Conway.

The V.R. the Dean of **Bittlesham** conducts the wedding service of Adrian Mulliner and Lady Millicent Shipton-Bellinger in 31SW.

Lord **Bittlesham**: see Mortimer Little.

Franklyn **Bivatt**, father of Margaret in 13JW, is an unpleasant little millionaire with a weak digestion, a taste for dogmatic speech, and the personal appearance of a pterodactyl. Small and shrivelled, lives on hot water, triturated biscuit, and pepsin tabloids. Promises /to let Freddie Bingham marry Margaret if he can hold down a job long enough to earn $500. Has an idle son named Twombley.

Margaret **Bivatt**, daughter of Franklyn Bivatt, is engaged to Freddy Bingham in 13JW. Her elder sister is two years married to the idle Earl of Datchet.

Squiffy **Bixby**, Lord Tidmouth, once married to Lottie Higginbotham in DS42, four times married.

Blagdon is captain of the Hearty Lunchers' Cricket Club in 09RR.

Cosmo **Blair**, successful playwright in SF48. Short and tubby unwanted guest at Beevor Castle, proposes to Clare Cobbold.

Mr. **Blaize**, science & chemistry master at St Austin's in 03SA.

Audrey **Blake**, Mrs. Sheridan in LN13, a widow who before her marriage had jilted Peter Burns. Onetime governess to Ogden Ford, sent to Sanstead House by Mr. Burns to guard Ogden from kidnappers. Small, graceful, about 25, pretty and brisk.

Jno. **Blake**, 6th Avenue tobacconist, a hearty, red-faced Englishman, organizes a pie-eating contest in 20WM/IA21.

Rupert **Blake**, golfer in 23CF.

Susan **Blake**, the vicar's daughter at East Wobsley, a crossword puzzle addict, cures Mr. Mulliner's nephew George of stammering and consents to marry him in 26TA.

Thomas **Blake**, brother to Malim's wife Kit in NG07. Proprietor and skipper of a pair of barges, the *Ashlade* and the *Lechton*, lives at Fenny Stratford with wife Ada. A dipsomaniac, agrees to act as one of Cloyster's three pseudonym-agents in return for 10% of the fee.

Henry **Blake-Somerset**, a small and slender young man of singular but frosty good looks, attached to the British Embassy in Paris in BM64. Enameled elegance: light, sleek hair, aristocratically arched nose, thin lips, pale, chilly blue eyes. Engaged to Kay Christopher.

Lady **Blake-Somerset**, mother of Henry in BM64. Relict of the late Sir Hubert Blake-Somerset of Lower Barnatoland and The Cedars, Mafeking Road, Cheltenham.

Crispin **Blakeney**, brother of Felicia in 23CF, odious reviewer and essayist, was at school with Chester Meredith.

Felicia **Blakeney**, 23, sister of Crispin, daughter of authoress Wilmot Royce, courted by Chester Meredith in 23CF.

Blatherwick, headmaster of Harrow House, a grim mansion on the outskirts of Dover in 09OS. A long, grave man, brother-in-law to Bertie Baxter, employer of James Datchett.

Blaythwayt, sportsman and acquaintance of Robert Ferguson in 10MM.

Roland **Bleke**, 22, employed at the beginning of MM14 as second clerk at the Bury St. Edwards Seed Company, wins £40,000 in the Calcutta Sweepstake and unwittingly builds a £250,000 fortune. Becomes entangled with a succession of women: Muriel Coppin, Billy Verepoint, Maraquita, Lady Eva Blyton, and Maud Chilvers.

Blenkinsop[1], a member of Jephson's house at Beckford in 04BB, now curate at a village in Somersetshire which you will not find on the map.

Blenkinsop[2] is Eustace Mulliner's man in 32OH.

Mr. **Blenkinsop** is an officer of the London and Oriental Bank in MK09.

Blenkinsop's is publisher of Roland Attwater's essays in 24SS.

Robert **Blenkinsop** is knighted in JF54.

Mrs. Alderman **Blenkinsop**, Mrs. Trotter's rival in Liverpudlian society in JF54.

Rupert **Blenkinsop-Bustard**, horsewhipped on the steps of the

Junior Bird Fanciers by Major-General Sir Masterman Petherick-Soames for trifling with the affections of the latter's niece Gertrude, as recalled in 28OO.

Joseph or Rodney Widgeon, Lord **Blicester**, third Earl of Blicester, resides at Blicester Towers, Blicester Regis, Kent in 31FA, 34NO, 36MT, 58FL, IB61; Freddie Widgeon's uncle who provides his quarterly allowance; school friend of Mavis Peasemarch's father Old Bodsham in 31FA. Old friend of Lady Carroway in 35TD, of Lady Pinfold in 36MT. Winner of the Fat Uncles competition at the Drones in 58FL (where his name is given as Rodney). Becomes engaged a second time to Leila Yorke in IB61.

Lady Gwendolyn **Blinkhorn**, Lady Beatrice Bracken's Aunt Gwendolyn in HW32.

Maurice, Vicomte de **Blissac**, New York friend of Packy Franklyn in HW32.

Blizzard, Bradbury Fisher's English butler, the finest in Long Island, radiates port and popeyed dignity; splay feet, three chins. Staked against three railroads in a golf match in 25HS. In 26KI he has been replaced in the Fisher household by Hildebrand Vosper.

General Sir Hector **Bloodenough**, V.C., K.C.I.E., M.V.O., chairman of the Harchester College Board of Governors in 27BM.

Squire **Bloomenstein** supplies the handsome pewter cups given to winners of the Lawn Tennis Championships at Wambledon in 29PW. His son Oscar is tutored by George Murgatroyd.

Joe **Blossom** is one of Sally Preston's many suitors in 13ST.

Lotus or Lottie **Blossom**, born a Murphy of Hoboken, Hollywood actress with red hair and large, shining eyes. Owns a pet alligator named Wilfred. Friend of Reggie Tennyson, engaged to his brother Ambrose in LB35.

Joseph, Earl of **Blotsam**, maternal uncle of Mervyn Mulliner in 31KQ. A heavy uncle living at Blotsam Castle and 66a Berkeley Sq.

Mr. **Blumenfield**, a large, round, flat, overflowing bird, American theatrical manager in 18JC/IJ23, 29JD. Follows the opinion of his stripling son on what will please the general public in the theater.

Maxie **Blumenthal**, music publisher, swept off his feet by Wilson Hymack's song "It's a Long Way Back to Mother's Knee" in 20MK/IA21.

Lady Julia **Blunt**, née Coombe-Crombie, daughter of the tenth Earl of Dreever and wife of Sir Thomas, statuesque aunt of Lord Dreever in IJ10; talks as if she were biting at you.

Sir Thomas **Blunt**, a small, pink, obstinate man with a genius for trade and the ambition of a Napoleon, self-made millionaire and owner of Dreever Castle in IJ10. Chairman of Blunt's Stores. Married to Lord Dreever's aunt Lady Julia. London address 6A Eaton Square.

Lady Eva **Blyton**, daughter of the late Earl, niece of Lord Evenwood and Lady Kimbuck in MM14, is engaged to Roland Bleke but wants to marry her penniless cousin Gerry O'Rion.

Wilkinson **Bodfish** is not Reginald's weekend host in 15SP.

Col. **Bodger**, a tottery golfer of advanced years in 23AR, for the last decade a martyr to lumbago. See also FM47, where he participates in Brown's Club and the Loyal Sons of Shropshire.

A.B. **Bodger**, a Wrykyn Old Boy in 23LA, awarded Mutt-Spivis Gold Medal for Geological Research at Oxford.

Sir Joseph **Bodger**, K.C., attorney for the defense of Clarence Mulliner in 27RB.

Stuyvesant **Bodger**, explorer recently back from West Africa in 15DP, claims to have seen and spoken to Robert Podmarsh among the M'Pongo.

Mr. Aubrey **Bodkin** of the National Theater is offended by something in *Candor* in 06BJ.

Harold **Bodkin**, pal of Reggie Pepper, devoted to his first wife Amelia's memory in 15TC.

Hilda **Bodkin**, Ann Selby's sister, Harold's second wife in 15TC.

Montague or Montrose "Monty" **Bodkin**, second-richest Drone, nephew of Sir Gregory Parsloe; there is also an Uncle Percy. Son of a solicitor with a small country-town practice, he inherited his money from an aunt who married a Pittsburgh millionaire visiting London when she was in the chorus of a musical entertainment at the Adelphi Theatre. His uncle Lancelot was jugged for passing bad cheques the year Hot Ginger won the Cesarewitch. Tall, slender, and lissom, with butter-colored hair and a voice containing something of the tonal quality of a bleating sheep combined with a suggestion of a barking prairie wolf. Tries to hold down a job in HW33, editing *Tiny Tots* in the Mammoth Publishing Co. during the absence of Aubrey Sellick. Will be allowed to marry Gertrude Butterwick if he can hold a job for one year. Fired from Tilbury House for giving improper advice to tiny tots, engaged by Constance Keeble as Lord Emsworth's secretary in HW33. Still engaged to Gertrude in LB35, where he has purchased a position in the Argus Enquiry Agency from Percy Pilbeam for £1,000 and is on his way to Montreal, where his family have sent him to work in an office. Once engaged to Sue Brown for a period of two weeks, during which he had had her name tattooed on his chest. Finally escapes from his engagement to Gertrude in PG72, where he gives up the job as Llewellyn's Adviser for Productions which he obtained by blackmail in LB35 and obtains honest work helping Llewellyn write a history of Superba-Llewellyn, and agrees to marry his former secretary Sandy Miller.

Jno. **Bodmin**, the world-famous hatter of Vigo Street in 33AH, blindly trusted Bespoke Hatter to the Royal Family, Percy Wimbolt, and Nelson Cork.

Old **Bodsham** or Old Bodders: see Peasemarch.

B. Brewster **Bodthorne**, fat first vice-president of Amalgamated Tooth-Brushes in SB27; rolling in money, friend of Lady Waddington.

Stultitia **Bodwin**, authoress of *Offal* in 30BS.

Joe **Boffin**, famous invalid in 37RD, uncle of Annabel Purvis.

Bishop of **Bognor**: see Rev. J. G. Smethurst and Theophilus Mulliner.

Paul **Boielle**, waiter at Bredin's Parisian Café and Restaurant in Soho, aspiring painter in love with waitress Jeanne in 10RH.

Pierre Alexandre **Boissonade**, Commissaire of Police at Roville-sur-mer in FL56.

Constable **Boker** is punched in 30GN by Percy, Bishop of Stortford, in a dive called the Home From Home.

Bolt is the chauffeur at the late Eustace Carmody's Rudge Hall in MN28.

Bombito, one of those outsize, hasty-looking men, is a member of Maraquita's entourage in MM14. A royalist counter-revolutionary from Paranoya, driven out by the Infamy of '05, he wishes to return Alejandro XIII to the throne.

Alice **Bond**, daughter of Wall Street power Paul Bond, is Desmond Fendall's fiancée in 06TP.

Isobel **Bond**, sister of the late Hugo Bond, laid up with a leg broken in a motor accident in DB68, nursed by Jill Willard.

Mike **Bond**, nephew of the late Sir Hugo Bond of Bond's Bank in Wallingford, Worcestershire. Master of Mallow Hall, phone Wallingford 834. Slim and wiry, a graduate of Cambridge and a well-known amateur rider, in love with Jill Willard in DB68.

Paul **Bond**, father of Alice in 06TP, the Wall Street power who has amassed a large fortune through a series of increasingly shady deals.

Cosmo **Booch**, press agent to Joey Cooley in LG36.

Freddy **Boot**, tennis champion, one of Annabell Sprockett-Sprockett's seven suitors in 34FW.

Clarissa **Boote**, only daughter of Col. Anstruther Boote, D.S.O. and Mrs. Boote of Simla Lodge, Wimbledon Common. Formerly engaged to Biffy Wix-Biffen, marries Joe Peabody in 58UK.

Mrs. **Bootle**, postman's wife at Totleigh-in-the-Wold, owns the cottage where Stinker Pinker lives in SU63.

Genevieve **Bootle**, screenwriter for Perfecto-Zizzbaum's production of *Scented Sinners*, affianced to Ed. Murgatroyd in 33CA.

Mrs. Carrie Melrose **Bopp**, American novelist in 37AW.

Lord **Bosham**, courtesy title of Lord Emsworth's elder son. See George Threepwood.

Bosher, Ivor Llewellyn's estranged butler in BA73.

Plug **Bosher**, a fat all-in wrestler managed by Jas Waterbury and Oofy Prosser in 48FO.

Major-General Sir Wilfred **Bosher**, D.S.O. served on the north-western frontier of India. One of the high spots of Bertie Wooster's youth came when Sir Wilfred was distributing prizes at the school where young Bertie Wooster and Gussie Fink-Nottle were students. Dropping a book which he was about to bestow, he stooped to pick it up and split his trousers up the middle (as fondly remembered in RH34).

Sir Aylmer **Bostock**, uncle to Bill Oakshott in UD48, father of Hermione. Was at school with Lord Ickenham, where he was known as Mugsy. Formerly governor of Lower Barnatoland, a crown colony, where he collected a hideous, futile and valueless collection of African curios. Soup-strainer moustache makes him look like Clemenceau. Lives in his nephew's house, Ashenden Manor, Ashendon Oakshott, Hants., with his wife Emily.

Emily, Lady **Bostock**, wife of Sir Aylmer and mother of Hermione in UD48, a woman in the late forties who looks like a horse starting at a hundred to eight in the two-thirty race at Catterick Bridge.

Hermione **Bostock**, daughter of Sir Aylmer and Lady Emily in UD48, cousin of Bill Oakshott. Tall and dark, with large, flashing eyes, firm chin, perfect profile and figure, and rich contralto voice, writes novels under the pseudonym Gwynneth Gould. Engaged for a time to Pongo Twistleton.

J. Gladstone **Bott**, golfing rival of Bradbury Fisher in 25HS. Handicap of 24. Was at Sing-Sing with Fisher, where they ran neck and neck for the prizes which that institution had to offer. Exchanges the baffy used by Bobby Jones in his first important contest (the Infants' All-In Championship of Atlanta, Ga.) for Bradbury Fisher's English butler Blizzard.

Bottles, dog of uncertain breed owned by Beefy Bingham in 31GG.

Cosmo **Botts**, son of Ponsford and Lavender in 56JB, a civil servant who reviews books for various weekly papers in his spare time and gives advice freely.

Irwin **Botts**, juvenile son of Ponsford and Lavender Botts in 48EX.

Mrs. Lavender **Botts**, author of *My Chums the Pixies*, *How to*

Talk to the Flowers, and *Many of My Best Friends Are Mosqui- toes* in 48EX. Wife of Ponsford, mother of Irwin and Cosmo. Aunt of Angela Pirbright in 56JB, where her works include a book on field mice titled similarly to her opus on mosqui- toes.

Ponsford **Botts**, resident in neighborhood of the golf club in 48EX, tells dialect stories about Irishmen named Pat and Mike. Uncle of Vera Witherby and Angela Pirbright. Father of Cosmo in 56JB, of Irwin in 48EX.

Elizabeth **Bottsworth**, small and dainty girl courted by Percy Wimbolt in 33AH; becomes engaged to Nelson Cork.

Bowden plays centre three-quarters for the St Austin's Second Fifteen in 02HP.

Frederick **Bowdon**, a smallish, wiry boy with a cheerful, pleasant face, is at Alderton College in LS08, where he befriends Jimmy Stewart.

Bowles, an ex-butler like all proprietors of furnished rooms in the Sloane Square neighborhood, landlord of James Corcoran in 23DB, 23UD, 24UR, 25BD, 31UH, and other Ukridge sto- ries. For many years butler to the Earl of Oxford, now performs various butlerine services for his tenant. Roman Emperor features; portly aspect, bald head, prominent eyes of a lightish green. His wife is Scotch by birth.

Claude Nutcombe "Nutty" **Boyd**, long spare brother of Elizabe- th in UM16. Receding chin, never reads or thinks; has a drinking problem.

Elizabeth **Boyd**, 21, sister of Nutty in UM16, niece and benefici- ary of the late Ira J. Nutcombe. Small and capable, rents Flack's farm at Brookport, L.I. and keeps bees for a living (cf. Kate Trent in FL56).

James Renshaw **Boyd**, New York playwright from Chicago in 15BL, son of Boyd's Premier Breakfast-Sausage and Boyd's Excelsior Home-Cured Ham.

Millicent **Boyd**, anxious fiancée of Mitchell Holmes in 19OG.

Capt. Cuthbert Gervase **Brabazon-Biggar**, white hunter in RJ53, wins a large bet booked by Bill Belfry and Jeeves. Tough, square, chunky, weatherbeaten, with a very red face and small bristly moustache. In his middle forties, lives at the

United Rovers Club on Northumberland Avenue. Hunts with a .505 Gibbs. In love with Rosalinda Spottsworth.

Major **Brabazon-Plank**, leader of expeditions into the Amazon in UD48, known in school as Bimbo. A pear-shaped man with a pugnacious, sunburned face.

Lady Beatrice **Bracken**, daughter of the Earl of Stableford, of Worbles, Dorsetshire: spectacularly beautiful, never smiles; engaged at the beginning of HW32 to Packy Franklyn.

Evangeline **Brackett**, fiancée of Angus McTavish in 35FL, takes a shine to Legs Mortimer.

Ronald **Bracy-Gascoigne**, of the Berkshire Bracy-Gascoignes, young man of independent means engaged to Hypatia Wace in 30GN.

Capt. **Bradbury**, large and beefy officer in the Indian Army, veteran on the North-Western Frontier; rich tan, natty moustache, Freddie Widgeon's rival for April Carroway in 35TD.

J. Bashford **Braddock**, cousin to Mabel Petherick-Soames and Osbert Mulliner's rival for her hand in 28OO. Explorer in central Africa.

J. Willoughby **Braddock**, a pinkish, stoutish, solemn young man in SS25, was at Wrykyn with Sam Shotter (with whom he shared a study) and Claude Bates. Lives on John Street, Mayfair under the supervision of his former nurse Martha Lippett, now his housekeeper. Has an Aunt Julia. His valet is named Sleddon.

Frederick Wackerbath **Bradshaw**, St Austin's trickster, tells a little story to account for his grade of 4% in a Euripides exam in 02BL; evades a Thucydides exam in 03SA. An early manifestation of the Ukridge type, but more successful in his intrigues. Cf. PGW's English friend and correspondent Leslie Havergal Bradshaw.

Dr. **Brady**, physician to Rose Maynard in 25HC.

Kid **Brady**, title character of 05BL, 05BB, 06BW, 06BA, 06BJ, 06BF, and 07BT, Bowery orphan who defeats Jimmy Garvis to become U.S. lightweight champion. British born, his real name is Edward Darrall. Revived as a 133-pound boxer from Wyoming whose pugilistic career is sponsored by *Peaceful Moments* in PA12, *Cosy Moments* in PJ15.

Ted **Brady** of the Glencoe Athletic Club courts Katie Bennett in 15CH.

Braithwaite of St Austin's Upper Fourth lives in Merevale's in 02OT.

Bill **Bramble**, pugilist known to the boxing world in 13KI as "Young Porky," has a brainy son Harold. Short, stocky, red-headed.

Jane **Bramble**, the stupidest woman in Barnes and one of the best-tempered, wife of Bill the pugilist in 13KI and mother of brainy Harold. Her brother is Maj. Percy Stokes.

Harold **Bramble**, 10, son of Bill and Jane in 13KI, is brainy in defiance of the laws of genetics.

Jane **Brandon**, the vicar's daughter, wooed and won by Augustine Mulliner in 26MB. See Jane Brandon Mulliner.

The Rev. Stanley **Brandon**, vicar at Lower Brisket-in-the-Midden where he is assisted by Augustine Mulliner in 26MB, was at school (where he was known as "pieface") with Boko Bickerton. Father of Jane. A huge and sinewy man of violent temper, with red face and glittering eyes; former heavyweight boxer at Cambridge.

Lord **Brangbolton**: see R.A.M.J.B.T. Shipton-Bellinger.

Muriel **Branksome**, only daughter of Sir Redvers Branksome: one of those hearty, breezy girls who abound in the hunting counties of England, engaged to Sacheverell Mulliner in 31VP.

Lieut. Col. Sir Redvers **Branksome** of Branksome Towers, father of Muriel in 31VP.

Eunice **Bray**, tyro golfer wooed by Ramsden Waters in 20RS.

Wilberforce **Bray**, noisome younger brother of Eunice in 20RS.

Daphne **Braythwayt**, Bingo Little's latest flame at the end of 22SO/IJ23.

Wilberforce **Bream**, a superior golfer in 36AG, wins club golf championship by a long putt in the beginning of 48EX.

Messmore **Breamworthy**, colleague of Freddy Threepwood at Donaldson's Dog Joy in Long Island City mentioned in SB77 and elsewhere.

M. **Bredin**, porcine owner of the Parisian Café in 10RH.

Godfrey Edward Winstanley **Brent**: see Lord Biskerton.

George **Brent**: see Earl of Hoddesdon.

Daniel **Brewster**, proprietor of the Hotel Cosmopolis in New York in the stories of IA21. Father of Lucille and William, reluctantly becomes father-in-law of Archie Moffam in 20MH/IA21; a massive grey-haired man who likes building hotels, including the summer hotel in the mountains named the Hermitage, 20RH/IA21.

Sgt. Herbert **Brewster** of the Wallingford Constabulary is in love with Ivy, parlourmaid at Mallow Hall, in DB68.

James Barr **Brewster**, only son of the late John Waldo Brewster, signatory to J.J. Bunyan's matrimonial tontine; spouse of Sybil Fanshawe-Chadwick in SF57. (A J.B. Brewster is cited in RH34 as Winner of an Exhibition for Classics at St Catherine's, Cambridge.)

Mabel **Brewster**, sister of the late millionaire oilman Wilmot Brewster, unwilling sister-in-law to Julia Brewster Gedge in HW32.

William **Brewster**, square-built son of Daniel, brother of Lucille, was at Yale. Just engaged to an English chorus-girl named Mabel Winchester in 20DF/IA21; in love with Spectatia Huskisson in 20MK/IA21.

Sergeant **Brichoux**, officer of the Monaco police force in 67GA.

Tubby, Lord **Bridgenorth**, sometime gossip writer in IW31, a Drone. Engaged to Luella Beamish.

Lord **Bridgworth**: see Digby Thistleton.

Briggs is butler at Norworth Court, Hampshire, rented by Richard Morrison in PB12.

Augustus **Briggs**, chauffeur to George Pyke, Lord Tilbury in BC24.

Sir Eustace **Briggs**, Mayor of the borough of Wrykyn in GB04, a hater of the Irish nation whose statue O'Hara covers with tar. Has resigned for ill-health in WF07.

Jeremiah **Briggs**, founder and proprietor of Briggs Breakfast Pickles, Lancelot Mulliner's uncle on his mother's side in 27CD. Has a villa at Chutney, Putney, town residence in Berkeley Sq.

Lavender **Briggs**, Lord Emsworth's secretary in SS61, formerly employed by Lord Tilbury of the Mammoth Publishing Co., wears harlequin glasses, speaks with an affected accent, is tall and ungainly with large feet and hair like seaweed.

Little **Briggs**, accountant at the New Asiatic Bank in PC10.

Paul Axworthy **Briggs**, the Boy Novelist who lives upstairs in 15BL, adopts the black cat Joseph for luck.

Stanley **Briggs**, actor for whom J.O. Cloyster writes lyrics in NG07.

Mrs. C. Hamilton **Brimble**, mother of Hermione Brimble[2] in BW52, a short, stout woman.

Hermione **Brimble**[1], daughter of the late Bishop of Stortford, niece to Mrs. Willoughby Gudgeon; courted by Augustus Mulliner in 47RA.

Hermione **Brimble**[2], daughter of well-known financial magnate C. Hamilton Brimble of King's Point, Long Island, fiancée of Mervyn Potter in BW52. A tallish product of Miss Finch's School and Vassar, with a complexion the color of marble in starlight.

Percy **Brimble**: see Bishop of Stortford.

Brinkley, demented leftist valet to Bertie Wooster who replaces Jeeves in TY34 after a rift caused by Bertie's playing on a banjolele. A melancholy man with a long, thin, pimplestudded face and deep, brooding eyes. Burns down Bertie's cottage at Chuffnell Regis and chases him with a carving knife during a drunken fit. See Rupert Bingley.

Eustace **Brinkley**, member of the golf club in 21SG.

Beulah **Brinkmeyer** (Brinkwater in U.S. edns.), sister of T.P. Brinkmeyer in LG36, a tall, rangy, light-heavyweight, severe manager of Brinkmeyer's home and his child star Joey Cooley.

Theodore P. **Brinkmeyer** (Brinkwater in U.S. edns.), stout, billowy head of the Brinkmeyer-Magnifico Motion Picture Corporation in LG36. Formerly in the cloak and suit business, wears horn-rimmed spectacles.

Angelica **Briscoe**, daughter of the Rev. P.P. or Ambrose Briscoe in 35TF and AA74; in the latter she persuades Billy Graham to steal Pop Cook's cat.

Col. Jimmy **Briscoe** of Eggesford Hall, Somerset, brother of Rev. Ambrose Briscoe and husband of Elsa, host of Dahlia

Travers in AA74. Chairman of the Eggesford board of magistrates, has fined his neighbor and horseracing rival Mr. Cook for moving pigs without a permit. Owner of a racehorse named Simla.

The Rev. P.P. **Briscoe**, of Maiden Eggesford, Somersetshire, father of Angelica in 35TF; in AA74 his name is Ambrose; his brother is Col. Jimmy Briscoe.

A Mr. **Briscoe**, second cousin and fiancé to Angelica Briscoe in 35TF.

Bristow, a flashy dresser in the Postage Department of the New Asiatic Bank, PC10.

Sampson **Broadhurst**, godfather and benefactor of Dudley Fish in 25AG and 40DI, owns a sheep ranch in western Australia.

Eddie **Brock**, a rising lightweight boxer in 05BL, is Kid Brady's first opponent.

Brodie, friend of G. Montgomery Chapple in 05PP, advises him on how to avoid oversleeping.

Lord **Bromborough** of Rumpling Hall, Lower Rumpling, Norfolk; owner of a moustache named Joyeuse in 36BT.

Muriel **Bromborough**, daughter of foreg., courted by Brancepeth Mulliner in 36BT.

Brookfield, an old friend of Jeeves, butler to the Rev. Francis Heppenstall at Twing Vicarage in IJ23/22SH, 22MT.

Alf **Brooks**, milkman for York Mansions, Battersea, in 15RU, courts Ellen Brown.

Broster, golfer who plays for high stakes in 25HS.

Reggie **Broster**, Ogden Ford's erstwhile tutor at Eastnor in LN13.

Annette **Brougham** writes waltzes in a Chelsea apartment below Alan Beverley's in 10MU.

Brown, a boy at St Austin's in 03HP, hit in the side of the head by a drive hit by Babington. Has his eye on the form prize in 03SA.

Arthur **Brown** is one of Sally Preston's many suitors in 13ST.

Ellen **Brown**, serving girl charged with theft in 15RU, courted by Alf Brooks and P.C. Edward Plimmer.

Percival **Brown**, a betting member of the golf club in 19WW.

Phil **Brown**, friend of Nelly Bryant in LW20, plays straight man opposite Joe Widgeon on a jazz-and-hokum team on the Keith circuit.

Polly **Brown**, a small (105 pounds), fragile American girl with piquant features, works as a manicurist for Syd Price in IW31; wooed and won by Anthony, Lord Droitwich.

Reginald **Brown**, golfing detective hired by William Bates in 25PR.

Rev. Septimius **Brown** teaches Math 4B at St Austin's in 01AU.

Sue **Brown**, daughter of the late Dolly Henderson in SL29, FP29 and HW33: a tiny thing, mostly large eyes and a wide happy smile; her late father, Jack Cotterleigh, was in the Irish Guards. For a time in the chorus at the Regal Theatre, engaged to Monty Bodkin for a period of two weeks, during which he has her name tattooed on his chest. Wooed by Ronnie Fish in FP29, still betrothed to him in HW33, his wife in LB35.

Jack **Bruce**, a day-boy on the engineering side at Wrykyn College in WF07, quiet, self-sufficing son of mayoral candidate Sir William Bruce.

Nannie **Bruce**, family retainer and onetime nurse of Johnny Pearce in CT58, a tall, gangling light-heavyweight in residence at Hammer Hall. Engaged to constable Cyril McMurdo.

Sir William **Bruce**, an Old Wrykynian, governor of the school, and Conservative candidate for mayor of Wrykyn in WF07. Father of Jack.

Mme. **Brudowska**, a tragic actress in 20DO/IA21, owns a snake named Peter given her by a Russian prince.

Vladimir **Brusiloff**, famous Russian novelist specializing in grey studies of hopeless misery where nothing happens till p. 380, when the moujik decides to commit suicide. His face is almost entirely concealed behind a dense zareba of hair; believes P.G. Wodehouse and Tolstoi not bad. Golf enthusiast in 21UC.

Nelly **Bryant**, New York chorus girl in LW20, falls in love with Freddie Rooke after he gives her £50 to get back to New York from London.

Bryce, Roland Attwater's manservant in 24SS.

Anthony Claude Wilbraham **Bryce**: see Lord Droitwich.

Robert **Bryce**, police-constable, stops a fight between Arthur Welsh and Skipper Shute in 10WD.

Buchterkirch: see Grusczinsky & Buchterkirch.

George **Budd**, bookie to whom Pongo Twistleton owes £200 in UF39.

James "Spider" **Buffin**, pickpocket in 10MI.

Pvt. William **Buggins**, a Boy Scout in SW09 and 15MI, helps Clarence Chugwater defeat the invading Germans and Japanese.

Ike **Bullett**, turf commission agent in BC24.

G. **Bullett**, cited as being awarded the Lady Jane Wix Scholarship at the Birmingham College of Veterinary Science in RH34.

Freddie **Bullivant**, a Drone engaged to Elizabeth Vickers in 11HF.

Sam **Bulpitt**, brother of Alice Abbott and uncle of Jane Abbott in SM37. A round, small, rosy man who chews gum, started his career as a singing waiter, continued as a traveler in patent floor sweepers, now America's foremost process server.

Bulstrode[1], Mrs. C. Hamilton Brimble's English butler in BW52.

Bulstrode[2], Col. Wyvern's pimply sixteen-year-old butler in RJ53. Chinless, sucks toffee.

Mr. **Bulstrode**, Mabel's father in 25BL, runs some sort of immensely wealthy business in Singapore. A member of George Tupper's club, is looking for a secretary.

J.G. **Bulstrode**, resident of Valley Fields whom Uncle Fred Twistleton impersonates in 35UF.

Mabel **Bulstrode**, title character loved and lost by Ukridge in 25BL. Lives in Onslow Square.

Percy **Bulstrode**, chemist on High Street, Market Blandings in PW52 and BG65.

Mr. **Bunbury**, orange-haired producer of *The Primrose Way* in AS22.

Sir Percy **Bunt** of the English Civil Service is Hermione Pegler's dinner guest in FL56.

Cyril **Bunting** of Bunting, Satterthwaite & Miles, Lord Tilbury's dyspeptic legal advisor in BM64, looks like a vulture but lacks its strong digestion: his diet consists of glasses of milk, spinach, and hot water. Assumes role of Jorkins the butler at The Oaks at the request of Lord Tilbury. In 66LF his law firm is Bunting & Satterthwaite; now well stricken in years, his lunches consist solely of a glass of warm water. Represents Mr. Donaldson the dog biscuit magnate and Judson Phipps in his breach-of-promise suits.

George **Bunting** is a contender for the club golf championship in 40SM.

A Mr. **Bunyan** drinks stout from a tankard and squashes a wasp in the bar parlour at the Angler's Rest in 32MB.

J.J. **Bunyan**, New York millionaire in SF57 with a summer house in Meadowhampton, L.I., makes up a matrimonial tontine at a dinner on Sept. 10, 1929, the beneficiary of which will be the last son of the ten signatories to remain unmarried.

Roscoe **Bunyan**, son of J.J. Bunyan in SF57, inherited $20 million after taxes from his father's estate. Rents Shipley Hall from Lord Uffenham. A singularly unattractive young man who bulges freely in all directions.

Lester **Burdett**, a garment manufacturer who withdraws his $20,000 investment in *Sacrifice* when Mervyn Potter gives him a hot foot in BW52.

P. **Burge** of Blackburn's house at Eckleton throws a Bradley Arnold's Latin Prose Exercises at Shearne in 08GU and suffers for it when Shearne returns it to his midriff at a range of two yards.

Mary **Burgess**, niece of old Heppenstall, only daughter of the late Matthew Burgess of Weatherly Court, Hants., courted simultaneously by Bingo Little and Hubert Wingham in 22MT/IJ23.

Wilfred **Burgess**, Mary's kid brother in 22MT/IJ23, wins a weight-for-age eating contest.

William B. **Burgess**, captain of the Wrykyn 11 in MK09; the school fast bowler, genial giant, head of the school.

Michael **Burke**, older brother of Tim; Irish immigrant from Skibbereen, now a New York policeman in 13ML.

Tim **Burke**, Michael's younger brother in 13ML, a gigantic, red-haired man with a vast jaw. Manages Red Dan Magee's hotel out west in Wistaria.

Dolly **Burn**, loved by Tom, Dick, & Harry in 05TD.

Cecil **Burns**, a rat-faced, sinister-looking boy, brother to Flossie Burns in 23RB.

Flossie **Burns**, spectacular blonde affianced to Wilberforce Billson in 23DB and 23RB; barmaid at the Crown in Kennington. See also Flossie Dalrymple.

Peter **Burns**, narrator of 13EC and LN13, one of the two assistant masters at Sanstead House; thirty years old with not much of a degree from Oxford, in LN13 he is engaged to Cynthia Drassilis, having once been jilted by Audrey Blake.

Lester **Burrowes**, a small man of sporting exterior, once a famous featherweight boxer, now manager of Bugs Butler in AS22.

Corporal Sam **Burrows** served under Col. Stewart in the North Surreys on the Indian Frontier. Entrusts The Tear of Heaven (The Luck Stone) to Col. Stewart's nipper Jimmy in LS08.

Jake **Burt** is a seaman on the *May Moon* in 07BT.

B.K. **Burwash**, dentist to Joey Cooley in LG36.

Hortensia **Burwash**, Empress of Molten Passion, temperamental female star at Perfecto-Zizzbaum, on an orange juice diet ·in 33JO because of a weight clause in her contract.

Twombley **Burwash**, son of the Dwight N. Burwashes, rejected by Ann Frisby in BM31 because he refuses to hit a policeman.

J. Mortimer **Busby**, publisher of Sir Buckstone Abbott's *My Sporting Memories* in SM37, sometime employer of J.J. Vanringham.

Lieutenant-Colonel J.J. **Bustard**, neighbor of Bertie Wooster's at Berkeley Mansions who objects to his banjolele in TY34.

Bugs **Butler**, a singularly repellent lightweight boxer managed by Lester Burrowes in AS22, defeated by Lew Lucas by a knockout in round 3.

Edith **Butler**, author of *White Roses* in 11PO (see Mr. Prosser).

Rabbit **Butler**, eminent member of the Frith St. Gang in 10MI.

Alfred **Butt**, town constable in MK09.

Comrade **Butt**, small shrivelled revolutionary in 22CB/IJ23 who looks like a haddock with lung trouble, Bingo Little's rival for Charlotte Corday Rowbotham, takes over after Comrade Little's discomfiture at Goodwood; remembered in 22SH.

Butterfield, Sir Watkyn Bassett's butler at Totleigh Towers in CW38, well stricken in years by SU63.

Gertrude **Butterwick**, a beefy girl with large feet, fiancée of Monty Bodkin in HW33, LB35, where she is on her way to America as a member of the England Hockey Team, and PG72, where she finally breaks off the engagement and announces her intention to marry Wilford Chisholm. Cousin of Reggie and Ambrose Tennyson.

J.G. Butterwick of Butterwick, Price, & Mandelbaum, export and import merchants. Lives at 11 Croxted Road, W. Dulwich, London S.E. 21. Dyspeptic father of Gertrude, imposes on Monty Bodkin the test of holding a job for an entire year as a precondition of his daughter's hand in HW33. Conspires to get this engagement broken in PG72, where in fact it does end.

Buxton is a member of Mr. Appleby's house, Wrykyn in 04HT and 05CL. A member of the Lower Fifth in 04HT, shares study eight with Liss. Owns a Dr. Giles crib to Euripides' *Medea*, likes scents such as *Simpkins Idle Moments* and *Riggles's Rose of the Hills*.

Sarah **Byles**, Bingo Little's onetime Nannie, retained by the Littles in 50SP as nurse for young Algernon.

Lady Caroline **Byng**, née Marsh, daughter of the 6th Earl of Marshmoreton; sister of John Belpher, Lord Marshmoreton Chatelaine of Belpher Castle in DD19. Widow of Clifford Byng, a very wealthy colliery owner; stepmother of Reggie Byng.

Reginald **Byng**, son of the late Clifford Byng, stepson of Lady Caroline. A long young man, devoted to cars and golf. Elopes to Paris with Alice Faraday in DD19.

Stephanie "Stiffy" **Byng**, courted by Stinker Pinker in CW38 and SU63. Cousin to Madeline Bassett, lives at Totleigh Towers, where she is the ward of her uncle, Sir Watkyn Bassett. Owns an Aberdeen terrier named Bartholomew. In

CW38 she induces fiancé Stinker Pinker to steal Constable Oates' helmet. Referred to in MO71 as Mrs. Stinker Pinker.

Wilmot **Byng**, tall, red-headed, impatient golfer who woos Gwendoline Poskitt in 36LL.

Chas. **Bywater**, chemist in Rudge-in-the-Vale, Worcestershire in MN28, has a daughter in the post office.

C

George **Caffyn**, New York playwright and friend of Bertie Wooster, author of *Ask Dad* in 18JC/IJ23.

Cakebread, faux butler at Shipley Hall in MB42. See George, Lord Uffenham.

Alexandra or Sandy **Callender**, trim redhead in BG65 with tortoise-shell-rimmed glasses which seem to cover most of her face. Daughter of the late Ernest Callender. Once secretary to the late Chet Tipton, she leaves post of secretary to Lord Emsworth to marry S.G. Bagshott. Galahad Threepwood persuades her to destroy her spectacles.

George Barnert **Callender**, a powerful swimmer, author of *Fate's Footballs*, a comedy in four acts playing at Marvis Bay in 10DW. Falls in love with Mary Vaughan.

Aurelia **Cammarleigh**, a tall, superbly handsome girl, lives in Park Street with her potty aunt who thinks Bacon wrote Shakespeare; daughter of Sir Rackstraw. Wooed and won by Archibald Mulliner in 28RW. Still his fiancée in 35AM and 35CM.

Sir Rackstraw **Cammarleigh**, Aurelia's father, a tough, hardbitten retired Colonial Governor of the type which comes back to England to spend the evening of its days barking at club waiters. Resides at 36a Park St.; cured of repetitive storytelling in 35CM.

Mary **Campbell**, courted by Jack Wilton in 15WH, is moved to affection by pity, fear, or a chilly breeze.

Captain Kettle is Prater's larcenous cat in 02TT.

Letitia **Carberry**, head of the Anti-Tobacco league, former employer (for two years) of Sally Fitch in BA73.

Brenda **Carberry-Pirbright**, only daughter of Mr. & Mrs. B.B. Carberry-Pirbright, subject of a portrait being painted by Lancelot Mulliner in 32SW.

Bobbie **Cardew**, married to Mary Anthony in 11AT, plagued by a bad memory to the degree that he forgets his wife's birthday.

Joe **Cardinal**, nephew of Arnold Pinckney in 66LF and heir to an aunt's estate held in trust by Pinckney, has given up his painting and gone to work for the New Asiatic Bank. Lives in a Chelsea studio, falls in love with Dinah Biddle.

Mycroft (Mike) **Cardinal**, friend of Stanwood Cobbold in SF48. Wealthy junior partner in a motion-picture agency, continually proposes to Teresa Cobbold.

Gertrude "Sweetie" **Carlisle**, Gordon's wife and confederate in HW32 and CT58. A strapping young woman with bold hazel eyes and a determined chin, likes to bean people with vases and bottles.

Gordon "Oily" **Carlisle**, tall, dark, slender, beautifully dressed specialist in the Confidence Trick in HW32, tries to blackmail Beefy Bastable in CT58.

Hugh or Hugo **Carmody**, son of the late Eustace Carmody of Rudge Hall, Worcestershire, nephew of Lester Carmody, cousin of John Carroll in MN28, where he needs money from uncle Lester, his trustee, for his partnership with Ronnie Fish in The Hot Spot, a night club just off Bond Street. Lord Emsworth's secretary in FP29, after the failure of The Hot Spot, in love with his cousin Millicent Threepwood. A Drone, friend of Monty Bodkin in HW33, still engaged to Lord Emsworth's niece Millicent.

Lester **Carmody**, trustee of Rudge Hall and his nephew Hugo's estate in MN28. Second son of a second son, went into business at an early age, spent his youth and middle age on the London Stock Exchange, now a man of ample proportions.

Lady Monica "Moke" **Carmoyle**, sister of W.E.O. Belfry in RJ53, wife of Sir Roderick. Small and vivacious, an Old Cheltonian.

Sir Roderick "Rory" **Carmoyle**, husband of Monica Belfry Carmoyle in RJ53. Large and stolid, like a more than ordinarily stolid buffalo, works as a floorwalker at Harrods.

Bruce **Carmyle**, cousin to Ginger Kemp in AS22, son of Carmyle, Brent & Co with coal mines up in Wales. Master of Monk's Crofton, Much Middleford, Shropshire. Wants to marry Sally Nicholas.

Frederick "Butch" **Carpenter**, a large young man with bright red hair and a freckled face, majority stockholder in Fizzo, the well-known sparkling table water. Owns an enormous yacht, the *Belinda*, in FL56, where Hermione Pegler manages his engagement to Mavis Todd.

John **Carroll**, nephew of Lester Carmody in MN28, manager of Rudge Hall, his uncle's estate. Played rugger for Rugby, Oxford, and England. In love with Pat Wyvern.

April **Carroway**, courted by Freddie Widgeon and Capt. Bradbury in 35TD; daughter of Lady Carroway, sister of Prudence. Loves Tennyson's poetry.

Lady **Carroway** of Tudsleigh, Worcestershire, old friend of Lord Blicester, mother of April and Prudence Carroway in 35TD.

Prudence **Carroway**, April's young sister, plays Lady Godiva in 35TD.

Col. **Carteret**, guardian of Rose Maynard in 25HC.

Mabel **Case**, fiancée of George Potter in 56JB.

Tim **Cassidy**, New York police officer in 21SE/IA21.

Walter **Catfield** is the comic in *Ask Dad* in 29BG.

Sir Edward **Cave**, a nasty little man in 05WP who has made a great deal of money somehow or other and been knighted for it. Takes a great deal of trouble about cricket: fields a team called Castle Cave or The Cave.

Celestine: see Maggie O'Toole.

Chadwick of Appelby's house is an absolute outsider at Wrykyn in 05IA.

Chaffinch, actor-butler for T.P. Brinkmeyer in LG36.

The Hon. Freddie **Chalk-Marshall**, younger brother of Lord Droitwich in IW31, monocled second son of John, late fourth Earl of Droitwich; A Drone and a fastidious dresser.

Challis, a first eleven man at Blackburn's, Eckleton, in HK05.

William Fitzwilliam Delamere **Chalmers:** see Lord Dawlish.

Willie **Chambers,** one-time winner of Choirboys' Hundred Yards Handicap in 22PT.

G. Montgomery **Chapple,** of Seymour's house at Wrykyn in 05PP, specializes in being late for breakfast.

Charles[1], second footman to Lord Wickhammersly in 22PT.

Charles[2], footman at Langley End in IW31.

Charles[3], footman at Blandings in UF39 and FM47.

Charles[4], footman at Claines Hall in QS40.

Charlie brings a motor to the Weary Willies-Marvis Bay cricket match in 05LB.

Charteris, a prefect in Merevale's house at St Austin's, is founder, editor, and publisher of the *Glowworm,* an unofficial and highly personal paper a great deal more in demand than the *Austinian* in PH02, 02BD (where he bowls for the School-house), 03MC, and 11PP. In 03MC he is in the sixth form, plays half on the School 15, and is out to break school rules. Called the Alderman because he is inclined to stoutness. Loquacious, plays the banjo, a poor student; shares a study with Welch. In IJ10, he is a Cambridge graduate and a member of the Footlights with a monomania for amateur theatricals.

Tom **Chase,** a lieutenant in the Royal Navy, engaged to Norah Derrick in LC06.

Mrs. Beatrice **Chavender,** widow of Mabel Steptoe's brother Otis in QS40, once engaged to J.B. Duff.

Otis **Chavender,** late brother of Mrs. Howard Steptoe in QS40.

G. D'Arcy (Stilton) **Cheesewright** was at private school, Eton, and Oxford with Bertie Wooster. Captain of Boats at Eton, rowed assiduously at Oxford. Beefy of frame, with a head like a pumpkin and a face like a slab of pink dough. His uncle is magistrate at the Vinton St. police court. Employed as a policeman in Steeple Bumpleigh in JM46, where he is engaged for a time to Florence Craye. Member of the Drones in JF54, where he is again affianced to Florence but breaks off his engagement by telegram and falls in love with Daphne Dolores Morehead.

Julia **Cheever,** sister of Judson Phipps in 66LF; divorced, now engaged to Arnold Pinckney.

Howard **Chesney**, American friend of Freddie Threepwood and visitor at Blandings Castle in PB69; a slender young man of medium height, distinctly ornamental in appearance.

Wallace **Chesney** is engaged to Charlotte Dix in 22MP, where he buys a pair of prismatic Plus Fours from the Cohen Brothers. Reappears briefly in 23AR with his Plus Fours.

Chester, personal maid to Lady Ann Warblington in SN15.

Ann **Chester**, red-haired daughter of Hammond Chester and niece of Peter Pett in PJ17, courted by Jimmy Crocker.

Hammond **Chester**, a massive, weather-beaten traveler, explorer, and big-game hunter, father of Ann in PJ17.

Sidney **Chibnall**, Mrs. Steptoe's butler, a lissome, athletic young butler of the modern type (dignified but sinewy) in QS40.

Miss Maud **Chilvers**, Roland Bleke's hired past in MM14, niece of Lord Evenwood's butler Teal in MM14, lives at the Goat and Compasses in Aldershot. Presents a passionate correspondence from Roland Bleke in time to save him from his engagement to Lady Eva Blyton. Has dyed yellow hair, done all frizzy.

Elmer **Chinnery**, paying guest at Walsingford Hall in SM37. A large, spreading American with a smooth face and very big horn-rimmed spectacles. Partner in a fish-glue business, enormously rich and often married.

Chippendale, acting butler at Mellingham Hall in GB70, actually a broker's man for the firm that does the repairs at Mellingham Hall. A small man of muddy complexion with ears like the handles on a Greek vase and the beak and eyes of a farmyard fowl.

Wilfred "Cheeser" **Chisholm**, son of Sir Wilberforce Chisholm, Assistant Commissioner of Scotland Yard. Played hockey at Eton and Oxford, now plays for England. Was at school with Monty Bodkin. Gertrude Butterwick breaks her engagement to Monty to become Chisholm's fiancée in PG72, where he is employed as a plainclothesman.

The Duke of **Chiswick**, Bicky Bickersteth's rich and stingy uncle in 17JH, is a hard-boiled egg.

Edmund Biffen "Biff" **Christopher**, 29, brother of Kay in

BM64, godson of the late Edmund Biffen Pyke, whose fortune he will inherit at the age of 30 according to the terms of a spendthrift trust. Onetime reporter, aspiring novelist, looks like a dachshund, with a longish nose and not much chin. Twice engaged to Linda Rome.

Katherine or Kay **Christopher**, a small, trim, alert girl with a tiptilted nose, bright hazel eyes and brisk manner, an American on the Paris staff of the New York Herald Tribune in BM64. Sister of Biff Christopher, with whom she shares a flat at 16 Rue Jacob. Engaged to Henry Blake-Somerset.

Marmaduke, "Chuffy" **Chuffnell**, fifth Baron Chuffnell, of Chuffnell Hall, Chuffnell Regis, Somersetshire. Nephew of Myrtle, Dowager Lady Chuffnell, from whose late husband he inherited his title. Attended private school, Eton, and Oxford with Bertie Wooster. Member of the Drones. Suitor of Pauline Stoker in TY34, her husband in SU63. See also 65JG.

Myrtle, Dowager Lady **Chuffnell**, relict of the late 4th Baron Chuffnell, aunt to Marmaduke, mother to Seabury in TY34 by an earlier marriage, one of those women who look like female Masters of Hounds. Betrothed to Sir Roderick Glossop in 65JG but refuses to marry as long as Honoria Glossop remains unmarried: nothing will induce her to share a home with Miss Glossop.

Clarence Breamworthy **Chugwater**, Pride of the Boy Scouts in 15MI, works as office boy at the *Sentinel* and masterminds the expulsion of German and Japanese forces from New York.

Clarence MacAndrew **Chugwater**, 14, one of Gen. Baden-Powell's Boy Scouts in SW09. Lives in Nasturtium Villa, Essex with his parents, brothers Reggie and Horace, and sisters Grace and Alice.

Reggie **Chugwater**, Clarence's eldest brother in SW09, is an agent for the Come One Come All Accident and Life Assurance Office.

J. Chichester **Clam**, American tycoon in JM46, managing director of the Clam Line who comes to Steeple Bumpleigh to consummate a secret business deal with Lord Worplesdon.

Clarkson, J. Wendell Stickney's English valet in PP67. Small, pale, skinny, 36, with lemon-colored hair. Once employed by a Mr. Waddington in Old Westbury, Conn.

Ada **Clarkson**, "Clarkie," formerly English mistress at Wayland House, runs a domestic employment agency on Shaftesbury Avenue patronized by Eve Halliday and Psmith in LP23.

Bessy **Clay**, disqualified in Girls' Egg and Spoon Race in 22PT/IJ23.

Spencer **Clay** likes to tell sad tales about himself in 15WH, where he is the first to hear of Jack Wilton's supposed bereavement.

Bernadette "Barney" **Clayborne**, relict of the late pet of the sporting set Wally Clayborne, sister of Homer Pyle in GB70. A large, cheerful, friendly woman given to shoplifting.

Clayton tries to conduct a court-marshall of Sheen at Seymour's in WF07.

Mrs. **Cleghorn**, cook at Shipley Hall in MB42.

Clementina, title character of 30JK, Bobbie Wickham's thirteen-year-old cousin. A quiet, saintlike fiend, student at St. Monica's, whose headmistress is Aunt Agatha's oldest friend Miss Mapleton.

Clephane is a day-boy who comes into Shield's house at Wrykyn owing to the departure of his parents for India. A member of the second eleven, a fast bowler, he makes a century in 05SC. See also 05LP (where he is described as a erratic bowler) and MK09.

Clowes, a tall, dark, thin Wrykynian with a pensive eye in GB04; Trevor's study-mate at Donaldson's, Wrykyn, in 04RS, 05LP and MK09. A member of the Oxford A team playing football against Wrykyn in WF07.

James Orlebar **Cloyster**, Wodehouse alter ego, chief narrator of NG07. Took a 3rd class degree in the classical tripos, now making his living as a writer in London, engaged to Margaret Goodwin.

Clunk, J.B. Duff's osteopath in QS40.

G.G. **Clutterbuck**, chartered accountant injured in an auto accident on Fulham Road, successfully represented by John Halliday in PB69 at the expense of the latter's engagement with Linda Gilpin.

J. Russell **Clutterbuck**, Oswald Stoker's eccentric American publisher in 47RA, partner in Clutterbuck & Winch, publishers of the book beautiful. Owner of a summer home in Bensonburg, L.I. in FL56, and a customer of the Trents' honey business who is displeased with the price he is charged for honey. His home town is Niles, Michigan. Thrice married, he bulges opulently in all directions; his round face, round eyes, and round spectacles give him the look of an owl which has done itself too well on field mice. Publishes Jefferson Auguste's novel.

Constable **Cobb** is the village policeman at Millbourne in 13ST.

Adela **Cobbold**, eldest daughter of the Earl of Shortlands in SF48, wife of Desborough Topping. The tall, handsome imperious chatelaine of Beevor Castle who controls her father's spending and other activities.

Lady Clare **Cobbold**, second daughter of Lord Shortlands in SF48, looks like her father. The sort of girl who goes about in brogue shoes and tweed and meddles vigorously in the lives of the villagers. Courted by Cosmo Blair.

Claude Percival John Delamere **Cobbold**, fifth Earl of Shortlands in SF48. A stout, smooth-faced man of 52 who looks like a discontented butler. Master of Beevor Castle, Kent, but financially dependent on his daughter Adela, who makes him live all the time at his castle. Wants to borrow £200 to buy a public house and marry Mrs. Punter, his cook.

G. Ellery **Cobbold**, of Great Neck, L.I., stout economic royalist in SF48. A distant relation of the Beevor Castle Cobbolds, father of Stanwood Cobbold.

Stanwood **Cobbold**, son of G. Ellery Cobbold in SF48. A mass of muscle and bone, the bone extending to the head. Onetime All-American football player, in love with Eileen Stoker. Friend of Mike Cardinal, was kind to Teresa Cobbold in London.

Lady Teresa (Terry) **Cobbold**, youngest daughter of the Earl of Shortlands in SF48. Persistently courted by Mike Cardinal; worked briefly but unsuccessfully as a showgirl in London, where she was jilted by an actor named Geoffrey Harvest.

C.D. Codger, a Wrykyn Old Boy in 23LA, appointed to the sub-junior deanery of Westchester Cathedral.

Count Fritz von **Cöslin,** equerry to his Serene Highness the Prince of Saxburg-Liegnitz, arrives in time to save George Lattaker in 12RR.

Jack **Coggin** is a Marvis Bay bowler in 05LB.

Coggs, butler at Ickenham Hall in UF39, CT58, UD48. A large, stout, moon-faced man with an eye like that of a codfish. Taught Bert Peasemarch how to buttle.

The **Cohen** brothers Isadore, Lou, and Irving run a second-hand clothing establishment near Covent Garden (cf. the Moses Brothers in 23UA, and the real-life Moss Bros. of Covent Garden, mentioned in SS61). In 22MP (where the first brother's name is spelled Isidore) they sell Wallace Chesney a pair of prismatic Plus Fours allegedly made for Sandy McHoots. In SS25 they sell ready-made clothing and outfit Sam Shotter in a bold tweed suit. In 28OO they outfit Osbert Mulliner in secondhand traveling clothes. In JM46 they supply Bertie Wooster with a Sinbad costume. In BM64, they are called on to supply trousers for Biff Christopher.

Alice **Coker,** imperious fiancée of Bill West in BC24; sister of Judson, daughter of J. Birdsey. Marries a wealthy young man from Pittsburgh.

J. Birdsey **Coker,** father of Judson and Alice in BC24, lives on East 61st Street.

Judson **Coker,** son of J. Birdsey Coker, best friend of Bill West, with whom he went to school and college, in BC24. Brother of Alice Coker. Tall and homely, with a prominent arched nose and plaintive green eyes. Founder of the Fifth Avenue Silks.

Eustace **Coleman** is butler at Mallow Hall at the beginning of DB68.

Sergeant **Collard,** an ex-sergeant of his Majesty's army, served in India until disabled by sunstroke; school sergeant at Sedleigh in MK09 and 10SW. W.J. Stone, whom he catches smoking, calls him "Boots." Has a son named Ernie.

Aloysius **Connolly,** a large, stout, square-faced man of commanding personality, labor leader and friend of Daniel

Brewster in 20MK/IA21.

John Beresford "Berry" **Conway**, 25, old school friend of Lord Biskerton in BM31, living at The Nook, Mulberry Grove, Valley Fields with his former nurse Hannah Wisdom. Raised by a rich aunt, widow of a man in the jute business, now employed as private secretary to Paterson Frisby. Lean, athletic-looking, in love with Ann Moon.

Mr. **Cook**[1], late sergeant in a line regiment, 6' 3", disposition amiable, left leg cut off above the knee by a spirited fuzzy in the last Soudan war, runs Cook's, a little confectioner's shop in the High Street of Wrykyn with his wife in 05IA and WF07.

Mr. **Cook**[2], short and elderly father of Vanessa in AA74, lives at Eggesford Court, Somerset. Rival of neighbor Col. Jimmy Briscoe and owner of a racehorse named Potato Chip who is emotionally attached to a black and white cat.

Charles Mereweather **Cook**, 14, a day boy at Wrykyn in GB04.

Vanessa **Cook**, daughter of Mr. Cook[2], a large and radiant beauty engaged to Orlo Porter and (briefly) to Bertie Wooster in AA74; studying Art at the Slade in London, active in political demonstrations.

J. Mereweather **Cooke**, a day boy, lives in the town of Wrykyn in 05RR.

Joey **Cooley**, child film star, mutinous Idol of American Motherhood in LG36, comes from Chillicothe, Ohio; Little Lord Fauntleroy type complete with curls.

Hildebrand Spencer ("Spennie") Poyns de Burgh John Hannasyde **Coombe-Crombie**, twelfth Earl of Dreever and nominal master of Dreever Castle, Shropshire in IJ10. Light-haired, weedy, in the twenties, nephew of Lady Julia Blunt.

Lancelot **Cooper**, junior partner in Caine & Cooper, house agents, High St., Market Blandings; shows Sunnybrae in PW52.

J.G. "Looney" **Coote**, superstitious friend of James Corcoran, was at Wrykyn School with him. A Drone rich beyond the dreams of avarice, as crazy a bimbo as ever went through life one jump ahead of the Lunacy Commissioners. Loud laugh, wide grin, sunny disposition. Owns a Winchester-Murphy auto which Ukridge steals in 23LA. Raids the Cedars dressed as a policeman in 47SS.

Ada **Cootes**, short and stocky daughter of a retired butler, secretary to Mike Bond in DB68, wooed and won by Horace Appleby.

Eddie **Cootes**, onetime cardsharper on the Atlantic Lines, at Blandings with Smooth Lizzie in LP23.

Myrtle **Cootes**, a kitchen maid in Green St., Mayfair, hired by Oofy Prosser in 48FO as training-camp cook for Porky Jupp and Plug Bosher. Niece of Jas Waterbury.

Frank and Percy **Coppin** are Muriel's permanently unemployed brothers in MM14.

Muriel **Coppin**, the landlord's daughter in MM14, is courted by Albert Potter. She is the first threat to Roland Bleke's happiness and independence.

Sir George **Copstone**, guest of Ponsford Botts in 48EX, business client of R.P. Crumbles—one of those tall, thin, bony Englishmen who seem to be left over from the 1860's, a slow golfer known as The Frozen Horror.

Bruce "Corky" **Corcoran**, aspiring portrait painter in New York in 16AC, commercial artist and cartoonist who creates "The Adventures of Baby Blobbs" for the comic section of the *Sunday Star*.

James "Corky" **Corcoran**, narrator of the Ukridge stories, an alter ego of the early PGW; writes articles for *Interesting Bits* and footling short stories about girls who turn out to be missing heiresses. Boyhood chum (at Wrykyn School) of S.F. Ukridge, who continues to prey upon his good nature. A graduate of Cambridge, he now rents a bedroom on Ebury Street, where he is attended by his landlord, the ex-butler Bowles. Frequent source of petty loans and articles of clothing pressed into service by Ukridge.

Mrs. Adela Shannon **Cork**, Hollywood relict of the late Alfred Cork in OR51. Sister of Wilhelmina Shannon. Owner of the Carmen Flores place in Hollywood; onetime Empress of Stormy Emotion in silent films, she retains her tall and stately figure, imperious look and formidable demeanor.

Clarissa **Cork**, widow of Wellesley Cork, a large, powerful, handsome woman in the middle forties; explorer and big-game huntress, author of *A Woman in the Wilds*. Runs a colony for the promotion of plain living and high thinking at Shipley Hall, which she has rented furnished from Lord Uffenham in MB42. Aunt of Lionel Green.

Nelson **Cork**, a member of the Drones, built like a minor jockey with a head like a peanut. Hat owner who courts Diana Punter and becomes engaged to her friend Elizabeth Bottsworth in 33AH. Has a cousin Fred, and an Aunt Clarissa who was involved in a scandal in 1922—the jury gave her the benefit of the doubt. Reappears as a Drone in 58FL.

Smedley **Cork**, brother of Mrs. Cork's late husband Alfred in OR51. A large, stout, elderly gentleman who looks like a Roman emperor who has been doing himself too well on starchy foods. Supported by his sister-in-law Adela in accordance with the terms of brother Alfred's will. Sought in marriage by Bill Shannon.

Corker is Oofy Prosser's man is 39SB.

Percy **Cornelius** of The Nook, Mulberry Grove, Valley Fields (cf. W. Dulwich), London S.E. 21, house agent in SS25, BM31, IB61. His office is on Ogilvy St. in SS25, where he rents Mon Repos to Sam Shotter. His firm is named Matters & Cornelius in BM31, where he lets Peacehaven to Lord Biskerton. White beard and bushy eyebrows, with the voice and appearance of a druid priest. Has lived all his life in Valley Fields, and does not get around much. Has been compiling a history of Valley Fields for a considerable time. Favorite author: Leila Yorke. Has a rich brother Charles who lives in America and falls out of his aeroplane during the course of IB61, leaving a $3-4 million fortune to his brother Percy, who then lends £3000 so that Freddie Widgeon can start his coffee plantation in Kenya.

Mrs. **Cornelius**, wife of the prec. in IB61, née Bulstrode of the Happy Haven Bulstrodes, a stout, comfortable woman.

Frederick Altamont **Cornwallis**: see Twistleton.

Sue **Cotterleigh**: see Sue Brown.

Reggie **Cracknell**, backer of *The Primrose Way* in AS22, in love with Mabel Hobson.

Sidney **Crane**, baritone, plays the hero in *The Girl from Brighton* in 15BB; his wife hires Henry Pifield Rice to watch him on tour.

Edwin **Craye**, Lord Weeting, elder son of Lord Worplesdon, is ten years younger than his sister Florence and six years older than his brother Percy. A mild, hopeless sort of ass in 12DO, spends all his time at Weeting and has never been known to come to London. He is writing a history of the family or something, but falls in love with Dorothea Darrell. Subsequently demoted to a ferret-faced juvenile, he is a pestilential stripling of 14 and Boy Scout in 16JT and JM46.

Lady Florence **Craye**, only daughter of Percy, Earl of Worplesdon, thereby becoming stepdaughter to Bertie Wooster's Aunt Agatha about eighteen months before JM46. First appears in 12DO, where she is head of the household at Eaton Square and the terror of her brothers Edwin, ten years her junior, and Percy, sixteen years her junior. Author of *Spindrift*, engaged to practically everybody at some time or another: Bertie Wooster in 16JT, JF54, and AA74, Stilton Cheesewright in JM46 and JF54, Percy Gorringe in JF54, Ginger Winship in MO71 and AA74, Boko Fittleworth, and an unnamed jockey: England is strewn with ex-fiancés whom she bounced because they did not come up to her expectations. Her eyes are bright and black, and have a way of getting right inside you and running up and down your spine. Tall and willowy, with a terrific profile and luxuriant platinum-blond hair, with as many curves as a scenic railway (cf. Daphne Dolores Morehead). One of those intellectual girls, steeped to the gills in serious purpose. Imperious as a traffic cop, she has what is called a presence. Hates a loser above all else and breaks off engagements as soon as a fiancé loses a race, an election, or any other contest.

Percy **Craye**[1], father of Florence, Edwin, and Percy[2], marries Dorothea Darrell in 12DO. Just prior to JM46, he marries Bertie Wooster's Aunt Agatha, thereby becoming Bertie's uncle by marriage. In the *Colliers* version of 12DO he is an American who made his fortune in the Soup Trust. Elsewhere he is Lord Worplesdon, q.v.

Percy **Craye**[2] (named Douglas or Duggie in the *Colliers* version of 12DO), younger son of Lord Worplesdon, is Reggie Pepper's dear old pal and a member of the Guards. Brother of Florence and Edwin, he is the first of his family to become entangled with Dorothea Darrell.

Adela **Cream**, wife of Homer and mother of Wilbert and Wilfred in HR60. Tall and thin with a hawk-like face, writes mystery stories, e.g. *Blackness at Night*.

Homer **Cream**, big American tycoon who suffers from ulcers, husband of Adela and father of Wilbert and Wilfred in HR60.

Wilbert or Willie **Cream**, elder son of Homer Cream and brother of Wilfred in HR60. Teaches romance languages at one of the great American universities, in England on sabbatical, in love with Phyllis Mills. Willowy bird with ginger hair and a small moustache, about the tonnage and general aspect of David Niven. Collects old silver.

Wilfred **Cream**, younger brother of Wilbert in HR60, New York playboy known as Broadway Willie, notorious for his escapades and thrice divorced.

The Rt. Hon. the adenoidal Marquess of **Cricklewood** makes a speech for candidate B.V. Lawlor at the Associated Mechanics' Hall, Redbridge, in 23LA.

Bingley **Crocker**, 50, once a small-part actor in New York, now five years married to Eugenia, sister of Nesta Ford Pett, and living in Drexdale House, Grosvernor Square. Misses baseball. Father of Piccadilly Jim in PJ17, plays Skinner the butler in the Pett household.

Eugenia **Crocker**, ambitious sister of Nesta Ford Pett, five years married to Bingley in PJ17 and determined to become a leading figure in London society. Previously married to the late G.G. van Brunt, the well-known Pittsburgh millionaire.

James Braithwaite **Crocker**, title character of PJ17, son of Bingley Crocker; suitor of Ann Chester.

Croome buttles for the unnamed narrator of 06FM.

Barbara **Crowe**, junior partner in Edgar Saxby & Sons, literary agents in CT58, widow of a friend of the Earl of Ickenham who was killed in a motor accident. Once engaged to Beefy

Bastable; undeniably attractive, with a wide, humorous mouth and a kindly briskness of manner.

Crowinshaw is Charteris' fag in 03MC.

Algernon P. **Crufts**, a Drone, was at Oxford with Clifford Gandle. Tennis partner of Bobbie Wickham in 26PT, crony of Ambrose Wiffin in 28PA.

R.P. **Crumbles**, purveyor of Silver Sardines (the Sardine With A Soul) in 48EX, vainly orders Horace Bewstridge to play Customer's Golf against Sir George Copstone.

Edwin **Crump**, a young man of extraordinary gravity of countenance, private secretary and French interpreter to Benjamin Scobell in PA12 and PB12.

Charles Percy **Cuthbertson**, the Old Stepper, Ukridge's supposed Uncle from Australia (married Ukridge's late stepmother's stepsister Alice), title character in 28UO. A professional scrounger, acquires a sundial, a summer house, and several dozen roses from Col. Bayliss to aid Ukridge's courtship of Myrtle Bayliss.

Cyril is the boy who cleans the knives and spoons at Blandings in 36CW.

D

Joseph **Dacre**, housemaster in 02HP, 02BD, 02WM, 03HS, and other tales of St Austin's, has a finished gift of sarcasm. Engaged to Florence Beezley in 02BD. In 05LB he is curate of a parish and a cricket team at Marvis Bay, Devonshire. Played for Cambridge in the nineties, and is still a sound and pretty bat of the Jimmy Douglas type.

Bertie Wooster's Aunt **Dahlia**: see Dahlia Wooster.

Daintree is House-prefect at Merevale's, St Austin's in PH02, 03MC.

A Miss **Dalgleish**, daughter of Old Colonel Dalgleish, is a dog girl in 30TC: largish, corn-fed.

Dalgliesh is a member of the Heath Hall cricket team in 05BI.

John **Dalgliesh**, a middle-aged bounder in loud checks who digs up the turf of the cricket pitch at St Austin's with his walking stick, is Richard Venables' Uncle John in 01AF.

Dallas, a student at Ward's house, St Austin's College in PH02, shares a study with Vaughan and Plunkett.

Reginald **Dallas**, successful suitor of Sylvia Reynolds, outshoots her father Col. Reynolds in 01WP.

Flossie **Dalrymple**, barmaid at the Blue Anchor in Knightsbridge who marries Battling Billson in 35CB; identical to Flossie Burns in 23DB, 23RB. In SF57 her family name is changed once again to Keggs.

Vera **Dalrymple**, actress in Joseph Pickering's *Cousin Angela* in BA73.

Jasper **Daly**, Bill West's uncle in BC24, is brother-in-law to Cooley Paradene and one of his many poor relations. An unsuccessful inventor.

Joe **Danby**, father of Ray Denison in 15EY, won't let her marry outside vaudeville. Formidable old boy with thick eyebrows and a sort of determined expression, usually looks like a cross between a Roman emperor and Napoleon Bonaparte in a bad temper. Long an ardent admirer of Bertie Mannering-Phipps' Aunt Julia, with whom he worked in the music halls.

Danvers, a worthless student at Beckford College in PU03, allies himself with Jack Monk and Waterford.

Mae **D'Arcy**, "The Duchess," member of the ensemble of *The Rose of America* in LW20.

Dorothea **Darrell**, widow of a soldier in a line regiment, works as a palmist in the beginning of 12DO, where after a flirtation with Percy Craye[2] and his brother Edwin, she marries their father, Lord Worplesdon, and becomes Florence Craye's stepmother.

Edward **Darrell**: see Kid Brady.

James **Datchett**, aspiring writer just out of Oxford, assistant-master at Harrow House in 09OS.

Horace **Davenport**: see Horace Pendlebury-Davenport.

Joe **Davenport**, friend of Bill Shannon in OR51, with whom he worked on the Superba-Llewellyn lot, blacklisted for throwing a richly-bound copy of the *Saturday Evening Post* at Ivor Llewellyn's head. Back from New York with the remains of a $24,000 radio jackpot. Loves Kay Shannon.

Eustace **Davenport-Simms**, ex-fiancé of Clarissa Binstead in 51HT.

Davies shares Study Sixteen at Donaldson's house, Wrykyn, with Bellwood in 04RS. A slacker like Bellwood, who shelters behind a doctor's certificate and enjoys tormenting Dixon.

Mrs. **Davis** is cook at Mallow Hall in DB68.

Polly **Davis**: see Pauline, Countess of Wetherby.

Dawkins[1], St Austin's Gym Instructor in PH02.

Dawkins[2] is former coach of the First Trinity Crew in NG07.

Dawlish is the grocer at Lyme Regis in LC05.

William Fitzwilliam Delamere Chalmers, Lord **Dawlish**, beneficiary of the late Ira J. Nutcombe in UM16 (cured him of his slice). A large, penniless young man in excellent condition, with a pleasant, goodhumoured, brown, clean-cut face. Engaged to Claire Fenwick, in love with Elizabeth Boyd.

Elaine **Dawn** (SF57): see Emma Billson.

Mr. **Dawson**, not of Scotland Yard, Stuttering Sam's accomplice in 25BD.

Mr. **Day** is master of the Wrykyn Lower Fifth in 04HT; a serious man without a spark of humour in his composition, and a tremendous enthusiasm for fairness. Henfrey's housemaster at Wrykyn in 04JE, P.A. Dunstable's housemaster at Locksley in 05CL (where he collects autographs) and 05AH.

Pearl **Delahay** has escaped from an upstate town near the Canadian border named Franklin, where she is married to Brewster Gooch and has a three-year-old son Elmer. In 29BG, she has a place on the chorus of *Ask Dad*.

Ferdinand James **Delamere**, 6th Earl of Wivelscombe, superstitious father of Geraldine Spettisbury in 33LS, kicks Stiffy Stiffham 11' 2" (a record for the midland counties) when he sees him locked in a close embrace with his daughter Geraldine.

George Francis Augustus **Delamere**: see Murgatroyd.

Cyril **Delancy**, golfing detective hired by William Bates in 25PR.

Loretta **Delancy**, a widow from Pittsburgh who met Horace Prosser on the boat in 58FL.

Vera **Delane**, Prosser's fiancée in 11PO.

Mr. **Dencroft**, one of the most popular masters at Eckleton in HK05, takes over Mr. Kay's house.

Lois **Denham**, Jill Mariner's special friend on the chorus of *The Rose Of America* in LW20; her boy friend's name is Izzy.

Ray **Denison**, daughter of Joe Danby in 15EY, New York vaudeville performer loved by Gussie Mannering-Phipps.

Dent shares a study with Hammond next to Rigby's in Seymour's house at Wrykyn in 05RR.

Eddie **Denton**, Mortimer Sturgis' best friend in 20MT where he is an explorer just back from central Africa, marries Betty Weston.

Kay **Derrick**, daughter of the late Col. Eustace Derrick of Midways Hall, Wilts., 22, works as secretary-companion to Mrs. Winnington-Bates in SS25 until driven off by the attentions of her son Claude. Lives with uncle Matthew Wrenn; courted by Sam Shotter.

Norah **Derrick**, daughter of Prof. Derrick, engaged to Lieut. Tom Chase in LC06.

Prof. Patrick **Derrick**, short-tempered father of Phyllis and Norah in LC06, teaches at Dublin University and owns a summer house at Combe Regis, Dorsetshire.

Phyllis **Derrick**, sister of Norah, consents to Jeremy Garnet's proposal of marriage in LC06.

Ronny **Devereux** is one of Freddie Rooke's London friends in LW20.

Charlotte, Emmeline, Harriet & Myrtle **Deverill**: see Esmond Haddock.

Aubrey Rockmetteller **Devine**, known to the world of 15AA as I-forget-his-name, Adelaide Brewster Moggs' husband, rescues Genevieve O'Grady from the whirling waters of the Hudson River.

Raymond Parsloe **Devine**, rising young American novelist but no golfer, a pale young man in horn-rimmed spectacles. Cuthbert Banks' rival for Adeline Smethurst in 21UC.

Mr. Robert **Dexter** runs the most lawless of the houses at Wrykyn in GB04; in 04JE, he regards his house as a warder might a gang of convicts. Fives is his one relaxation. He is

O'Hara's house master in 04JE and 05DE. G. Montgomery Chapple's form-master in 05PP, still a house-master in WF07.

The Rev. Cuthbert **Dibble** of Boustead Parva, Glos., starter in the Great Sermon Handicap in 22SH/IJ23.

Ferdinand **Dibble**, a sensitive and introspective goof in love with Barbara Medway in 23HG, has permitted gold to eat into his soul like some malignant growth.

Pauline **Dicey**, a coquette in 10WD.

Mrs. **Digby**, housekeeper at Belpher Castle in DD19.

Dimsdale, one of the two School House fags in PH02.

Steve **Dingle**, 28, retired prize-fighter, friend and sparring partner of Kirk Winfield in WH14, godfather of William Bannister Winfield. Physical instructor at the New York Athletic Club; in love with William's nurse Mamie.

Charlotte **Dix**, long-suffering fiancée of Wallace Chesney in 22MP.

Rev. W. **Dix**, vicar of Little Clickton-in-the-Wold, starts at 9-2 odds in the Great Sermon Handicap in 22SH/IJ23.

Dixon[1] lives in Donaldson's house at Wrykyn in 04RS. A mild, spectacled youth who does an astonishing amount of work, as much a hermit as anyone can be in a public-school house. Has a large collection of Greek plays.

Dixon[2] is Arthur Mifflin's valet in IJ10.

Rupert **Dixon**, an unpleasant young man but a suave golfer, candidate for treasurer of the Paterson Dyeing & Refining Co. in 19OG.

Wall-Eyed **Dixon** runs a big boxing-place in the East End in 35CB.

P.C. Ernest **Dobbs**, the local rozzer at King's Deverill in MS49 and the village atheist, engaged to Queenie Silversmith. Chunky and nobbly.

Dobson is Sir Roderick Glossop's butler in 65JG.

Constable **Dobson**, tall, lean, and stringy nephew to Constable Voules in TY34, keeps company with Mary, redheaded parlourmaid at Chuffnell Hall.

Jacob **Dodson** of Detroit is Daniel Rackstraw's rival in collecting baseball memorabilia in 10PP. He puts up his Hans Wagner bat against Rackstraw's Neal Ball glove that the

Giants will beat the Tigers in a private game at the Rackstraw country estate. In 12GK he is a rugby football fan from Manchester, his pet team is Manchester United, and he competes with Rackstraw in collecting football memorabilia.

Elsa **Doland**, a pretty girl with big eyes who lives in Mrs. Meecher's boarding house in AS22, actress in *The Primrose Way*. Briefly married to Gerald Foster.

Daphne **Dolby** of the Eagle Eye Detective Agency is betrothed to Sir Jaklyn Warner in BA73. Hired to monitor Sally Fish's smoking.

Officer **Donahue**, New York cop in 21SE/IA21, believes the Shannon will one day flow in blood to the sea.

Donald, uncle of Ginger Kemp and Bruce Carmyle in AS22, lives at Monk's Crofton, Much Middlefold, Shropshire. 62, weighs 240 pounds, mackerel-eyed, highly respected in the National Liberal Club but has a personality which would have cast a sobering influence over the orgies of the emperor Tiberius at Capri.

Mr. **Donaldson**, father of Aggie in 24CP, a tall, handsome, smooth-faced gentleman of authoritative appearance with rimless glasses. A firm believer in President Roosevelt and the New Deal, though his fortune has shrunk to $9-10 million. Founder and head of Donaldson's Dog-Biscuits.

Niagara or Aggie **Donaldson**, Freddie Threepwood's American fiancée, later his wife, daughter of Donaldson's Dog-Biscuits, cousin to Angus McAllister in 24CP. Named after the Niagara Falls Hotel, where her parents spent their honeymoon; now living in Great Neck, NY.

Penelope **Donaldson**, younger sister of Niagara in PW52; a small, slender girl with fair hair, in love with Jerry Vail.

M. **D'Orby**: see Orby.

Billie **Dore**, one of the chorus of George Bevan's musical comedy *Follow the Girl*, playing at the Regal in DD19. Daughter of an Indiana nursery gardener, marries Lord Marshmoreton.

Earl **Dorm** of the Hills, a small, elderly man with a furtive air and six daughters in 12SA.

Mr. **Dorman**, Shropshire farmer, old acquaintance and host of

Owen Bentley in 11PO.

Mrs. **Dorman** tells Owen Bentley's fortune in 11PO.

George **Dorman**, son of the above in 11PO.

Dorothy, the Head's niece at St Austin's, is the twelve-year-old girl with the bicycle rescued by Charteris from the two Rural Hooligans at Rutton in 03MC.

Lady Chloe **Downblotton**, beautiful daughter of the 7th Earl of Choole, related on her mother's side to the Somersetshire Meophams, the Brashmarleys of Bucks, the Widringtons of Wilts, and the Hilsbury-Hepworths of Hants. Her second cousin Adelaide is married to Lord Slythe and Sayle; among the branches of the family are the Sussex Booles and the ffrench-ffarmiloes of Sorsetshire; engaged to an artist named Claude in 29SC.

Mr. **Downing**, Adair's housemaster at Sedleigh in MK09 and games-master in 10SW, is a short, wiry little man with a sharp nose and a general resemblance to an excitable bullfinch; head of the school Fire Brigade and keen promoter of cricket at Sedleigh.

Drake beats Jim Thomson in the mile at the College races in PH02.

Sir Hugo **Drake**, a Harley Street nerve specialist in DS32, uncle of Bill Bannister.

Cynthia **Drassilis**, a tall, strikingly handsome girl with a rather hard and cynical cast of countenance in LN13. Daughter of the Hon. Hugo Drassilis, younger brother of the Earl of Westbourne. Engaged to Peter Burns, she induces him to participate in a scheme to kidnap Ogden Ford from Sanstead House.

Lord **Dreever**: see Hildebrand Spencer Poyns de Burgh John Hannasyde Coombe-Crombie, twelfth Earl of Dreever.

Rev. Henry **Drew**, cricketing curate, captain of the side and engaged to Dolly Burn in 05TD.

Mrs. **Driver**, James Orlebar Cloyster's landlady at 93A Manresa Road, Chelsea, in NG07.

Anthony Claude Wilbraham Bryce, Lord **Droitwich**, fifth Earl of Droitwich and master of Langley End, Worcestershire in IW31. Phone Langley 330. A massive young man on the borderland of thirty. A changeling as in the story of the "Baby's Vengeance" in the *Bab Ballads*, he was born to Bella Price over a barber's shop in Mott Street, Knightsbridge. His alter ego is Syd Price, q.v. In love with Polly Brown.

Drummond, a featherweight boxer at Wrykyn in GB04, lives in Seymour's in 05AB and WF07; winner of the Feather Weights at Aldershot, a member of the first fifteen and the second eleven.

Drusilla, man-eating girl with whom Freddie Widgeon is infatuated in 34NO.

Claude **Duff**, nervous young junior secretary to Sir James Piper in SB77; shared a study at Wrykyn with Jeff Bennison. Nephew of Daphne Winkworth and of Duff & Trotter, the provision people. Tall, aggressively good-looking, impeccably dressed.

James Buchanan **Duff** the Ham King, creator of the Paramount Ham and trustee of the fortune of Lord Holbeton in QS40. Managing Director of Duff & Trotter, London's leading provision merchants. A large, dyspeptic man, once engaged to and still in love with Beatrice Chavender.

Clarence **Dumphry**, son of J. Mortimer Dumphry, rejected suitor of Ann Frisby in BM31. A stiff.

Robert **Dunhill**, employee of the New Asiatic Bank in 23UA.

T. Mortimer **Dunlop**, business associate of Franklyn Bivatt in 13JW, is a bald, purple-faced millionaire and a dead-game sport who wheezes when he speaks.

Detective **Dunn** of the Metropolitan Police force is felled by Kid Brady as he tries to arrest Grace Grant in 06BA.

Alaric Pendlebury-Davenport, Duke of **Dunstable**, was at Eton and Cambridge. A large, stout, bald-headed man with an unpleasantly loud voice, jutting nose, prominent eyes and a bushy white moustache of the type favored by regimental sergeant majors and walruses, which he is always blowing at, causing it to leap like a rocketing pheasant. Large outstanding ears like those on a Greek amphora. Uninvited guest at Blandings in UF39, SS61, PB69. An opinionated, arbitrary, autocratic resident of Wiltshire, where his standing among his neighbors is roughly that of a shark at a bathing resort; considers everybody he encounters to be "potty." Uncle to Horace Pendlebury-Davenport, Ricky Gilpin, and Linda Gilpin, his court-appointed ward in PB69. In UF39 displays tendency to destroy rooms with a poker when angry. Nervous of fire; invites himself to Blandings in PB69 following a fire at his Wiltshire house. A onetime suitor of Constance Keeble, who continues to show a certain fond tolerance of him (Alaric ended their engagement because her father refused to meet his terms in the matter of a dowry). Once tried to get himself elected to the old Pelican Club, was heavily blackballed. Long a widower, once married to a rich girl who was the daughter of one of those rich chaps up North who make cups and basins and things; her death left him twice a millionaire but always on the lookout to become richer.

P.A. Dunstable of Day's, Locksley School, Founder-President of Locksley Lines Supplying Trust, Ltd. in 05CL, autograph hunter in 05AH. A Wrykyn boy in 05LP and a loyal customer of Cook's in the town of Wrykyn in 05IA, where he laces the buckwheat cakes at Ring's with sal ammoniac. A resident of Day's at Wrykyn in WF07, friend of Linton.

Dunster is the boy who paints Mr. Downing's bull terrier Sampson red in MK09.

Heloise, Princess von und zu **Dwornitzchek**, relict of the late Franklin Vanringham, divorced wife of Prince v. u. z. Dwornitzchek in SM37. Stepmother of Tubby and Joe Vanringham; her first husband was a Mr. Spelvin, Elmer Chinnery's partner in the glue business. A large, sinuous woman, described as the sand in civilization's spinach.

E

Edmund is the boot-boy at Outwood's, Sedleigh, in MK09.

Joseph Edwardes, defeated pugilist in 10WD.

Egbert[1], a cousin of Jeeves, constable at Beckley-on-the-Moor in 25WO.

Egbert[2], one of two swans resident at Mulberry Grove, Valley Fields in BM31.

Egbert[3], cousin of Barmy Phipps in 36MT and CT58, student at Harrow and a dead shot with a catapult.

Blair **Eggleston**, angry young novelist, author of *Worm i' the Root* and *Offal*, is engaged to Jane Opal at the beginning of HW32. In 65JG he is in love with Honoria Glossop, and doing a series on the Modern Girl for *Milady's Boudoir*.

Ellen is cook at Towcester Abbey in RJ53.

Mrs. **Ellis**, Mabel Steptoe's cook at Claines Hall in QS40, is discovered to have a natural aptitude for craps.

Aline **Ellison**, courted by Lord Bertie Fendall and John Barton in 10LM, loves John's bulldog Reuben.

G.B. **Ellison**, inseparable friend of Selwicke in 05LP, is in the Sixth and a house prefect at Donaldson's. Becomes Selwicke's rival for the last place on the Wrykyn 11.

Tom **Ellison**, friend of Dick Henley and his rival for Dolly Burn, plays cricket for love in 05TD.

Miss **Elphinstone**, lady receptionist at the Gish Galleries in SF57.

Mrs. **Elphinstone** broke up her brother's courtship of Eve Hendrie in 11BS.

Hildebrand **Elphinstone** was Eve Hendrie's previous charge in 11BS.

George **Emerson**, suitor of Aline Peters in SN15, sturdy young man with a small moustache and wiry red-brown hair; second-in-command of the Hong Kong police.

Emily is John Carroll's Welsh terrier in MN28.

Empress of Blandings, the black Berkshire sow owned by Lord Emsworth in nine Blandings novels, introduced in 27PH. The only pig that has ever won the silver medal in the Fat Pigs class three years in succession at the eighty-seventh, eighty-eighth, and eighty-ninth annual Shropshire Agricultural Show. Resembles a captive balloon with ears and a tail. Her keepers are variously George Cyril Wellbeloved, Percy Pirbright (last heard of in Canada), Edwin Pott (retired into private life after winning a football pool), and Monica Simmons (who elopes with Wilfred Allsop).

The Empress under the admiring gaze of
Lord Emsworth and Wellbeloved

Lord **Emsworth**: see Clarence Threepwood.

Trevor "Catsmeat" **Entwhistle**, Headmaster of Harchester in 27BM, onetime schoolmate and particular crony of Boko, later Bishop of Stortford.

Epstein, art agent and picture-dealer in 10MU.

Erb, collector for bookie George Budd in UF39; attached to Percy Stout in the same capacity in 67US.

'Erbert is the potboy at the Emsworth Arms in FM47.

Erbut[1], plug-ugly who works for Oofy Prosser's bookie in 37AW.

Erbut[2] cleans the knives and boots at Bumpleigh Hall in JM46.

Erbut[3] cleans the boots at the Bull's Head in UD48.

Ern is Gladys' little brother in 28EG.

Ernest, second quarrelsome burglar in 28OO.

Jefferson Auguste, Comte d'**Escrignon**: see Jefferson Auguste.

Madame **Eulalie**: see May Stubbs.

Eustace, monkey kept by Polly Wetherby in UM16 on the advice of her publicist, Roscoe Sheriff. Shot by Dudley Pickering.

Evans, Morrison's fag at St Austin's in 01PP; a small, stout youth with a rich uncle, loses a sovereign in 10PD.

Police Constable **Evans** maintains order in Market Blandings in 27PH (where he arrests pigman George Cyril Wellbeloved for being drunk and disorderly in the taproom of the Goat & Feathers) and PW52; assisted in BG65 by brother-in-arms Officer Morgan.

Llewellyn "Basher" **Evans**, colossal safe-cracker in Horace Appleby's entourage in DB68, gets religion and retires.

Lord **Evenwood**, master of Evenwood Towers and brother of Lady Sophia Kimbuck, tries to marry his niece, Lady Eva Blyton, to Roland Bleke in MM14.

Sir Everard **Everett** becomes British ambassador to Washington in JF54.

Eva **Eversleigh**, niece of the Gunton-Cresswells, cousin of Julian Eversleigh in NG07. Petite, dark, brown hair, very big blue eyes, retroussé nose, rather wide mouth; briefly engaged to James Orlebar Cloyster.

Julian **Eversleigh**, cousin of Eva Eversleigh, one of the narrators of NG07. Friend of James Orlebar Cloyster; went to Oxford with Malim. Green eyes, red hair, writes advertisements for Skeffington's. One of nature's slackers until energized by love for his cousin Eva. Modeled on Herbert W. Westbrook, eccentric assistant master at a small preparatory school called Emsworth House. Cf. S.F. Ukridge.

F

Sally **Fairmile**, poor relation of Mrs. Steptoe in QS40, the orphan daughter of distant cousins. Small and slight with blue eyes; engaged to George Trotter, wooed by Joss Weatherby.

Jane **Falconer**, friend of Bobbie Wickham in 28PA and 40DI.

Col. **Fanshawe** of Marling Hall, a frequent host of Freddie Threepwood in 66FA. Fox-hunter, local Master of Hounds, father of Valerie Fanshawe.

Valerie **Fanshawe**, daughter of above in 66FA, a dish and a pippin.

Col. & Mrs. R.G. **Fanshawe-Chadwick**, parents of Sybil in SF57.

Faraday, a light-haired young man in charge of the London office of a New York dramatists' representative in PB12, was at Cambridge with John Maude.

Alice **Faraday**, secretary to Lord Marshmoreton in DD19, marries Reggie Byng.

Prof. Pepperidge **Farmer**, author of a book on hypnotism in 65ST; gaunt-faced, looks like Count Dracula.

Reginald **Farnie**, title character of PU03, Gethryn's juvenile uncle who is four years younger than his nephew. Enters Lower Fourth at Beckford College after being sacked from Harrow and Wellington, lives in Leicester's, where his nephew is prefect.

Belinda or Bunny **Farringdon** of Plunkett Mews, Onslow Square, South Kensington, engaged to Johnny Pearce in CT58.

Maxwell **Faucitt**, oldest inhabitant of Mrs. Meecher's boarding-house in AS22, a former actor and emigrant from England; inherits his brother's dress-making place in Regent Street, Laurette & Cie.

Gladys "Toots" **Fauntleroy**, girl friend of Lancelot Topham in OR51.

Dame Flora **Faye**, the actress, relict of the late Charles Upshaw of Upshaw's Diet Bread, mother of Vera Upshaw in GB70 and author of *Theatre Memories* (as told to Reginald Tressilian).

General Sir Frederick **Featherstone**, trustee of Bond's Bank in DB68, a guffin; tall lean stringy white-moustached ex-officer approaching the seventies.

Felstone is a member of the Heath Hall cricket team in 05BI.

Lady Angelica **Fendall**, remembered by Keggs[1] as a romantic and a lover of poetry in 10GA, daughter of Lord Stockleigh.

Lord Bertie (for Herbert) **Fendall**, son and heir of the Earl of Stockheath, Angelica's brother remembered in 10GA, is interested in Aline Ellison in 10LM. A buzzer with a high-pitched voice, afraid of dogs.

Desmond **Fendall**, an Oxford Blue at cricket, lives with his parents in Ovington Square in S.W. London in 06TP. Son of a man with no profession and considerable fortune, now mostly lost in mining stock purchased from Paul Bond. Becomes a pro for Middlesex under the pseudonym Gray. Engaged to Alice Bond.

Robert Mowbray **Fenn**, an exceptional all-around cricketer, is also a musician who plays the piano; head of Kay's house, Eckleton in HK05. Has an older brother who was at Cambridge.

Claire **Fenwick**, tall and willowy actress engaged to Lord Dawlish at the beginning of UM16. Large grey eyes, strikingly handsome, lives with her mother in a West Kensington flat. Friend of Daisy Leonard, who arranges her meeting with Dudley Pickering.

Percy **Fenwick**, Claire's vile ten-year-old brother in UM16.

Mr. **Ferguson** is head of Locksley School in 04AD.

Archie **Ferguson**, a Futurist painter with a studio in Chelsea and a dear old friend of Reggie Pepper, does a good imitation of an Irish cook talking to an Italian organ-grinder. Hasn't sold a single picture in three years as a painter, but does the Doughnut family for a weekly paper called *Funny Slices*. Marries Eunice Nugent in 15CA.

Rev. Cyril **Ferguson**, curate at Little Weeting, Hants. in DD19.

Robert **Ferguson**, former employer of Roland Bean in 1MM.

Etienne **Feriaud**, intrepid French aviator in MM14, helps Roland Bleke escape the Coppins.

Charles **Fermin**, editor of the *Orb* in NG07.

Ferris[1], an agent of the usurper Maharajah of Estapore in LS08, tries to get The Tear of Heaven, a.k.a. The Luck Stone. Probably a broken army man who has got mixed up in shady affairs. His partner is a Major Marshall.

Ferris[2] is valet to Percy, Lord Stockheath in SN15.

Andrew **Ferris**, the large, ponderous, and gloomy butler employed for Ashby Hall in PP67. Rubicund, balding, 54; formerly employed at Brangmarley Manor, Little-Seeping-in-the-Wold, Shropshire. A widower who disapproves of marriage and posterity.

Charlie **Ferris** owns a drug store in Ashley, Maine and thinks New York is the life in 15AG.

Mary **Ferris**, neglected wife of Charlie in 15AG, wins the Lover-ly Silver Cup with some help from Mrs. John Tyson.

Rupert Antony **Ferris**, butler to the Waddingtons in SB27, formerly butler at Brangmarley Hall, Little-Seeping-in-the-Wold, Salop. Forty-six inches in the waist, disapproves of Swedes because their heads are too square, of Irish because they are Irish.

Sir Jasper **ffinch-ffarrowmere**, Bart., of ffinch Hall, Yorkshire, a very stout man with a broad pink face, guardian of Angela Purdue in 26SL.

Percy **ffinch-ffarrowmere**, son of the above in 26SL.

Sally **Field** is a chorus girl for Mason & Saxby in FP29, where Sue Brown saves her job by quitting her own.

The Right Hon. A.B. **Filmer**, pres. of the Anti-Tobacco League and a Cabinet Minister, is Aunt Agatha's guest and victim of Thos in 26JI, where he and Bertie Wooster are chivvied by an angry swan onto the roof of a shack known as the

Octagon on the island in the lake at Woollam Chersey.

Sgt. **Finbow**, police officer at Valley Fields in BM31, engaged to Hannah Wisdom.

Colonel **Finch**, a stolid individual with a bald forehead and a walrus moustache, one of a delegation of four gamblers to John Maude, Prince of Mervo, in PB12.

Dudley **Finch**, a Drone who suffers for his infatuation with Bobbie Wickham in 25AG, is cousin to Roland Attwater. In 40DI he is back in London after two years of sheepfarming in western Australia for his godfather and benefactor Sampson Broadhurst. Engaged to Ellabelle "Stinky" Prebble, he again falls (briefly) under the malign influence of Bobbie Wickham.

Ernie **Finch**, former suitor of Mabel Price in 23NW, gives S.F. Ukridge a black eye.

George **Finch**, originally from East Gilead, Idaho, title character and resident of a small bachelor apartment on top of the Sheridan Apartment House near Washington Square in SB27. Slim and slight, with pleasant, undistinguished face, brown eyes, and chestnut hair. The worst painter in New York, heir to the fortune of his late uncle Thomas of Finch, Finch, Finch, Butterfield & Finch, the Corporation Law firm. In love with Molly Waddington.

Rollo **Finch**, nephew and designated heir of millionaire Andrew Galloway of Pittsburgh in 11AS. Cf. Barmy Barminster in 57WT.

Julian **Fineberg**, head of the Bury St. Edwards Seed Company, is Roland Bleke's employer at the beginning of MM14.

Edward "Finky" **Finglass**, recently deceased in Buenos Aires, took $2 million from the New Asiatic Bank and hid it in Mon Repos, Valley Fields, where it is found in SS25.

Augustus **Fink-Nottle**, fish-faced newt-keeper in RH34, CW38, MS49, SU63. Small and shrimplike, a teetotaler (but also a Drone), pre-eminent subnormal who wears horn-rimmed glasses. Engaged to Madeline Bassett in CW38. Chinless recluse who can't stand London, spends his time in a remote village in Lincolnshire; Nature's final word in cloth-headed guffins, he prefers company of newts, which he keeps in a glass tank.

Gussie Fink-Nottle

In RH34 after drinking a large amount of Aunt Dahlia's whiskey in order to muster courage to propose to Madeline Bassett, he drinks a pitcherful of orange juice (his customary beverage) spiked with two tumblers of gin immediately prior to making a speech and distributing prizes at Market Snodsbury Grammar School. Still engaged to Madeline Bassett in MS49, where he impersonates Bertie Wooster. Elopes with Emerald Stoker in SU63.

Firby-Smith, called the Gazeka, is head of Wain's at Wrykyn in MK09; all spectacles and front teeth.

Firman, a member of the Lower Fifth at Wrykyn in 06DS, sees Merrett cheating in his French exam.

Lady Julia **Fish**, relict of the late Major-General Sir Miles Fish, C.B.E., late of the Brigade of Guards, a man whose wild days are featured in Galahad's memoirs. One of the twelve Threepwood scions, including Lady Constance, Galahad, and Clarence, Lord Emsworth. Mother of Ronnie. First mentioned in FP29, joins Lady Constance's efforts to suppress Galahad's memoirs in HW33. A handsome middle-aged woman of the large blonde type, with a breezy and commanding personality; once bit a governess in two places.

Ronald Overbury **Fish**, Lord Emsworth's nephew, son of Lady Julia Fish and Miles Fish, cousin to George Fish. A small, pink Drone of extraordinary solemnity, the last of the Fishes. Went to Eton and Trinity with Hugo Carmody, his partner in a night club called The Hot Spot just off Bond Street in MN28. This enterprise has failed in FP29, where he is the title character and woos Sue Brown. Still engaged to Sue in HW33, where he must overcome Lady Constance Keeble's objection to his marriage. His valet is named Bessemer.

Isadore **Fishbein** is President of Perfecto-Fishbein, a motion picture corporation, in 33RM.

Bradbury **Fisher**, of Goldenville, L.I., one of America's most prominent tainted millionaires (Sing-Sing # 8,097,564), golfing rival of Gladstone Bott in 25HS. Handicap of 24. Misspent youth in the pursuits of commerce, now no halfhearted enthusiast of golf and collector of golfing relics. In 26KI, where his particular friend and fellow Sing-Sing graduate is

Rupert Worple, he makes sacrifices to keep in favor with his new butler Vosper.

Evangeline Maplebury **Fisher**, wife of Bradbury, daughter of Mrs. Lora Smith Maplebury, acquires Vosper in 25HS, does everything to keep in with him in 26KI.

Jerry **Fisher**, a little, ferret-faced man, is Bill Bramble's trainer in 13KI.

Smooth Sam **Fisher** poses as butler-detective White at Sanstead House in 13EC and LN13; his object is to kidnap Ogden Ford and retire from the kidnapping profession with the proceeds. His first attempt to do this (in New York in 1906) miscarried.

Sir Abercrombie **Fitch**, headshrinking colleague of Sir Roderick Glossop in FM47 (where his surname is reduplicated) and PB69.

Clarice **Fitch** becomes Mrs. Ernest Plinlimmon and a golfer of queenly dignity as a result of developments in 36AG.

Sarah or Sally **Fitch**, daughter of Rev. Herbert Fitch, vicar of Much Middlefold, Worcestershire; twice engaged to Sir Jaklyn Warner, reporter in BA73, formerly secretary-companion to the late Letitia Carberry, from whom she inherits an apartment at 3A Fountain Court and £25,000 on condition she never smoke. In love with Joe Pickering.

Freddie **Fitch-Fitch** is affianced to Annabel Purvis in 37RD.

George Webster "Boko" **Fittleworth**, friend of Bertie Wooster and author of wholesome fiction for the masses, engaged to Nobby Hopwood in JM46. A Drone, once engaged to Florence Craye. In appearance a cross between a comedy juggler and a parrot that has been dragged through a hedge backward. One-time flatmate of Ginger Winship in MO71.

Agnes **Flack**, distant cousin of Mr. Mulliner of Angler's Rest, a tournament golfer in 27TP, one of the Devonshire Mulliners. By 40SM she has been the undisputed female champion of the club. In 48TH she is still the female club champion and owns a wolfhound. A fine, large, handsome girl built rather on the lines of Popeye the sailor: 160 pounds, all muscle, with a voice that sounds like the down express letting off steam at a level crossing. Niece of millionaire Josiah

Flack; engaged to Sydney McMurdo in 50FC, where she becomes briefly infatuated with Captain Jack Fosdyke. Still intermittently engaged to McMurdo in 65ST, where she has written a novel.

Josiah **Flack**, uncle of Agnes Flack in 50FC; old and frail with one foot in the grave, one of the richest men in America. Host of Captain Jack Fosdyke at Sands Point.

Egbert **Flannery**, assistant to Dr. Twist at Healthward Ho in MN28. An ex-sergeant-major with a long, blonde and bushy waxed moustache with needle-point ends. Six feet two in his socks with broad shoulders and prawn-like eyes.

G.J. **Flannery**, author's agent, member of Bachelors Anonymous in BA73.

Harry **Fletcher**, theatrical agent for *Oh, Mabel!*, recruits May Gleason in 20GF.

Merwyn **Flock**, New York actor engaged to Kitchie Valentine in BM31, marries an actress while Kitchie is in England.

Aunt **Flora**, one of Joan Romney's muddling Aunts in 09AC, not nearly so nice as Aunt Edith but not perfectly awful like Aunt Elizabeth.

Wentworth **Flood** dresses well, looks neat, never breaks things, plays a number of card games with more than average skill, acts in theatricals, and plays the mandolin. Small and soft-spoken, he is liked by women in 05BI but cordially disliked by his male peers, including Peter Baynes.

Major **Flood-Smith**, resident of Valley Fields in BM31 and SF57, lives next door but one to The Nook, Mulberry Grove.

Harold **Flower**, messenger at the Planet Insurance Company in 12TM, one of the most assiduous money-borrowers in London, a bibulous individual of uncertain age. Calls George Balmer a vegetable.

Orlando **Flower**, red-headed spotty-faced child actor, rival of Joey Cooley in LG36.

Klaus von der **Flue**, a Swiss chimney sweep who loves mixed biscuits in WT04.

Sir Hercules **Foliot-Foljambe**, new husband of Myrtle Beenstock in 65SS; bald, about the color of tomato ketchup, and enormously stout.

Reggie **Foljambe** once offered Jeeves double the salary Bertie Wooster was paying, as recalled in 17JH.

Tony **Fontelli**, restaurant owner in New York, ordered by Bat Jarvis to hire Betty Silver as cashier in PA12.

Elmer **Ford**, New York multimillionaire father of Ogden Ford in 13EC, LN13. A massively built man of middle age with powerful shoulders and a face like a Roman emperor's; a typical American merchant-prince.

Mrs. Elmer **Ford**, sometimes-divorced wife of prec., named Ruth in 13EC, Nesta in LN13 and in PJ17, where she is two years married to Peter Pett, Elmer Ford having perished suddenly of an apoplectic seizure. A tall, formidably handsome woman, originally from Mechanicsville, Illinois, more recently from New York and smothered in furs. Author of sensational fiction, e.g. *A Society Thug*. The type of woman whom small, diffident men seem to marry instinctively, as unable to help themselves as cockleshell boats sucked into a maelstrom. Protective mother of Ogden; aunt of Willie Partridge in PJ17. Her sister Eugenia is Mrs. Bingley Crocker in PJ17.

Ogden **Ford**, singularly repellent son of Elmer and Mrs. Ford in 13EC, LN13, and PJ17. The first of a series of young male horrors in PGW, he is about fourteen, bulgy, overfed, and spoiled, considered the El Dorado of the kidnapping industry.

Mr. **Forman**, master of Dunstable's new form at Locksley in 05CL, is editing a new edition of the *Bacchae*.

Grace **Forrester**, loved by James Todd and Peter Willard in 19WW, plays tennis.

Fosberry is vicar at Market Blandings in HW33, where he is succeeded by James Belford..

Captain Jack **Fosdyke**, famous explorer engaged to superintend the Perfecto-Zizzbaum production of *Black Africa* in 32MB; guest of Josiah Flack in 50FC, where he rescues an unwilling Agnes Flack from the ocean at East Bampton. Family seat at Wapshott Castle, Wapshott-on-the-Wap, Hants. Tall, slender, and willowy, twice winner of the Grand National steeplechase and a scratch golfer, but believes golf is only a game.

Gerald **Foster**, an English playwright in the middle twenties, author of *The Primrose Way* in AS22. Engaged to Sally Nicholas and Elsa Doland, marries the latter.

Sally **Foster**, secretary to Leila Yorke in IB61, in love with Freddie Widgeon. A small girl with blue eyes, copper hair, and a nose which twitches like a rabbit's and tilts slightly at the tip.

Aubrey **Fothergill**, a Drone in 16JT, gives up a beloved pair of brown shoes because his man Meekyn disapproves of them.

Cornelia **Fothergill**, the novelist, lives at Marsham Manor, Marsham-in-the-vale, Hampshire. Specializes in rich goo for the female trade. A large, spreading woman with horn-rimmed spectacles, Dahlia Travers' hostess in 59JM.

Edward **Fothergill**, father of Everard, an unskilled painter who hates cats in 59JM.

Everard **Fothergill**, son of Edward, husband of Cornelia; small, thin artist in 59JM with a beard of the type that causes so much distress.

Jimmy **Fothergill**, golfer in 19WW, 23HG and 23CF.

A policeman named **Fotheringay** is imagined by Bertie Wooster, arresting the latter during a dark moment in JF54.

Fotheringay, butler to the Earl of Biddlecombe in 27CD; in 32CC he is Lady Widdrington's butler at Widdrington Manor, Bottleby-in-the-Vale, Hants.

Another Mr. **Fotheringay** is on the staff of Perfecto-Zizzbaum in 33CA, one of many writing a screenplay for *Scented Sinners*.

Cyril "Barmy" **Fotheringay** (pron. Fungy)-**Phipps**, son of Ruby Poskitt, a tall, willowy Drone with hair the color of creamery butter. Nephew to Theodore, Lord Binghampton. A graduate of Eton and Oxford, has inherited a small fortune from his maternal grandfather, American P. Middlemass Poskitt. Has an open, engaging face which arouses the maternal instinct in women. Present at Gussie Fink--Nottle's pre-nuptial feast in CW38; in JM46 it is recalled that he was pinched in Leicester Square on Boat Race Night by his brother George, a policeman. Sometime desk clerk at J.G. Anderson's hotels in BW52, where he courts Dinty Moore. See also 31FA, 35TF (where he is in a cross-talk act at the Drones with Pongo Twistleton-Twistleton), RJ53, JF54.

Bertram **Fox**, author of *Ashes of Remorse* and other unproduced movie scenarios, partner in Ukridge's accident syndicate in 23UA.

Hugo Percy de Wynter **Framlinghame**, sixth Earl of Carricksteed in 14OT, has married Mae Elinor Birdsley, daughter of J. Wilmot Birdsey.

Francis, janitor in Elizabeth's Herrod's apartment house in 15BL.

Desmond **Franklyn**, William Mulliner's rival for the hand of Myrtle Banks in 27SW: one of those lean, keen, hawk-faced, Empire-building sort of chaps you find out East.

Patrick B. "Packy" **Franklyn**, well-known young American millionaire and sportsman, all-American halfback from Yale, engaged to Lady Beatrice Bracken at the beginning of HW32, where he falls in love with Jane Opal.

Fred, barman in 15TM, son of the caretaker of a country house.

Frederick[1], a supercilious young man with long legs, is footman at the Keiths' in 10LM.

Frederick[2] is a chauffeur employed by a man named Fillimore in 23NW; met S.F. Ukridge in a pub, persuaded by same to drive him around in millionaire style.

Ellen Tallulah **French**, a tall, good-looking girl, housemaid at Towcester Abbey in RJ53.

Horace **French**, a square-faced, freckled boy with short, sandy hair and sardonic eyes, in cahoots with Professor Appleby and Joe the Dip in BC24 as Cooley Paradene's newly-adopted son.

Friesshardt (pron. Freeze-hard), one of Hermann Gessler's bodyguards in WT04.

Bernadine **Friganza**, one of Ivor Llewellyn's five ex-wives in BA73, Empress of Stormy Emotion who ran through three directors, two assistant directors, and a script girl during a filming of *Passion in Paris*.

Algy **Fripp**, big-game hunter, one of Annabell Sprockett-

Sprockett's seven suitors in 34FW.

Miss **Frisby** is secretary to Mrs. Waddeseley Peagrim in LW20.

Nathaniel **Frisby**, George Pennefeather's golfing partner in 22MP.

T. (for Torquil) Paterson **Frisby**, brother of Josephine Moon and employer of Berry Conway in BM31. Comes from Carcassone, Illinois, now resident at Grosvernor House, London. Dyspeptic president of Horned Toad Copper Corp. Inc. A little man, looks as if was made of some leathern materials and then pickled.

Oscar **Fritchie**, assistant manager of the Mayflower Hotel, Syracuse in BW52. A stoutish, stage-struck young man with a vacant face and large, myopic eyes, like a sheep with horn-rimmed spectacles.

Major Augustus "Tubby" **Frobisher**, a friend of Capt. Brabazon-Biggar out East. Red face, small bristly moustache, glass eye, and a slight stammer. Marries Cora Rita Rockmettler, widow of Sardine King Sigsbee Rockmettler in RJ53.

Fry is head of West's at Wrykyn in 11EA. A large, stout, placid boy with a broad, good-natured face, but quite incompetent to be head of a house.

Walter **Fürst**, Swiss envoy to Hermann Gessler in WT04, has red hair and looks fierce.

G

Ephraim **Gadsby**, The Nasturtiums, Jubilee Rd., Streatham Common, police-court pseud. of Bertie Wooster in SF57.

Samuel **Galer**, New York detective employed from Dodson's Private Inquiry Agency (Bishopsgate Street, London E.C.) by John McEachern in IJ10. A small wooden-faced man.

Andrew **Galloway**, portly Pittsburgh uncle of Rollo Finch in 11AS, world-famous Braces King, inventor of "Tried And Proven" Braces. Afflicted with an indian summer, he is in love with Marguerite Parker, as is his nephew Rollo and Rollo's man Wilson. Portly uncle of Barmy Barminster in

57WT, thrice-divorced owner of half the restaurants in America, now in love with Mabel Parker.

M. **Gandinois**: see Gaudinois.

M. **Gandinot**, ugliest man in Roville-sur-Mer, pawnbroker in 12RE.

Clifford **Gandle**, MP, one of Bobbie Wickham's luckless suitors in 26PT, was President of the Oxford Union. A long, thin young man with a curved nose, author of a book of political essays entitled *Watchman, What of the Night?*.

Raymond **Gandle**, golfing artist who objects to Wallace Chesney's plus fours in 22MP.

Lady Dora **Garland**, relict of the late Sir Everard Garland, K.C.B., one of Clarence and Galahad Threepwood's ten sisters, mother of Prudence Garland, aunt of Wilfred Allsop in FM47, PW52, BG65. Lives on the fourth floor of Wiltshire House, Grosvenor Square. Acutely alive to the existence of class distinctions, she vigorously opposes her daughter's association with Bill Lister in FM47. By PB69 never leaves London except to go to fashionable resorts on the Riviera and in Spain.

Prudence **Garland**, only daughter of Dora; trim, slim, and blue-eyed, in love with Bill Lister in FM47, married to him in BG65; they run a sort of roadhouse place near Oxford.

Jeremy **Garnet** writes novels and things in 05WP. Narrator of LC06, author of *The Outsider* and *The Manoeuvres of Arthur*. Only son of the late Henry Garnet, vicar of Much Middle-fold, Salop. Hobbies: cricket, football, swimming, golf. Clubs: Arts. Friend of S.F. Ukridge, whom he helps to start a chicken farm; successfully courts Phyllis Derrick.

Officer **Garroway**, policeman at one of New York's popular police stations, learning how to write poetry from Hamilton Beamish in SB27, where he poses as a richly-dressed Delancy Cabot in order to cop pinches. Befriends Tipton Plimsoll and Wilfred Allsop in BG65. Long and stringy, with three to four extra inches of neck, flows out of his uniform at odd spots.

Tom **Garth**, a long, thin young man with a dark, clever face and a humorous mouth, sometime reporter for the *Manhattan Daily*, was at school and Oxford with Lord Whitfield.

Writes a tongue-in-cheek fruitarian article that fools Kid Brady in 05BB. In 06BJ he starts a New York scandal sheet with Lord Whitfield called *Candor.*

Jimmy **Garvis**, U.S. lightweight boxing champion, loses his title to Kid Brady in 06BW; he loses a rematch in 06BF.

Gascoigne, butler to Ferdinand James Delamere, 6th Earl of Wivelscombe, in 33LS.

Gates, friend of Bill Dawlish and Nutty Boyd in UM16, London correspondent for a New York newspaper with an apartment in the 40s of E. 27th Street, member of the New York Players' Club. Long face, not unlike a pessimistic horse.

M. **Gaudinois** or Gandinois is French master at Wrykyn in GB04, 04JE, and 06DS, at Locksley School in 05CL.

M. **Gautier**, a brown, dried-up little man, is a French master at Locksley School in 04AD.

Mme. **Gavarni**, breezy old lady with a military moustache, runs a dancing school in 16TL.

Geake plays cricket for the Weary Willies in 05LB. He was at Malvern.

J. Wellington **Gedge**, a tubby little Californian from Glendale with a receding chin and bulging eyes, unhappy occupant of the Chateau Blissac in HW32.

Julia **Gedge**, a solidly built, handsome woman with a forceful manner, widow of a multimillionaire oil man named Wilmot Brewster, two years married to J. Wellington Gedge in HW32. Onetime inside worker for Soup Slattery.

Gentleman Jack, a member of Burke's gang in PJ17, alias Lord Wisbeach, trying to steal Willie Partridge's worthless explosive Partridgite.

Genevieve, a tall, blonde beauty in 15CH, friend of Katie Bennett and destroyer of masculine peace of mind. Cloak-model at Macey's (*sic*) in New York.

George[1], groom at Col. Stewart's Gorton Hall in LS08.

George[2], Freddie Widgeon's cousin in IB61, a beefy chap with red hair who shares Peacehaven, Valley Fields with Freddie. Boxed for Oxford as a heavyweight, now a policeman, engaged to Jennifer Tibbett.

M. **Gerard**, French master at St Austin's in 03HP, 03SA.

Hermann **Gessler**, not a nice man, Governor of Switzerland for the Emperor of Austria in WT04. Likes to tax things and forbid things that people enjoy.

Alan **Gethryn**, head of Leicester's house, Beckford College in PU03, known as the Bishop. Member of the first fifteen and the first eleven, second best bowler in the school. Nephew of Reginald Farnie. Recruited by Joan Romney (a sort of cousin, about twice removed) to pitch for Much Middlefold in 07PC, where he is still in Leicester's house at Beckford.

Gwendoline **Gibbs**, secretary to Lord Tilbury in BM64, a sensational beauty, blonde and willowy, thinks mostly about motion pictures and hairdos. Cousin to Percy Pilbeam.

Tankerville **Gifford**, a sleek-haired, pale young man in LN13, onetime dissolute suitor of Cynthia Drassilis.

Alaric (Ricky) **Gilpin,** Archibald's brother, cousin of Horace Pendlebury-Davenport, nephew to the Duke of Dunstable, son of William Gilpin of the Connaught Rangers. Beefy poet with red hair and freckles, engaged to Polly Pott in UF39, where he is trying to raise money to buy an onion-soup bar off Leicester Square. In SS61, he supplements his income with the proceeds of that business.

Archibald **Gilpin**, younger brother of Ricky, nephew of Alaric, Duke of Dunstable, employed by the Mammoth Publishing Co. An artist formerly engaged to Millicent Rigby, he woos Myra Schoonmaker in SS61: tall and slim and elegant, he looks like a film star of the better type.

Linda **Gilpin**, sister to Archie and Ricky Gilpin, niece and courtappointed ward of Alaric, Duke of Dunstable in PB69. Slim and blue-eyed, with chestnut-colored hair; problematically engaged to John Halliday.

Lew **Ginsberg** is the advance man for the Number Two company of *Ask Dad* in 29BG.

Leonard **Gish**, proprietor of the Gish Galleries in SF57: small, dark, irascible, rather like a salamander in temperament and appearance. Employer of Linda Rome in BM64.

Gladys, title character of 28EG, of Drury Lane, is a Fresh Air London visitor at the Blandings Parva School Treat.

May **Gleason**, manicurist at the Hotel Cosmopolis in New York, comes from an unconscious town in Ohio called Ostoria and is courted by Lancelot Purvis in 20GF. Small and pretty, with a soft, brooding cloud of dark hair. Cf. Maud Peters in 10WD.

Magnolia **Glendennon**, from South Carolina: one of those quiet, sympathetic girls whom you could tell your troubles to in the certain confidence of having your hand held and your head patted. The little mother, in short, with the added attraction of being tops at shorthand and typing. Onetime secretary to Boko Fittleworth, hired as Ginger Winship's secretary in MO71 and becomes engaged to him.

Mr. **Glossop** is a master at Sanstead House in 13EC and LN13; a dismal man of nerves and mannerisms and an amateur Life Insurance agent.

Basil **Glossop**, a onetime disguise of Pongo Twistleton (SS61).

Hildebrand or Tuppy **Glossop**, nephew of Sir Roderick in 27JY, 29JS, 30TC, RH34, and MO71, a friend of Bertie Wooster's since boyhood who was at Magdalen with him. Frequently mentioned as the fellow Drone who bet Bertie he couldn't swing himself across the swimming pool at the Drones by the rings and looped back the last ring, giving Bertie no option but to drop into the water in faultless evening dress (some time prior to the action of 27JY). In 29JS as a result of singing "Sonny Boy" at the Oddfellows' Hall in Bermondsey East he drops his courtship of Cora Bellinger and takes up again with Angela Travers, Aunt Dahlia's daughter. Still betrothed to Angela in 30TC, RH34 and MO71. His late father invented a headache cure marketed as Runkle's Magic Midgets, which has earned huge profits for Runkle Enterprises. An Old Austinian who still plays football; light hair, a Cheshire-cat grin, a high, squeaky voice, in build and appearance somewhat resembling a bulldog.

Honoria Jane Louise **Glossop**, daughter of Sir Roderick and Lady Glossop (née Blatherwick), one-time flame of Bingo Little with whom he falls in love while tutoring her younger brother Oswald at Ditteredge in 22SO/IJ23, where she decides to marry Bertie Wooster and make something of him. Still engaged to Bertie in 22SR/IJ23; in 24RA and 27JY she is engaged to Biffy Biffin. Went to Girton where she went in for every kind of sport and developed the physique of a middleweight catch-as-catch-can wrestler; one of those robust, dynamic girls with the muscles of a welterweight and a laugh like a squadron of cavalry charging over a tin bridge, or like waves breaking on a stern and rock-bound coast. Brainy, moreover. A ghastly dynamic exhibit who reads Nietzsche, courted by Blair Eggleston in 65JG.

Oswald **Glossop** is Honoria's pestilential little brother and Bingo Little's tutee in 22SO/IJ23, where Bertie Wooster pushes him off the bridge into the lake at Ditteridge Hall.

Sir Roderick **Glossop**, Harley Street loony-doctor in 22SR/IJ23, 24RA, 25WO, 27JY, UF39, HR60, and 65JG; widowed father of Honoria, uncle of Tuppy. Master of Ditteredge Hall, Hants. A formidable old bird with a bald head, outsize eyebrows, and eyes that go through you like a couple of Death Rays, he believes Bertie Wooster is insane; he himself is nervous about fires (27JY, where Bertie puts a hole in his hot water bottle with a knitting needle). A large list of his phobias appears in 22SR /IJ23: he is President of the West London branch of the Anti-gambling league; he drinks no wine, strongly disapproves of smoking, has impaired digestion, disapproves of coffee, and has a particular dislike for cats. Known to Lord Emsworth as Pimples when they were boys at school, and remembered as a most unpleasant boy with a nasty, superior manner and an extraordinary number of spots on his face. Usually ranked #2 gargoyle of the Demosthenes Club, second to Howard Saxby. A widower of two years in TY34, wants to marry Myrtle, Dowager Lady Chuffnell, but runs afoul of her foul son Seabury. Lord Ickenham impersonates him in UF39. Has a clinic at Chuffnell Regis, Somersetshire in HR60, where he visits Brinkley Court in the role of Swordfish, a substitute butler, in order to observe Willie Cream. Still engaged to Lady Chuffnell in 65JG (where she refuses to marry him until Honoria marries out of his household), and running his clinic at Chuffnell Regis.

Jacob **Glutz** of Medulla-Oblongata-Glutz hires James Phipps to play butler roles in OR51.

Sir Roderick Glossop

Sigismund or Sam **Glutz** is head of a motion picture corporation named Medulla-Oblongata in 33RM. Head of Perfecto-Wonderful in 67GA, where he is the victim of a mugging.

Isaac **Goble**, New York theatrical manager in LW20, partner of Jacob Cohn, producer of *The Rose of America*.

The Bishop of **Godalming** is a house guest at Blandings in SN15.

Sam **Goldwyn**, a shaggy dog of mixed parentage belonging to Corky Pirbright in MS49. Looks like Boris Karloff made up for something. A South London dog, definitely of the people.

Gooch[1] fags for Fry at West's (Wrykyn) in 11EA.

Gooch[2], rent-collector on Broster Street in PA12, on Pleasant Street in PJ15; a smallish, pale-faced man with protruding eyes and teeth which give him a certain resemblance to a rabbit.

Gooch[3], Ukridge's sad-looking grocer at Sheep's Cray in 23UD, is owed £6 three and a penny.

Mrs. **Gooch**, cook at Ashenden Manor in UD48.

Brewster **Gooch**, a long, skinny, freckled, lantern-jawed bozo with big feet, mail-order clothes, and one of those small-town haircuts that leave the back of the neck looking as if it had been peeled, runs the Always Open Garage on Main St. in Franklin, N.Y. Husband of Pearl Delahay and father of a three-year-old son Elmer in 29BG.

Constable **Gooch**, guardian of the law in a small English town in 14ST.

Gloria **Gooch**, film actress in 25PR.

J.G. **Gooch**, second-class passenger on the R.M.S. *Atlantic* who sings the Yeoman's Wedding Song in LB35.

John **Gooch**, writer of detective stories in 27TP.

Mortimer **Gooch**, Horace Bewstridge's golf antagonist in 48EX.

Rev. Sidney **Gooch**, vicar of Rising Mattock in 37AG.

Jimmy **Goode**, contender in Choirboys' Hundred Yards Handicap in 22PT/IJ23.

Margaret **Goodwin**, James Orlebar Cloyster's fiancée and one of the narrators of NG07, lives at St Martin's, Guernsey. Only daughter of the late Eugene Grandison Goodwin, LL.D. Writes hit play, *The Girl Who Waited*, which Cloyster has produced under his own name.

Gorrick, a member of the lower fourth at Eckleton in HK05, is a stout youth in 08GU.

Percy **Gorringe**, son of Emily Trotter, stepson to L.G. Trotter. Wears short side whiskers and tortoise-shell-rimmed spectacles; about 6' 2" tall, speaks with a bleating voice. Infatuated with Florence Craye in JF54, where he dramatizes her novel *Spindrift*; writes detective stories (e.g. *The Mystery of the Pink Crayfish*) under the pseudonym Rex West.

Samuel Wilberforce **Gosling**, a long, thin day boy in PU03, member of Beckford College's first eleven.

Gossett, Wall Street broker and nervous golfer in the Cape Pleasant Club in 10AB.

James J. **Gossett**, stout motion picture man with a bald head, is discovered eating with the Sausage Chappie's wife in 20AS/IA21.

Joe **Gossett** is an old man in 09AC who makes a little money winding up some of the big clocks in Much Middlefold. A plebeian antecedent to Lord Emsworth, he owns two pigs who are like sons to him. Loves talking about pigs and forgets all else while doing so.

Tony **Graham**, prefect in Merevale's, St Austin's, College champion middle-weight boxer in PH02; gets revenge on P. St H. Harrison in 02OT; an old and tried foe of Harrison in 03HS; breaks his collarbone in a football match against the Old Crockfordians in 03MC.

Herbert "Billy" **Graham**, king of the Eggesford poachers in AA74; uncle of Marlene, scullery maid at Eggesford Court. A man of educated diction and form-fitting tweeds, about the height and tonnage of Fred Astaire.

Grace **Grant**, pseud. Catherine Beaumont, jewel thief who escapes with Kid Brady's unwitting aid in 06BA.

Spenser **Gray**, a fat young man in love with Babe Sinclair in DD19.

Clarence **Grayling**, rabbit-faced rejected suitor of Ruth Bannister in WH14.

Montague **Grayson**, well-known writer of sunny and optimistic novels, flower-gardener in BC24.

The **Greaser**, boot-boy/butler in the school house at St Austin's in 10PD.

Lionel P. "Stinker" **Green**, nephew of Clarissa Cork, on whom he depends for his allowance in MB42, where he is engaged for a time to Anne Benedick and wants to enter a partnership with Orlo Tarvin. Was at school with Jeff Miller. An interior decorator, member of the Jr. Arts Club. Ornamental young man engaged—again unsuccessfully—to Jane Martyn in PP67. Tall and slender, with melting hazel eyes, perfectly modelled features, silky moustache, and flashing smile. Member of Tarvin & Green, interior decorators and dealers in antique furniture.

Greenwood is prefect of Appleby's at Wrykyn in 04HT.

Gregory is wicket-keeper for the Weary Willies in 05LB.

Mr. **Gregory**, truculent head of the Fixed Deposits Department of the New Asiatic Bank in PC10.

Gregson is a member of Day's, Wrykyn, in GB04.

Agatha **Gregson** tries to prevent nephew Gussie Mannering-Phipps from marrying a vaudeville singer in New York in 15EY by sending another nephew, Bertie Mannering-Phipps, to bring him to his senses. Sister of Gussie's late father Cuthbert, sister-in-law of Gussie's mother Julia. Subsequent to this story her maiden name becomes Wooster; see Agatha Wooster.

Spenser **Gregson** of Woollam Chersey, Herts., is a battered little chappie on the Stock Exchange in 15EY, married to Bertie Mannering-Phipps' Aunt Agatha. Still her husband and a successful member of the Stock Exchange in 26JI, after Agatha's family name has become Wooster. Deceased in CW38.

Thos **Gregson** is Aunt Agatha's loathly son, England's premier fiend in human shape, under Bingo Little's tutelage in 26JI; a chunky kid of fourteen in 29JL, often taken to the theatre at Agatha's request by a reluctant Bertie Wooster.

Gresham is co-author of "On Your Way" for the *Orb* in NG07.

Mr. **Grey** is Davies' form-master at Wrykyn in 04RS.

K. St H. **Grey** of Prater's house, St Austin's School, a naturalist in PH02. Captain of the first fifteen in 02HP; see also

03HS.

Greyson of Henry's house, St Austin's, is an early target of Pillingshot's paper *The Rapier* in 11PP.

Mr. **Grindlay** is S.F. Ukridge's persistent creditor in 23NW.

Pomona **Grindle**, a novelist whose latest work Aunt Dahlia hopes to serialize in *Milady's Boudoir* in CW38.

Constable **Grogan** is a large Southhampton policeman in 14DE.

Cyril **Grooly**, handicap 24, junior partner in the firm of Popgood & Grooly, publishers of the Book Beautiful, Madison Avenue, NY. Hermione Bostock's publisher in UD48, Leila Yorke's in IB61. Rejects Sir Raymond Bastable's *Cocktail Time* in CT58.

Grusczinsky & Buchterkirch, music publishers in 10MU.

Beatrice, Mrs. Willoughby **Gudgeon**, aunt to Hermione Brimble. A formidable woman of the heavy-battlecruiser class, girlhood friend of Theophilus Mulliner, Bishop of Bognor in 47RA.

Hilda **Gudgeon**, stout, athletic friend of Madeline Bassett in MS49, in love with Harold Anstruther. Won the tennis singles at Roedean in her school days.

Jack **Guffington**, Grand National winner, one of Annabell Sprockett-Sprockett's seven suitors in 34FW.

Dora or Dolly **Gunn**: see Dolly Molloy.

Capt. John **Gunner**, 55, retired sea captain living at the Excelsior Boarding House in Southhampton, corpse in 14DE.

Mrs. **Gunton-Cresswell** of #5, Kensington Lane, aunt of Eva Eversleigh in NG07, friend of James Orlebar Cloyster and Margaret Goodwin.

Ambrose **Gussett**, local doctor in 51UF who courts Evangeline Tewkesbury, a scratch golfer but no tennis player.

Gussie, mentioned in 16AC and 16JU as Bertie's cousin: see Augustus Mannering-Phipps.

H

Esmond **Haddock**, son of the late owner of a widely advertised patent remedy known as Haddock's Headache Hokies and

Esmond Haddock's Aunts: Charlotte, Emmeline,
Harriet and Myrtle Deverill and Daphne Winkworth

the late Flora Deverill, master of Deverill Hall, King's Deverill, Hampshire in MS49. Broad-shouldered, about 30, author of fruity and emotional sonnet sequences. Lives with his five imperious aunts: Charlotte, Emmeline, Harriet, and Myrtle Deverill and Daphne Winkworth. In love with Corky Pirbright. Jeeves' uncle Charlie Silversmith is his butler.

Alice **Halliday**'s photo is on Rutherford Maxwell's mantelpiece in his New York apartment in 11IA. She is his girl friend back in England.

Eve **Halliday**, daughter of a very clever but erratic writer who died some years ago; joyously impecunious, lives on a £150 annuity left her by her uncle Thomas. Very straight and slim, with a boyish suppleness of body. School friend of Phyllis Jackson, Cynthia McTodd, and Ada Clarkson in LP23, where she is hired to catalogue the Blandings library and courted by R. Psmith.

John **Halliday**, son of the late G.J. "Stiffy" Halliday of the old Pelican Club, rising young barrister in love with Linda Gilpin in PB69. Oxford friend of Joe Bender, in whose art gallery he is a sleeping partner. Heir to an aunt's fortune, lives in Halsey Chambers, Halsey Court, attended to there by Ma Balsam.

Hammond shares a study with Dent next to Rigby's in Seymour's house at Wrykyn in 05RR. Plays for the Sedleigh School fifteen in 10SW.

Frances **Hammond**, sister of Sir George Pyke in BC24 and SS25; wife of Sinclair Hammond. Has the same bright, compelling eyes, overjutting brows, high coloring, and breadth of forehead as her brother. Her first husband was a Herbert Shale of Harrod's Hose & Underwear Dept.

Sinclair **Hammond**, the well-known archaeologist, husband of Frances Pyke Hammond. Lives in Holly House, Wimbledon Common. Guardian of niece Flick Sheridan in BC24.

Thomas "Bill" **Hardy** of Mon Repos, a semi-detached villa on Burberry Road, Valley Fields, London S.E. 23 in PP67. A broken nose gives him the looks of a gangster. Ran away to sea and worked as an assistant ship's cook, later picked lemons in Chula Vista, California. An alter ego of Bill

Townend; author of *Deadly Ernest* under the pseudonym Adela Bristow.

The Hon. Louis **Hargate**, friend of Lord Dreever and guest at Dreever Castle in IJ12; a tall, thin billiards and card sharper, with cold eyes and tight, thin lips.

Harold[1], Joe Rendall's office boy in 11TD.

Harold[2], practically circular pageboy to Lord Wickhammersly at Twing Hall, expelled from choir in 22PT/IJ23.

Harold[3], quarrelsome first burglar in the home of Osbert Mulliner in 28OO.

Rudolph der **Harras** tries to eat the apple shot from Walter Tell's head in WT04.

Philip St H. **Harrison** umpires a cricket match at St Austin's in 02OT; a resident of Merevale's, runs afoul of Venables' little brother in 03HS; foe of Tony Graham in both 02OT and 03HS; see also 03MC.

Sir Sutton **Hartley-Wesping**, Bart., larcenous baronet in 31SW who invites Adrian Mulliner to his house in Sussex.

Geoffrey **Harvest**, actor and flippertygibbet in SF48 who jilted Terry Cobbold.

Harvey, friend of Renford at Wrykyn in GB04, keeps clandestine ferrets for rabbit hunting.

Leonard **Haskell**, attorney with Haskell & Green, lawyers to Biff Christopher in BM64. Phone MUrray Hill 1-4025.

Hassall plays for the Sedleigh School fifteen in 10SW.

Wally **Hatt**, American cartoonist, creator of the Steve Bracy comic strip in 54OB (cf. Wally Judd in 54LA), pays £100 to use Algernon Little's face as the model for a new comic-strip creature of the underworld. (Cf. U.S. cartoonist Al Capp and the comic-strip detective Dick Tracy).

Rev. John **Hatton** was at Trinity with Malim, lives at 62 Harcourt Buildings and runs a boys' club in South Lambeth in NG07. Agrees to publish James Orlebar Cloyster's writing under his own name for 15% of the take.

Reginald John Peter Swithin, third Earl of **Havershot**, 28, large, beefy Drone with brown eyes and hair a sort of carroty color, the living image of his gorilla-faced father. Master of Biddleford Castle, Biddleford, Norfolk. Got his boxing blue at Cambridge. Once engaged to Ann Bannister, in love with April June in LG36.

Harry **Hawk**, boatman at Combe Regis whom Jeremy Garnet pays to upset Prof. Derrick's boat in LC06.

Lord Arthur **Hayling**, caste-conscious younger son and brother of a Duke, unsuccessful suitor of Betty Silver and social "barker" for Mr. & Mrs. Richard Morrison in PB12. Pale moustache, blond eyebrows.

Rev. G. **Hayward**, nephew to Old Heppenstall in 22SH/IJ23, a sermon competitor from Lower Bingley at 100-8 odds, receiving twelve minutes.

Lord **Heacham** was engaged to Lord Emsworth's niece Angela prior to 27PH. A solemn young man in riding breeches whose rent roll runs into the tens of thousands of pounds. Unsound on pigs, speaks disparagingly and with oaths of pigs as a class.

Ella **Heath**, sister of Tommy in 05BI, is discouraged by Peter Baynes (who is in love with her) from watering the Hall pitch.

Tommy **Heath**, son of Sir John Heath, younger brother of Ronald and Jack and elder brother of Ella, was captain of cricket at Winchester and wants to go to Oxford in 05BI so he can add a third to the family list of Cricket blues.

Mr. **Hebblethwaite** is editor of *The Ladies' Sphere* in 19SF, where his privacy is guarded by George Mellon.

Hemmingway is a golf-lawyer in 21LH.

Aline **Hemmingway**, supposed sister of Sidney in 22AA/IJ23, looks as if she plays the organ at a village church; Aunt Agatha thinks she will be a fine wife for Bertie Wooster.

Sidney **Hemmingway**, a.k.a. Soapy Sid, confidence man posing as brother of Aline and curate at Chipley-in-the-Glen, Dorsetshire. A small round cove with a face rather like a sheep, wears a pince-nez and a benevolent expression; makes a fool of Aunt Agatha in 22AA/IJ23.

Wadsworth **Hemmingway**, Palsied Percy, golfing lawyer, competes for the President's Cup (minimum handicap of competitors is 24) in 36LL. Unpopular retired solicitor.

Dolly **Henderson**, Galahad Threepwood's only great love, the cause of his being sent off to South Africa some years before the Blandings novels. Sang at the Oxford and the Tivoli, eventually married Jack Cotterleigh in the Irish Guards. Now dead, she is the mother of Sue Brown in FP29, SL29, FP29, HW33.

J. D'Arcy **Henderson** of The Firs, one of 19 suitors sending pug dogs to Sylvia Reynolds in 01WP.

Marion **Henderson**, beautiful parrot-owner staying at the Hotel Jules Priaulx in 12MC, daughter of a rich English landowner with a London house in Eaton Square. Courted by Capt. Bassett and Jean Priaulx.

Eve **Hendrie**, paid companion to Mrs. Rastall-Redford, formerly governess to Hildebrand Elphinstone; courted by Peter Rayner in 11BS.

Henfrey of Day's is captain of cricket at Wrykyn in 04JE, 05SC, and 05LP.

Dick **Henley**, Tom Ellison's friendly rival for the hand of Dolly Burn in 05TD.

Henry, narrator of 15MM, is a waiter at Mac's.

Old **Heppenstall** (Rev. Francis), vicar of Twing and umpire in the annual village school treat in 22PT/IJ23; uncle of James Bates, to whom he lends a sermon in 22SH/IJ23; uncle of Mary Burgess in 22MT/IJ23, where we learn that his second son (unnamed) is home from Rugby.

Herbert[1] is the factotum at Seymour's in Wrykyn College, GB04, 05PP, WF07.

Herbert[2] is the gardener at George Tanner's private school in Kent; shot by Sir Godfrey Tanner in 14CI, using Tom Billing's air gun (cf. Beach in 36CW).

Reginald "Kipper" **Herring** was at Malvern House with Bertie Wooster. Cauliflower ear, looks like Jack Dempsey. On the staff of the *Thursday Review* and engaged to Bobbie Wickham in HR60.

Elizabeth **Herrold**, writer who adopts a black cat in 15BL, comes from a small town in Canada; sent to college by a rich and unexpected aunt.

Daphne **Hesseltyne**, secretary to J.B. Duff in QS40.

Lancelot **Hibbs**, lost baby in 58UK.

Charlotte or Lottie **Higginbotham**, ex-wife and future wife of Lord Tidmouth in DS32.

Mr. **Higgs**, a fat comic actor-manager at the local theatre in HK05. Cf. Seymour Hicks, actor-manager at the Aldwych Theatre in 1904, who in 1906 gave PGW his first regular job.

Herbert **Higgs**, alias Otis Fitzpatrick, alias Chauncey Cabot, alias Christopher Robin Cork, is sought for a $15,000 jewel robbery at the Pierre. Arrested in 1938 and again in 50MM by John McGee, house detective at the Hotel Delehey, after a chase and a gun battle.

Mrs. Horace **Hignett**, née Adeline Marlowe, sister of Sir Mallaby Marlowe, mother of Eustace in TM22; world-famous writer on Theosophy, author of *The Spreading Light*, *What of the Morrow*, and all the rest of that well-known series. Chatelaine of Windles, Hampshire.

Eustace **Hignett**, son of Adeline, a small, fragile-looking young man with a pale, intellectual face, one of the three suitors of Billie Bennett in TM22.

Mary **Hill** from Dunsterville, Canada, has large grey eyes and a slim figure; secretary to Joe Rendal in 11TD.

Minnie **Hill**, 26, a small, slim girl with large eyes in 16TL, lady instructress at a dance studio until she marries Henry Wallace Mills.

Wentworth **Hill**, the English actor, fired from *The Rose of America* in LW20.

Mabel **Hobson**, ambitious and temperamental lady friend of Reggie Cracknell in AS22, sometime female lead in *The Primrose Way*.

George Brent, sixth Earl of **Hoddesdon**, penniless father of Lord Biskerton in BM31, brother to Lady Vera Mace. Grey moustache. Married a chorus girl at the Gaiety Theatre.

H.J. **Hodger**, toastmaster at Old Wrykynians' dinner in 23LA.

J. Bernard **Hoke**, stout and florid yes-man to financiers, engaged in BM31 to buy Berry Conway's shares in the Dream Come True copper mine.

Lord **Holbeton** (QS40): see George Trotter.

Joseph **Hollister**, late father of Bill Hollister in SF57.

William Quackenbush **Hollister**, son of 1929 matrimonial

tontine signatory Joseph Hollister, assistant at the Gish Galleries in Bond Street in SF57; engaged for a time to Angela Murphrey, falls in love with Jane Benedick. Ginger-colored hair, cauliflower ear from amateur boxing.

Mitchell **Holmes**, in love with Millicent Boyd in 19OG, a short-tempered golfer employed by the Paterson Dyeing & Refining Co. Has an unquestioned ability to imitate a bulldog quarrelling with a Pekingese.

T.B. **Hook** is captain of rugby at Oxford in 06PI. He lives at Trinity or Oriel.

Josh **Hook** (handicap of 24) does tricks with string in 35FL.

Hopwood fags for Stanworth in West's house at Wrykyn in 11EA.

Zenobia "Nobby" **Hopwood**, 20, ward of Lord Worplesdon in JM46. A blue-eyed little half portion with an animated dial, daughter of the late Roderick Hopwood, one of a rackety set of writers in London who lived most of the time on what they could borrow. Engaged to Boko Fittleworth.

Percival Alexander **Hotchkiss**, eldest son of Gregory Hotchkiss, Esq. and Mrs. Hotchkiss, marries Dora Pinfold at the end of 36MT.

M. de la **Hourmerie**, director of the troisième bureau of the Ministry de Dons et Legs in Paris in FL56. A small, stout man of pug-dog appearance.

Jane **Hubbard**, a tall, handsome girl with large brown eyes, daughter of an eminent explorer and big-game hunter, she has frequently accompanied her father on his expeditions. An out-doors girl. Becomes engaged to Eustace Hignett in TM22.

Spike **Huggins**, safe blower remembered in 25HS, was at Sing Sing with Bradbury Fisher in his freshman year.

Reginald **Humby** is engaged to Margaret Melville in 09RR, where he makes 113 for Chigley Heath against the Hearty Lunchers.

Kitty **Humphries**, switchboard operator at the Mayflower Hotel, Syracuse in BW52.

Conrad **Hunn** hurts his toe while attacking Friesshardt in WT04.

Jane **Hunnicut**, an air hostess in love with Jerry West in GB70, heiress to a large fortune bequeathed her by a former passenger named Donahue which is taken for back income taxes.

Lord **Hunstanton**, parasite and advisor to Mrs. Waddington in SB27; tall, slight, and elegant, with frank blue eyes, monocle, and clipped moustache. For Hunstanton Hall, where PGW was a guest in 1926 and which he rented in the summer of 1927, see 6/26/26 letter to W. Townend and Jasen, *Portrait* 103ff. Cf. Lord Roegate.

Frank **Hunt**, a small youth with short-cropped hair, professional boxer and dog lover who works for Joe Bevan in WF07.

Spectatia **Huskisson**, aspiring singer from Snake Bite, Michigan in 20MK/IA21. Tall, blonde, constructed on substantial lines, with the musical diction of one trained to call the cattle home in the teeth of Western hurricanes.

Herbert **Huxtable**, opposition candidate for Parliament running against B.V. Lawlor in 23LA.

Wilson **Hymack**, aspiring composer and author of "It's a Long Way Back to Mother's Knee" in 20MK/IA21, first met Archie Moffam in the neighborhood of Armentières during the war.

I

Lord **Ickenham**: see Frederick Altamont Cornwallis Twistleton.

Jane, Lady **Ickenham**, off-stage American wife of Fred in 35UF, SS61; prevents him from revisiting the U.S. or going to London except for the Eton and Harrow match. Broke off her engagement to Fred six times before marrying him. Her visits to an ailing mother in the south of France or the West Indies give Frederick his opportunities for forays to London and Blandings Castle.

Inge, a junior at Jephson's, Beckford, in 04BB, participates in Blenkinsop's benefit.

James **Innes**, narrator of 06AB, is captain of the Weary Willies

Cricket Club.

Lord **Ippleton**: see G.F.A. Delamere Murgatroyd.

Ivy, parlourmaid at Mallow Hall in DB68, has been walking out with Sgt. Brewster of the Wallingford Constabulary for seven months.

J

Jack, a terrier mongrel on Peter's estate in 15MS belonging to Dick, one of the grooms.

Jackson[1], of Dawson's house, St Austin's College, contributes to *The Glow Worm* in PH02.

Jackson[2] exits M. Gautier's Upper Fifth French class at Locksley School for an afternoon dip in 04AD. In Dexter's (at Locksley) in 05CL, where he often teas with Linton.

Jackson[3] of Spence's house at Wrykyn first appears in 04JE. Apart from his cricket, he does not shine in school. In 05DE, he is the only Wrykynian who ever got three centuries in first-eleven matches and five extra lessons in the same term, and who ever got a double century in a house match and 400 lines in the same week. Head and shoulders above the other batsmen in the first eleven, with an average of 51.3 in 05SC; mentioned as a great bat in 05LP. In WF07, he loves warring against boys from St. Jude's in town.

Mr. **Jackson,** patriarch of the Jackson family in MK09, went to Wrykyn, owns vast tracts of land in the Argentine where sheep are raised; now retired from the management of his land, lives with his family at Crofton, Shropshire and hires the pro Saunders to coach his sons in cricket. At the beginning of PC10 he has lost a very large sum of money, with the result that he must move to a smaller house and cannot send Mike to Cambridge.

Bob **Jackson,** Mike's eighteen-year-old brother in MK09, is finishing at Wrykyn, living in Donaldson's. Still a cricketer in PC10.

Gladys Maud Evangeline **Jackson,** 3, is the youngest of the

Jackson children in MK09; her sisters are Ella, Phyllis, and Marjory, 14; her brothers, in ascending order of age, are Mike, Bob, Reggie, and Joe.

Joe Jackson, the eldest of the Jackson brothers in MK09, is the All England batsman J.W. Jackson who plays for the Marylebone Cricket Club.

John Jackson, Mike's uncle in MK09, formerly an Army surgeon in Afghanistan, now retired with an inheritance.

Mike Jackson, friend and companion of Psmith in MK09, PC10, PJ15, LP23. Age 15 at the beginning of MK09, enters Wrykyn from King-Hall's, a private school at Emsworth, Hampshire. Tall, thin, and wiry, the youngest of the Jackson brothers, all of whom are keen cricketers. Lives at Wain's house and earns a place on Wrykyn's first eleven when his father withdraws him for poor grades and sends him to Sedleigh, where he lives in Outwood's, meets Psmith, and at first declines to play cricket. After Sedleigh, his name is down for King's College, Cambridge, but because of his father's financial reverses at the beginning of PC10 he rents a bed-sitter in Dulwich and works at the New Asiatic Bank. At the end of PC10, he will attend Cambridge as Psmith's confidential secretary and adviser, later to take up a position as an agent on the Psmith estates. Touring America as a member of the Marylebone Cricket Club in PJ15 after his first year at Cambridge with Psmith. Loses his position as manager of the Smith estate when Psmith's father dies; works for a time as master at a school. Married to Joseph Keeble's stepdaughter Phyllis in LP23, where they need capital to buy a farm.

Phyllis, Mrs. Mike Jackson, stepdaughter to Joseph Keeble by a previous wife, cut off by Lady Constance when she abandoned her designated fiancé Rollo Mountford and eloped with Mike Jackson: small and fragile, one of those porcelain girls whom the roughnesses of life bruise instead of stimulating; gets working capital in LP23.

W.P. Jackson, 14, an ordinary fag at Wrykyn, takes Jackson[3]'s extra lesson in 04JE because of his guiltier conscience.

Samuel Jakes, 3rd messenger at the New Asiatic Bank in PC10.

James[1] is the narrator of 05LB, a member of the Weary Willies cricket club.

James[2] is footman or something in the household of the narrator of 06FM.

James[3] is Lord Emsworth's footman in SN15 and FP29 (the other is Thomas).

Jane[1] is one of Mr. Outwood's maids at Sedleigh School in 10SW.

Jane[2], Lord Emsworth's niece in 36CW, daughter of his sister Lady Charlotte, third prettiest girl in Shropshire, wants to marry George Abercrombie.

Jane[3], parlourmaid at Brinkley Court in RH34.

Jane[4], parlourmaid at Ashenden Manor in UD48.

Hank **Jardine**, old friend of Kirk Winfield in WH14, dies of fever on a gold mining expedition in Colombia.

Jarvis is Mrs. Elmer Ford's chauffeur in 13EC.

Bat **Jarvis**, leader of the Groome Street Gang in PA12 and PJ15, a cat-fancier who runs a pet shop on Groome St. in the heart of the Bowery. Short, stout, with small eyes set close together, wide mouth, and a prominent jaw.

Jeanne[1], a large, slow-moving Norman girl, stolidly handsome, waitress at Bredin's courted by Paul Boielle in 10RH.

Jeanne[2], maid-of-all-work for Eugene Warden in 12RE.

Jeeves, Bertie Mannering-Phipps' valet in 15EY, prototype of Reginald Jeeves.

Reginald **Jeeves**, Bertie Wooster's manservant in 16JT (his first appearance), 16AC, 16JU, 16AS, 17JH, 22PT, 22BC, 22SH, 22MT, IJ23, 24RA, 25WD, 25CR, 26FF, 26JI, 26IC, 27JY, 27JS, 29JS, 29JD, 29SA, 29JL, 30JO, 30IS, 30TC, 30JK, TY34, RH34, CW38, JM46, MS49, RJ53, JF54, 59JM, HR60, SU63, 65JG, MO71, and AA74. Tall and dark and impressive, like one of the better class ambassadors or the youngish High Priest of some refined and delicate religion. His eyes gleam with the light of intelligence, and his finely chiseled face expresses a feudal desire to be of service. Opens conversations with a gentle cough that sounds like a very old sheep clearing its throat on a misty mountain top. Has many relatives: an uncle Charlie Silversmith who buttles

Jeeves

at Deverill Hall for Esmond Haddock, a cousin Queenie, daughter of his uncle Charlie Silversmith, and several aunts, most of whom are notable for some mania. One was a martyr to swollen limbs until cured by Walkinshaw's Supreme Ointment; her mania, after sending in an unsolicited testimonial, was for seeing her picture in the daily papers in Walkinshaw's advertisements. Another aunt owns an almost complete set of Rosie M. Banks novels; another has a passion for riding in taxicabs. Three are known to History by name: Emily was interested in psychic research; Annie was disliked by all members of her family, and the third is Mrs. P.B. Pigott of Maiden Eggesford, Somerset. Other kinfolk: a cousin George, an uncle Cyril, a niece named Mabel to whom Biffy Biffen is engaged in 24RA, a cousin Egbert, a constable who lives in Beckley-on-the-Moor, and another cousin who passed on to him the knowledge of an expert jeweller. In 21JS/IJ23 he has an "understanding" with Mortimer Little's gourmet cook Jane Watson which she breaks off to marry her employer, and another "understanding" with a waitress named Mabel. Privately educated, with an encyclopedic knowledge, particularly of literary quotations. Has a fondness for Spinoza, but considers Nietzsche fundamentally unsound. First employed as a page-boy in a school for young girls. Admits in RJ53 to having dabbled in the First World War to a certain extent. Formerly employed by Lord Worplesdon, left because his employer dined in dress trousers, flannel shirt, and shooting coat. Other earlier employers include Digby Thistleton, the late Lord Brancaster, who owned a parrot to which he was greatly devoted, Lord Frederick Ranelagh, and a financier named Montague-Todd. Briefly employed as manservant to W.E.O. Belfry in RJ53 while Bertie attends a self-sufficiency school. Has a falling-out with Bertie in TY34 because of the latter's brief passion for the banjolele; enters service of Chuffy Chuffnell but resigns to rejoin Bertie because it is not his policy to serve in the household of a married gentleman. Serves briefly for Pop Stoker, and for Gussie Fink-Nottle in MS49 when Gussie impersonates Bertie. A member of the Junior

Ganymede, a club for butlers and gentlemen's personal gentlemen on Curzon Street whose Rule 11 requires members to keep a record at the club of their employers' personal oddities and peccadilloes. Jeeves' calling is to oversee the habit of Bertie and to extricate him and his intimates from all sorts of personal embarrassment, a task for which his large brain (encased in a size 14 cerebellum) and alleged diet of fish render him eminently fit. Specializes in solutions based upon the psychology of the individual. Remarkable for his quiet entrances: he doesn't seem to have any feet at all. He just streams in. Describes Bertie to Pauline Stoker in TY34 as "mentally somewhat negligible," and to a temporary understudy in 22AA /IJ23 as "mentally quite negligible." There is a keen sporting streak in Jeeves, and he is fond of fishing. Every year he downs tools about the beginning of July and goes off to Bognor Regis for the shrimping. On the origin of the name, PGW writes "I was watching a county match on the Cheltenham ground before the first war, and one of the Gloucestershire bowlers was called Jeeves. I suppose the name stuck in my mind, and I named Jeeves after him." –letter to a Mr. Simmons, 10/20/60. Percy Jeeves, son of Mr. & Mrs. Edwin Jeeves of Manuel St., Goole, died at the Battle of the Somme at the age of 28 on 8/4/16, the same year the first Jeeves story appeared.

Sir Leopold **Jellaby**, O.B.E., millionaire philatelist, father of Myrtle, buys Anselm Mulliner's stamp collection in 37AG.

Myrtle **Jellaby**, niece of Sir Leopold, affianced to Anselm Mulliner in 37AG.

Mr. **Jellicoe**, tobacconist at Ashby Paradene in PP67.

Tom G. **Jellicoe**, a light-haired youth with a cheerful, rather vacant face and a receding chin, is a student at Sedleigh in MK09; owns two Aberdeen terriers named Jane and John.

Walter **Jelliffe**, comedian and star of Alice Weston's company in 15BB, hires Henry Pifield Rice as the company mascot.

George **Jenkins**, an old army man, boxing instructor at Wrykyn in WF07.

Jenkinson, a goof observed by the Oldest Member at the

beginning of 23HG.

Rosie **Jenks**, disqualified in Girls' Egg and Spoon Race in 22PT.

Myra **Jennings**, a plain girl from Waterbury, Conn. employed in the office of a wholesale silk importer, lives in a flat on 69th Street, flat 4B; assisted by Freddie Widgeon in 31FA.

Mr. **Jephson** is housemaster at Beckford College in PU03 and 04BB, and coach of cricket.

Rev. Aubrey **Jerningham**, vicar at Valley Fields in SS25, author of a stout volume entitled *Is There a Hell?*

Jervis, agent for Parliamentary candidate Morley-Davenport in 06AB, sometimes plays for the Weary Willies.

Mr. **Jervis** is managing clerk at Shoesmith, Shoesmith, Shoesmith & Shoesmith in IB61.

Boko **Jervis** brought the white rabbit into chapel in 34NO.

Superintendent Ernest **Jessop** of the Wallingford constabulary, reluctant investigator of the Bond's Bank burglary in DB68, brother-in-law of Scotland Yard Sergeant Claude Potter.

Jevons, faithful manservant of Sir Godfrey Tanner for 15 years, is fired in 14CI when he puts a piece of ice down his employer's neck. Retires to 193 Adelaide St., Fulham Road, London. His relation to Chicago millionaire Horace Jevons, sometime employer of Rupert Baxter mentioned in 36CW, is unknown.

Jimmy is the vacant-faced office boy at *Squibs* in MM14.

Catharine **Jipson**, fourth daughter of the Rev. B.J. Jipson of the Rectory, Piggleston, Herts. Lancelot Hibbs' fired nanny in 58UK, marries Biffy Wix-Biffen.

Bella Mae **Jobson**, American writer of juvenile fiction sought for *Wee Tots* in 39ER.

Joe the Dip, plug-ugly, confederate of Horace French and Professor Appleby in BC24.

Joe the Lawyer, bookmaker who sells S.F. Ukridge half-interest in a moribund racing dog in 26LB.

John is footman to the Romneys in 09AC.

Johnson, bearded baseball fan in 14OT. See John Benyon.

Mrs. Heavenly Rest **Johnson**, J. Wendell Stickney's non-resident cook in PP67, makes her home in Harlem.

Joe **Johnson**, colored champion of Brooklyn, plans to throw his fight with Eddie Brook in 05BL.

Evan **Jones**, revivalist in 23EB preaching in Llunindnno, Wales.

John Jasper **Jones**, undertaker at Wambledon in 29PW and a leading contender for the Lawn Tennis Championship, is an ambidextrous player and serves nothing but foot-faults.

R. (for Richard or Dickie) **Jones**, infinitely the fattest man in the west-central postal district of London, a fixer of delicate matters in SN15. About 50, grey-haired, with a mauve complexion.

Agnes Parsons **Jopp**, a kind-looking motherly woman, former wife of Vincent Jopp in 21HA.

Jane Jukes **Jopp**, another former wife of Vincent in 21HA.

Luella Mainprice **Jopp**, a kittenish little woman with blonde hair and a Pekingese dog, another of the same in 21HA. Talks baby talk.

Vincent **Jopp**, American multimillionaire with massive head, jutting chin, and skinny legs who joins the Wissahicky Golf Club and nearly wins the American Amateur gold championship in 21HA.

Joseph, black cat adopted for luck and named by Elizabeth Herrold in 15BL.

Joyeuse[1], moustache belonging to Lord Bromborough in 36BT.

Joyeuse[2], bath sponge belonging to Frederick Altamont Cornwallis Twistleton, Earl of Ickenham, in UF39 and UD48.

Wally **Judd**, American cartoonist in 54HA, creator of Dauntless Desmond, syndicated in 1600 American papers.

Judson, valet to Freddie Threepwood in SN15, a smooth-faced, lazy-looking young man.

Walter **Judson**, golfer engaged to Angela Pirbright in 56JB.

Alfred **Jukes**, a superior golfer in 36AG, runner-up in club-champion golf match at beginning of 48EX.

Cyril **Jukes** is a foul-weather golfer who plays during a blizzard at the opening of 50FC.

Otis (or Arthur) **Jukes**, rival of Rollo (or Ralph) Bingham in golf and love in 21LH.

Rosie **Jukes**, disqualified finisher in the Girls' Egg & Spoon Race in 22PT/IJ23.

Jules[1], the French cook at Mac's in 15MM.

Jules[2], night clerk and lift-attendant at the Normandie Pension at Roville-sur-Mer in AS22.

Julie, maid to Molly Waddington in SB27.

April **June**, the movie star living on Linden Drive in Beverly Hills, wants to be Countess Havershot in LG36.

Porky **Jupp**, a goon who works for Jas Waterbury in 48FO and 65JG; all-in wrestler and plug-ugly.

K

Katie[1], girl friend of Spennie Coombe-Crombie in IJ10.

Katie[2], adopted daughter of Mr. MacFarland in 15MM: see Katie MacFarland.

Mr. **Kay** is the fussy and ineffectual house-master at Eckleton in HK05.

Constable **Keating**, police-officer in Clerkenwell, arrests Spider Buffin in 10MI.

Mrs. **Keating**, landlady to Cosmo Wisdom at #11 Budge Street, Chelsea in CT58. Brightens at word of fatal diseases; husband died of TB.

Lady Constance **Keeble**, née Threepwood, widow of the late Joseph Keeble, who made a packet out East; sister of Lord Emsworth and chatelaine of Blandings in LP23, 27PH, 28EG, FP29, 31GG, HW33, 36CW, UF39, PW52, SS61, BG65, 66SW. For a list of her nine sisters, see under Clarence Threepwood. A strikingly handsome woman in her middle forties in LP23 with a high, arched nose, admirably adapted for sniffing. Devoted admirer of the Efficient Baxter, also soft on the Duke of Dunstable, her one-time suitor and briefly her fiancé until he canceled his wedding plans because her father refused to meet his terms in the matter of a dowry. With these exceptions, strong men run like rabbits to avoid her: the sort of woman who makes you feel that no matter how suave her manner for the nonce, she is at heart a twenty-minute egg and may start functioning at any

Lady Constance Keeble

moment. Her efforts in HW33 are directed at the suppression of her brother Galahad's memoirs and the prevention of her nephew Ronnie Fish's marriage to Sue Brown. Shot her governess, Miss Mapleton, in the bustle with an air gun in her youth; in 36CW she fires same at Beach at a range of six feet, and misses. Married to New Yorker James Schoonmaker and no longer resident chatelaine of Blandings in PB69, where she revisits the old haunt and once again terrorizes Clarence. Last heard of living in America in SB77.

Joseph **Keeble**, elderly widower who married Lady Constance two years prior to LP23, where his wife prevents him from helping his stepdaughter Phyllis Jackson. Amassed a large fortune in South African diamond mines.

Keggs[1], butler to the Keiths for the last six years in 10LM and 10GA, formerly butler to the Earl of Stockheath.

Keggs[2], English butler in the house of John Bannister and later the Winfields in WH14: stout, dignified, pigeon-toed, fond of betting on sporting events. Drops some of his h's.

Keggs[3], butler to Lord Marshmoreton at Belpher Castle in DD19. A man of reverend years, portly and dignified, privately a Socialist.

Augustus **Keggs**[1], former butler to Lord Stockleigh, buttles at the Keiths in 10GA and runs the matrimonial sweepstakes. Aspirates his vowels. Pigeon-toed at the base, bulgy half-way up, bald at the apex. Manner restrained and dignified, voice soft and grave.

Augustus **Keggs**[2], retired butler in SF57 and IB61, made his fortune buttling for NY millionaire J.J. Bunyan and picking up market tips overheard at dinners. Former butler for Lord Uffenham, now his landlord at Mulberry Grove, a complex of three homes (Castlewood, Peacehaven, and The Nook). Brother of Flossie Keggs (Mrs. Wilberforce Billson). Absent from England on an extended vacation in IB61, having come into a great deal of money.

Mr. **Kegworthy**, an acquaintance of Bertie's aunt Agatha, is father of the infant boy Tootles and a daughter named Bootles in 26FF.

Mr. **Keith** is Aline Ellison's host in 10LM.

Elsa **Keith**, worshipped since boyhood by Martin Rossiter in 10GA, briefly infatuated with Aubrey Barstowe and his poetry. Friend of Betty Silver, still engaged to Marvin Rossiter in PA12, PB12.

Tom **Keith**, host and employer of Keggs[1] in 10GA.

Kelly, mere acquaintance and enemy of Spider Buffin in 10MI, corrected with a sandbag.

Captain **Kelly**, a smoothly shaven man of uncertain years and expressionless features, unsavory business associate of J.B. Hoke in BM31.

Lancelot "Ginger" **Kemp**, in love with Sally Nicholas in AS22, was at Cambridge until his father's death. Red-headed, a one-time boxer and rugby player, was at school with Gerald Foster. Buys a kennel on the south shore of Long Island.

Kendal shares a study with White, Bradshaw, and the narrator of 02BL.

Kennedy is second prefect at Blackburn's, Eckleton, until made head of Kay's in HK05, where the house becomes Dencroft's with a change of masters; he is head of Dencroft's house in 08GU.

Mary **Kent**, daughter of an old school friend of Mrs. Podmarsh in 23AR. Courted by Rollo Podmarsh.

Lady Sophia **Kimbuck**, sister to Lord Evenwood in MM14, spends a happy widowhood interfering in the affairs of the various branches of her family. Has an encyclopedic grip on the Evenwood family annals, gets her way by threatening to write a history of the family for publication.

Thomas **Kitchener**, a large, grave, self-sufficing young man, the strong and silent second gardener at Millbourne Hall in 13ST. One of the men engaged to Sally Preston.

Mr. **Knight** is master of the lower fifth at Locksley School in 04AD.

Winfield **Knight**, actor in Rutherford Maxwell's *Willie in the Wilderness* in 11IA.

Frederick **Knott**, uncle of James Datchett in 09OS, made a substantial fortune in Western Australia; has just enough brain to make a jay-bird fly crooked, and no more.

Mr. **Knox**, remembered by Keggs[1] in 10GA as Bertie Fendall's

Latin & Greek tutor, reads poetry to Bertie's sister Angelica.

Percy, Lord **Knubble** of Knopp, Grosvernor Square, luncheon host of Cedric Mulliner in 29SC, guest of Sir Sutton Hartley-Wesping in 31SW, godfather of Eustace Mulliner in 32OH, and tennis partner and suitor of Amanda Biffin in 52BB, where he is described as a horse-faced young man with large ears and no chin.

L

Elizabeth **Lakenheath**, relict of the late Sir Rupert Lakenheath, K.C.M.G., C.B., M.V.O., Millie's Aunt in 24UR, living in Thurlow Square. Tall, angular, and thin, with an appearance of a woman designed by nature to instil law and order into the bosoms of boisterous cannibal kings.

Millie **Lakenheath**, niece of Elizabeth Lakenheath, a small and bewilderingly pretty girl courted by S.F. Ukridge in 24UR.

Lana, one of two stenographers employed by Percy Pilbeam at the Argus Enquiry Agency in BM64. Her colleague is Marlene.

Mr. **Lanchester** is Cedric Mulliner's slow-thinking cab driver in 29SC.

Mr. **Langridge** is a form-master at Locksley in 05CL.

Alfred **Lattaker**, 25, fictitious twin brother of George in 12RR, lost or kidnapped in infancy and adopted by a wealthy South American. Cf. Alfred Mulliner in 67GA.

George **Lattaker**, 25, engaged to Stella Vanderley in 12RR, thinks he has assaulted his Serene Highness the Prince of Saxburg-Liegnitz. Cf. George Mulliner[3] in 67GA.

B.V. "Boko" **Lawlor**, Old Boy from Wrykyn's, stands for Parliament at Redbridge in 23LA with the aid of speeches by S.F. Ukridge and a song by James Corcoran.

Mr. **Langridge** is Dunstable's form-master at Day's in 05CL.

James Rupert **Leather-Twigg** of Seymour's, Wrykyn, also known as Shoeblossom, occupies study 7 in GB04; no athlete in 05AB, he catches chicken-pox in MK09.

Mrs. **Lee**, the infirmary nurse at St Austin's in 01PP, a lady of advanced years and energetic habits.

Lefty, member of Buck MacGinnis' gang in LN13.

Fanny **Lehman**, formerly Fanita the World's Greatest Juggler, now in her late thirties and wife of Joe Lehman in BW52.

Joe **Lehman**, formerly a vaudeville agent, now a theatre producer, partner with Jack McClure in Lehmac Productions in BW52. A large, forceful man, always wears a derby hat.

Mr. **Leicester**, a well-meaning but weak housemaster at Beckford College in PU03. Alan Gethryn's housemaster in PU03 and 07PC: a thin, elderly man with a mild, kind face, rather like a sheep. Keen on antiquities.

Leonard, Mrs. Lakenheath's parrot in 24UR, talks in six languages.

Daisy **Leonard**, small, demure New York showgirl, friend of Nutty Boyd and Claire Fenwick in UM16, lives in a hotel near Washington Square.

Leutold, bodyguard of Hermann Gessler in WT04.

Isadore **Levitsky** is a fellow-executive of Mr. Schnellenhamer in the Perfecto-Zizzbaum Moving Picture Corporation in 33NO and 33JO. Identified as Perfecto-Zizzbaum's chief business operative in 33CA.

Lickford, an artist and correspondent of Jeremy Garnet in LC06. Alter ego of Bill Townend.

Renshaw **Liggett** is American millionaire J. Bellingwood Brackett's sharp-faced attorney in 15CA.

Linton is an enthusiastic but unskillful amateur chemist in 05IA. A resident of Seymour's at Wrykyn in 05RR. In 06DS he rather leads the Lower Fifth life and thought at Wrykyn. Promising at all games and a hard worker in form, he makes up for it by creating disturbances whenever possible. Still a resident of Seymour's house at Wrykyn College in WF07.

Charles J. **Linton** (cf. prec.) of Seymour's, Locksley School, is co-founder (with P.A. Dunstable) of Locksley Lines Supplying Trust, Ltd. in 05CL; Dunstable's confederate again in 05AH.

Claire or Clara **Lippett**, stocky daughter of Martha; formerly lady's maid to Kay Derrick at Midways, now cook and maid-of-all-work to Matthew Wrenn at San Rafael, Valley Fields, in SS25.

Mrs. Martha **Lippett**, former nurse of Willoughby Braddock, now his housekeeper on John Street, Mayfair, in SS25; mother of Clara. One of the well-known Bromage family of Marshott-in-the-dale.

J. Bromley **Lippincott**, attorney-at-law, partner in Lippincott, Lippincott, Cohn, Mandelbaum & Lippincott in BW52. A tall, dark, cadaverous man who looks about sixty; claims two thirds of the profits of *Sacrifice* for his client, the original author.

Liss shares study eight with Buxton in Appleby's in 04HT. A member of the Wrykyn Upper Fourth, owns a Bohn's crib to Livy I.

William Galahad "Blister" **Lister**, godson of Galahad Threepwood, son of a sporting journalist and a Strong Woman on the music-hall stage. A magnificently ugly man with the broad nose, prominent ears, prognathous chin, and simple, orderly mind of a kindly gorilla. What a female novelist of the Victorian era would have called "a magnificent ugly man," he is a onetime Amateur Heavyweight Boxing Champion. Has inherited a pub on the outskirts of Oxford called the Mulberry Tree. A sometime artist engaged to Prue Garland in FM47, where his godfather arranges for him to go to Blandings as Messmore Breamworthy and again as Mr. Landseer to paint the Empress. Married to Prue Garland in BG65 and established in his road house outside Oxford.

Algernon Aubrey **Little**, infant son of Bingo and Rosie in 39SB, 40WS, 50SP, 54HA, 54OB and 65SS. In 40WS he is put up for membership in the Drones; in 50SP his nurse (briefly) is old Sarah Byles, his father's erstwhile nurse. In 54OB his appearance is described as that of a mass murderer suffering from a painful gumboil. Oofy Prosser is his godfather.

Mortimer **Little**, uncle of Bingo. Creator of Little's Liniment—It Limbers Up the Legs; retired with a goodish pile, he gives Bingo a goodish allowance. Has become a great recluse since retiring and now devotes himself almost entirely to the pleasures of the table; gouty as a result, and enormously fat. In

21JS/IJ23 he lives at 16 Pounceby Gardens and becomes engaged to his cook, Jane Watson. In 22CB/IJ23 he is Lord Bittlesham, married to Jane Watson, and owner of a sluggish racehorse named Ocean Breeze. Throughout IJ23 he is infatuated with the romances of Rosie M. Banks, which, Bingo has told him, is Bertie Wooster's pen name.

Richard P. "Bingo" **Little** attended kindergarten, Rev. Upjohn's private school, Eton, and Oxford with Bertie Wooster; during his bachelor years he lives on an allowance from his uncle Mortimer, Lord Bittlesham. Another uncle, Wilberforce, 76, is mentioned as his legator in 30JO and 37AW. Long and thin, with a well-known loathing for country life. A Drone who repeatedly loves and loses, when turned down by a girl he simply says "Well, bung-ho!" and toddles off quite happily to find another. Smarting (however) from his break with Cynthia Wickhammersley in 22PT, 22SH, and 22MT/IJ23 where he fails to snaffle Mary Burgess; marries Rosie M. Banks in 22BL/IJ23 while she is working as a waitress in the Senior Liberal Club gathering material for a novel; husband of Rosie in 25CR, 26JI, 30JO, 37AW, 37BP, 39ER, 39SB, 40WS, 50SP, JF54, 54HA, 54OB, 65BB, 65SS. Lives in Magnolia Road, St. John's Wood in 25CR, 40WS. Attends Gussie's prenuptial dinner at the Drones in CW38. Gets editorship of H.C. Purkiss' *Wee Tots* through Rosie's good offices in 37BP, a position he holds in 39ER, 50SP, 54HA, 54OB, 65BB, 65SS. The family live just off Wimbledon Common in the later stories. His penchant for betting (and always losing) is held in check by wife Rosie, who keeps him low on pocket money.

Rosie **Little**: see Rosie Banks.

Wilberforce **Little**, uncle of Bingo, alive at 76 in 37AW but recently dead in 30JO, leaving his estate near Norwich and his fortune to Bingo.

Grayce **Llewellyn**, sister of Mabel and George Spence and wife of Ikey in LB35 and PG72, fifth divorced wife of Ivor Llewellyn in BA73 and widow of Orlando Mulligan. Once a panther woman on stage and screen, now large but still formidable, with eyes inclined to bulge a little. Mother of Mavis Mulligan by Western movie hero Orlando Mulligan.

Ivor "Ikey" **Llewellyn**, a Welshman by birth, stout president of the Superba-Llewellyn Motion Picture Corporation of Llewellyn City, Hollywood in LB35, BM64, FA64, PG72 (where he is married to Mable Spence's sister Grayce), and BA73. A big advertiser in Lord Tilbury's Mammoth Publications, takes his secretary Gwendoline Gibbs to Hollywood for the pix in BM64. Five times divorced, hires Joe Pickering in BA73 to prevent further marriages.

Lorimer is Pringle's study companion at the School-house, Beckford College, in PU03. Has a sister Mabel, aged fifteen. Takes Gethryn's place on the cricket team.

Love in Idleness, moustache belonging to Sir Preston Potter in 36BT.

George **Lucas** is a betting member of the golf club in 19WW.

Lew **Lucas**, lightweight boxing champion in AS22.

Alfred **Lukyn**, onetime fiancé of Miss Postlewaite of Angler's Rest, assistant at the Bon Ton Drapery Stores in the High Street near Angler's Rest in 29SC.

Freddie **Lunt**, injured bicyclist in 23UA, collects benefits of a £5 accident insurance policy instituted by Ukridge's Accident Syndicate.

Sir Claude **Lynn**, Bart., M.P. for East Bittlesham, suitor of Bobbie Wickham in 24SS.

Lysander is Aurelia Cammarleigh's snoring bulldog in 28RW.

M

Mabel[1], waitress at a tea-and-bun shop near the Ritz in 21JS/IJ23, courted successively by Bingo Little and Jeeves.

Mabel[2], niece of Jeeves, engaged to Biffy Biffen in 24RA.

Mabel[3], title character of 25BL, courted by S.F. Ukridge.

Mabel[4], Willoughby Scrope's receptionist at Scrope, Ashby, & Pemberton in GB70.

Mac, stage-doorman at the Regal Theatre in DD19, Mason & Saxby's in FP29, back at the Regal Theatre in BA73.

Robert **MacArthur**, commonly known as the Babe, rugby football star in PH02 and 02BD. Like most Scotsmen, he can play football more than a little. Captain of St Austin's fifteen in 03MC, 03HS. A day boy, lives with his parents in a big house about a mile from the College. Becomes a boarder in 02BD, moves into Merevale's to avoid Dacre—whom he thinks rather a rotter—and Dacre's fiancée Florence Beezley. Has a sister at Girton who is a friend of Miss Beezley.

Mace, an unruly member of the Lower Fifth in Merevale's, St Austin's in 02OT, Harrison's friend in 03HS.

Lady Vera **Mace**, relict of the late Col. Archibald Mace, C.V.O., of the Coldstream Guards, sister of George Brent, sixth Earl of Hoddesdon in BM31, where she chaperones Ann Moon in London. Lord Biskerston's aunt, reduced to writing Glad articles for the evening papers. Occupies a flat in Davies Street, Mayfair; becomes engaged to T. Paterson Frisby.

Andy **MacFarland**, proprietor of Mac's in 15MM.

Katie **MacFarland**, adopted daughter of the founder of Mac's in 15MM, becomes a successful actress and dancer.

Buck **Macginnis**, a short, tough, clean-shaven American gangster with a broken nose, first tried to kidnap Ogden Ford in Chicago in 1907. He succeeds (with the aid of Smooth Sam Fisher) in 13EC and LN13.

George **Mackintosh** suffers from a severe case of loquacity in 21SG.

MacPherson[1] is a long, weak-looking boy at Hay's, Eckleton in HK05.

MacPherson[2] is gardener at Belpher Castle in DD19.

Mr. **MacPherson** manages the Jackson land in Argentina in MK09.

David Ossian **Macrae**, Cloyster's former tutor at St. Gabriel's College, Cambridge (NG07).

A Mr. **Mac Sporan** has a scheme for extracting gold from seawater in 51HT.

Mad Mullah, Somali invader of England in SW09.

Mae, narrator of 29BG, is a chorus girl with a small speaking part in *Ask Dad*. Her husband Jim manages the Number Two company on the same show.

Tommy **Mainprice**, one of Annabell Sprockett-Sprockett's seven suitors in 34FW.

Claude **Mainwaring** is a golfer in 21SG.

Peggy **Mainwaring**, daughter of a Professor Mainwaring, red-haired schoolgirl of about twelve with a snub-nose and an extremely large grin. Hitches a ride with Bertie Wooster & Jeeves in 22BC.

Mrs. **Makepeace**, the single employee of Henry Paradene's Ashby Hall in PP67, is the wife of a neighboring farmer.

Malim, friend of Julian Eversleigh and James Orlebar Cloyster in NG07, went to Eton and Oxford, where he earned a double first. Now in the Foreign Office, secretary to Sir George Grant. A man of delicate literary skill, a genuine lover of books and a severe critic of modern fiction. Married to Kit Blake, he keeps an apartment in Vernon Place and a conjugal home at Hampstead Place.

Kit **Malim**, née Blake, sister of Thomas Blake the bargeman, Malim's wife in NG07: a pretty, good-natured creature bred in the gutter, works in a fried fish shop on Tottenham Court Road and keeps house for Malim at Hampstead Place.

Clarice **Mallaby**, courted by Mervyn Mulliner in 31KQ, demands strawberries in December.

Toddy **Malling**, Ann Moon's escort at the Bassingers' ball in BM31.

Pugsy **Maloney**, 15, office boy at *Peaceful Moments* in PA12 and *Cosy Moments* in PJ15, cousin of gang leader Bat Jarvis.

Yvonne **Maltravers**, stout young actress in pink with peroxide hair, engaged to assist Archibald Mulliner end his engagement to Aurelia Cammarleigh in 35CM.

Lady **Malvern**, massive friend of Aunt Agatha in 16JU, lives in Much Middlefold, Shropshire: a very vicious specimen who writes books. Mother of Wilmot, Lord Pershore.

Mamie, 19, the last of a series of nurses to William Winfield, the White Hope in WH14. Little and mouselike, in love with Steve Dingle.

Herr von **Mandelbaum**, member of a delegation of four

gamblers to John Maude, Prince of Mervo, in PB12.

Kitty **Manders**, a rival of Eunice Bray in 20RS.

Mr. **Manglehoffer** is manager of Berkeley Mansions in TY34, where Bertie Wooster's way with the banjolele calls for stern measures.

Lady Clara **Mannering**, Reggie Havershot's aunt, mother of Eggy Mannering in LG36.

Egremont or Eggy **Mannering**, Reggie Havershot's cousin in LG36, tall and slender with butter-colored hair. A heavy drinker, engaged to Ann Bannister.

Augustus **Mannering-Phipps**, only son of the late Cuthbert Mannering-Phipps and Julia, scion of one of the best and oldest families in England. More good-looking than clever, has lost his head over a New York vaudeville performer named Ray Denison in 15EY, where Bertie Mannering-Phipps' Aunt Agatha sends him to New York to prevent the marriage; uses the alias George Wilson. Nephew of Agatha Gregson, cousin to Bertie Mannering-Phipps. Referred to in 16AC and 16JU, where he has married Ray and is involved in music hall productions.

Bertie **Mannering-Phipps** is sent by his Aunt Agatha Gregson to New York in 15EY to extricate his cousin Gussie (above). Has a valet named Jeeves; prototype of Bertie Wooster.

Cuthbert **Mannering-Phipps**, Gussie's late father, Bertie's uncle, husband of Julia; master of Beechwood, improvident gambler, long dead by the time of 15EY.

Julia **Mannering-Phipps**, Gussie's mother in 15EY, sister-in-law of Agatha Gregson, was a vaudeville artist playing in panto-mime at Drury Lane when Cuthbert first saw her. Pulled up her socks and did a lot of educative work, and with a microscope you couldn't tell her from a genuine dyed-in-the-wool aristocrat. Exudes dignity, like a stage duchess. Well preserved, with large brown eyes, a mass of soft grey hair, and the complexion of a girl of seventeen.

Manners plays cricket for the Heath Hall team in 05BI.

General **Mannister**, a middle-aged man with a face like a horse, was at Eton and Oxford with Archie Moffam; uncle of Squiffy, Lord Seacliff; attached to the British legation in

Washington in 20DO/IA21.

Mansfield is a member of the first eleven at Wrykyn in 05SC.

Lady Mildred **Mant**, daughter of Lord Emsworth in SN15, is the oldest of Clarence's three offspring; wife of Colonel Horace Mant. Her lady is a Miss Willoughby.

Maple, butler at Lord Worplesdon's Bumpleigh Hall in JM46.

Mrs. Lora Smith **Maplebury** is Mrs. Bradbury Fisher's regrettable mother in 26KI.

Lester **Mapledurham** (pron. Mum), explorer and big-game hunter, a tall, bronzed, handsome man with flashing eyes, guest of Lord & Lady Bassett in 32SS.

Miss **Mapleton**, Aunt Agatha's oldest friend, headmistress of St. Monica's in 30JK. Possibly identical to the governess of the Threepwoods shot in the bustle by Connie with an air gun as recalled in 36CW.

Maraquita, royalist exile from Paranoya in MM14, likes bloodshed. Pioneer of a dance called the Caout-Chouc. Large, flashing eyes, physique of a Rugby International forward, and the agility of a cat on hot bricks. The wife of Bombito, she exerts a brief but strong influence on Roland Bleke.

Bessie **March** of 27 Guilford St. is writer of the Women's page of *Squibs* in MM14. Exerts a strong but brief influence on Roland Bleke.

Margerison, doorman at the Junior Lipstick in 27CD.

Marie, maid to Lottie Higginbotham in DS32.

Elmer **Mariner**, brother of Jill's father in LW20, a tall, bleak, shambling man who lives in a place called Sandringham in Brookport, L.I.

Jill **Mariner**, title character of LW20, daughter of a deceased American father, niece of Christopher Selby and Julia Mariner. Vivid, sympathetic, small-boned, dainty. One-time fiancée of Sir Derek Underhill, courted by Wally Mason.

Tibby **Mariner**, eight-year-old daughter of Elmer in LW20.

Mark, boot-boy at Day's in 05AH.

Sid **Marks**, all-powerful leader of the Frith St. Gang in 10MI.

Marlene[1] is secretary at Edgar Saxby & Sons, literary agents in CT58.

Marlene[2] is one of two stenographers working for Percy

112

Pilbeam's Argus Enquiry Agency in BM64. Her colleague is named Lana.

Sir Mallaby **Marlowe**, father of Sam in TM22: a dapper little man, with a round, cheerful face and a bright eye, brother to Mrs. Horace Hignett (Adeline); eminent London lawyer.

Peggy **Marlowe**, Broadway chorus girl, companion of Bernie Sampson in BW52. Wears a long cigarette holder, likes Barmy Fotheringay-Phipps.

Sam **Marlowe**, Eustace Hignett's cousin, son of Sir Mallaby, title character in TM22 who wins Billie Bennett's hand.

Marriott shares a study at Leicester's, Beckford College, with Gethryn in PU03.

Lady Patricia Maud **Marsh**, 20, daughter of Lord Marshmoreton and title character of DD19, in love with Geoffrey Raymond. Wooed and won by George Bevan.

Percy Wilbraham **Marsh**, Lord Belpher, 21, son of John Belpher, Lord Marshmoreton in DD19. Pudgy, with a small moustache and an extra chin. A kind of stage heavy brother to Maud Marsh; educated at Eton (where he was known as "Boots") and Christ Church, Oxford.

A Major **Marshall** assists Ferris in attempts to steal The Luck Stone (or Tear of Heaven, sacred jewel of the Maharajahs of Estapore) in LS08. Both work for the lame Indian who turns out to be the would-be ursurper Maharajah.

Mr. **Marshall** owns the yacht *Circe* anchored off Monte Carlo in 12RR.

John Belpher, Lord **Marshmoreton**, 48, master of Belpher Castle, Hants. in DD19. Brother of Lady Caroline Byng, father of Percy Wilbraham Marsh, Lord Belpher. Working on a History of the Family, but vague and inattentive to everything except his hobby, gardening. Marries Billie Dore, a chorus girl at the Regal.

Ashe **Marson**, 26, son of Joseph Marson, minister, and Sarah, of Much Middleford, Salop. Holder of a sort of degree from Oxford, where he spent his time being a track star; author of *Adventures of Gridley Quayle, Investigator* (British Pluck Library) for the Mammoth Publishing Company under the pseudonym Felix Clovelly. Lives at 7A Arundell St., Leicester

Square. Tall, well-built, fit-looking, with a strong chin. Falls in love with Joan Valentine in SN15.

Dikran **Marsupial**, film director to Joey Cooley in LG36.

Martha is the Brambles' general maid in 13KI.

Algernon **Martyn**, friend of Freddie Rooke in LW20, Jane's idle brother in PP67, a Drone. Long, thin, unfailingly cheerful, nephew of Henry Paradene.

Jane **Martyn**, niece of Henry Paradene in PP67, a small fair-haired girl who looks like a well-dressed wood nymph. Works as a secretary in the London office of *Newsweek*, engaged to Lionel Green.

The **Marvellous Murphys**, two lissome young gentlemen who have an equilibristic act in vaudeville in AS22.

Mary[1], servant in the Reynolds household in 01WP.

Mary[2], parlourmaid to Peter and Nesta Ford Pett in PJ17.

Mary[3], redheaded parlourmaid at Chuffnell Hall, courted by P.C. Dobson in TY34.

Dora **Mason**, secretary-companion to Julia Ukridge in 23FA; once courted by S.F. Ukridge, opens a typewriting bureau (the Norfolk Street Agency), which she runs in 23US as a partner.

Mortimer **Mason**, stout senior partner in Mason & Saxby, Theatrical Enterprises, Ltd., Sue Brown's onetime employer in FP29.

Wally **Mason**, suitor of Jill Mariner in LW20, went to school at Haileybury. Playwright, author of *Follow the Girl* and (under the name John Grant) a serious and unsuccessful play *Tried By Fire*, which closes when the theatre burns down.

John **Maude**, orphaned son of the late Prince Charles of Mervo and Maude Westley; nephew of Andrew Westley, who raised him in total ignorance of his father's identity and gave him his mother's name as surname. A big young man, tall and large of limb, a football player in college. A graduate of Harvard in PA12, of Cambridge in PB12, briefly serves as Prince of Mervo in PA12 and PB12; in love with Betty Silver.

Nicolas, Marquis de **Maufrigneuse** et Valerie-Moberanne: see Nicolas Jules St Xavier Auguste.

Maundrell, an old actor at The Barrel in NG07.

Rutherford **Maxwell**, younger son of an Englishman, aspiring writer employed by the New Asiatic Bank (and a PGW alter ego), lives in a New York apartment house named Alcala (cf. the Hotel Earle in Greenwich Village, PGW's NY address in 1909-13); friend of Peggy Norton in 11IA.

May Queen, a beverage recommended in UF39 and SS61 by Lord Ickenham, consisting of a good, dry, champagne, liqueur brandy, armagnac, kummel, yellow chartreuse, and old stout to taste. Alleviates despondency. Its full name is Tomorrow'll be of all the year the maddest, merriest day, for I'm to be the Queen of May, mother, I'm to be Queen of the May.

Rose **Maynard**, literary pilgrim to Honeysuckle Cottage in 25HC.

Angus **McAllister**, the human mule from Glasgow, has been Lord Emsworth's head gardener for about ten years in LP23, 24CP, 27PH, 28EG, HW33, 36CW, FM47. A sturdy man of medium height, eyebrows that would have fitted a bigger forehead, and a red and wiry beard. Holds subversive views on hollyhocks, but understands roses. Cousin to Aggie Donaldson. Fired in anger and rehired with alacrity in 24CP.

Cora Bates **McCall**, eminent lecturer on Rational Eating in 20WM/IA21, wife of Lindsay McCall and mother of Washington.

Lindsay **McCall**, a little hunted-looking man, husband of Cora Bates, father of Washy, and former friend of Daniel Brewster in 20WM/IA21.

Washington or Washy **McCall**, title character of 20WM/IA21, sixteen-year-old son of Cora and Lindsay, a long, thin, red-haired boy with sandy eyelashes and long neck; all legs and knuckles.

Isadore **McCallum**, theatrical agent for Yvonne Maltravers in 35CM.

McCay, Cape Pleasant Club Secretary in 10AB; a romantic and sentimental chartered accountant, rather stout, also a member of the Sybarites' Club.

Jack **McClure**, partner with Joe Lehman in Lehmac Productions in BW52: the tall, gentlemanly half, attractive, athletic, and well-dressed.

Angus McAllister

Mrs. **McCorkadale** of River Row, Market Snodsbury, a barrister by profession and Ginger Winship's opponent for the Parliamentary election in MO71; a grim woman with beaky nose, tight, thin lips, and an eye that could be used for splitting logs in the teak forests of Borneo.

John **McEachern**, an English gentleman by birth named John Forrest, only son of Eustace Forrest, a onetime major in the Guards and younger brother of Edward Forrest. Expelled from Eton for stealing, sailed to New York and took a job as a policeman, changing his last name to sound Irish. A large man with a jaw like the ram of a battleship, enriched by graft and successful investments. Father of Molly in IJ10.

Molly **McEachern**, 19, daughter of John above, courted by Jimmy Pitt in IJ10.

Clarence **McFadden**, character in American folklore cited in 16TL, suffers from big feet and pays a professor $5 extra for teaching him to dance.

McGarry, bartender at the Drones in 58FL and 65SS, has the uncanny gift of being able to estimate the weight of anything just by looking at it.

John **McGee**, house detective at the Hotel Delehay in 50MM, has an encyclopedic knowledge of motion pictures and a big day when he retrieves film actress Minna Norcross's bag in the lobby of his hotel. He also helps capture jewel thief Herbert Higgs after a chase and a gun battle.

Mrs. John **McGee** has female relations who could walk straight into any side-show and no questions asked. Lives with her husband in a snug little house in Astoria in 50MM.

Aloysius St X. **McGuffy**, curate of the small bar at Barribault's Hotel, creator of McGuffy's special in SF48.

Sandy **McHoots**, champion pro who teaches Vincent Jopp how to play golf in 21HA. Author of a book on golf in 27TP, where his name is given as McHoot. Winner of previous year's British & American Open in 21HA; Open Champion in 22MP and 24RF, remembered in 21SG as a laconic speaker when he won the British Open.

McIntosh, title character of 29JD, an Aberdeen terrier of weak intellect owned by Aunt Agatha. He is successor to Robert,

Agatha's spaniel in 26JI.

Mr. McIntosh, bookie in 34NO.

Andrew **McKinnon**, senior partner in McKinnon & Gooch, literary agents for James Rodman in 25HC.

Cyril **McMurdo**, large, stolid police constable at Dovetail Hammer in CT58, in love with Nannie Bruce.

Sidney George **McMurdo**, a two hundred pound mass of muscle with a violent disposition, works for an insurance company when not golfing. Admirer of Agnes Flack in 27TP. A contender for club championship in 40SM, where it is remembered that Agnes once broke off their engagement when he used a #3 iron for a #4 iron shot. Quarrels with his fiancée over golf technique in 48TH; briefly engaged to Cory McGuffy Spottsworth in 50FC, but resumes his engagement to Agnes Flack. Club champion in 65ST, and still intermittently engaged to Agnes Flack.

Angus **McTavish**, a serious golfer in 35FL, courts Evangeline Brackett, goes to sleep at parties.

McTeague, commissionaire at Mario's who ejects Hugo Carmody in FP29.

Cynthia **McTodd**, school friend of Eve Halliday, Ada Clarkson, and Phyllis Jackson in LP23, where she is for a time abandoned by her husband Ralston.

Ralston **McTodd**, guest at Blandings in LP23. Well-known Canadian poet, author of *Songs of Squalor*; the powerful young singer of Saskatoon's most-quoted line is "Across the pale parabola of Joy...." A gloomy-looking young man with long and disordered hair and a sullen air, turbulently married to Cynthia.

Meadowes[1] was Bertie Wooster's valet just prior to the action of 16JT, fired for stealing Bertie's silk socks and other items; he was replaced by Jeeves.

Meadowes[2], Archibald Mulliner's valet in 28RW, is a leftist revolutionary and orator in 35AM and still in service to A. Mulliner.

Meadowes[3] is Gussie Fink-Nottle's valet in MS49.

Freddie **Meadowes** is Reggie Pepper's old college chum in 11HF and 15TC. In 11HF he is engaged to Angela West (cf.

Freddie Bullivant in 26FF).

Meadows, butler to Mayor J.W. Biggs in 27RB.

Archibald **Mealing**, 31, golfer in the Cape Pleasant Club, fiancé of Margaret Milson in 10AB.

Sir Jasper **Medallion-Carteret**, hero of a popular novel by a female writer, wears riding-boots and kicks the girl of his heart with them. Clarice Fitch's ideal of manhood in 36AG.

Mrs. **Medley** is Jeremy Garnet's landlady in LC06.

Barbara **Medway** takes measures to get goof Ferdinand Dibble to propose in 23HG.

Gertrude **Medway**, maid to Mrs. Gedge in HW32, trim and respectable young woman, also known as Gum-Shoe Gertie.

Mr. **Medwin**, whiskered father of Tootles and Bootles in 11HF (cf. Mr. Kegworthy in 26FF).

George Christopher **Meech**, a barber at Price's Hygienic Toilet Salon in IW31, has been engaged for eight and a half years and is beginning to talk about marriage. Plays the saxophone.

Mrs. **Meecher**, a former actress, keeps the boarding-house in AS22.

Meeker, landowner in 27PH.

Meekyn, Aubrey Fothergill's valet in 16JT, compels his employer to give up a favorite pair of brown shoes because he disapproves of them.

Mr. **Meggs**, 56, martyr to indigestion in 14ST, imagines himself to be at work on a book on British Butterflies.

Arnold of **Melchthal**, Swiss envoy to Hermann Gessler in WT04, has light yellow hair and is supposed to know a great deal about the law.

Melhuish is a member of the Heath Hall cricket team in 05BI.

Mr. **Mellish**, master of the Upper Fourth at St Austin's in 02BL, 03SA, teaches Greek & Latin in 03HP, sets an examination on Thucydides Bk. II in 03SA.

George **Mellon**, 25, works in the ante-room at the offices of *The Ladies' Sphere* in 19SF, preventing people from seeing Mr. Hebblethwaite, the Editor. He is in love with Rosie.

Brewster **Melville** is the loutish brother of Reginald Humby's fiancée Margaret in 09RR.

Margaret **Melville** of Chigley Heath, fiancée of Reginald

Humby in 09RR, plays regularly in the ladies' cricket match.

Mennick, a wiry little man with grey hair and spectacles, is Elmer Ford's private secretary in LN13.

Menzies[1], a boxer at St Austin's in 03MC, in training for the Aldershot Boxing Competition.

Menzies[2] is a Wrykyn boy living at Seymour's in 05RR; in WF07 he has an older brother (Samuel?) on the Oxford A team.

Samuel **Menzies** (=prec.?) is a member of Seymour's house at Wrykyn in GB04.

Sidney **Mercer,** Henry Mills' fellow-cashier in 16TL, throws up his job to join the chorus of a musical comedy. Practically chinless face; becomes a professional dancer at Geisenheimer's.

Meredith is cited as the defendant in litigation successfully brought by Schwed in BW52; he is also one of J. Sheringham's Adair's fictitious operatives in IB61 (his partner is named Schwed). Cf. PGW's New York literary agent Scott Meredith.

Chester **Meredith** forgets himself during a round of golf in 23CF, where he is Felicia Blakeney's successful suitor.

Mr. **Merevale,** housemaster at St Austin's in 02BD, 02OT, 02WM, PH02, 03HS, and 11PP, rugby football coach in PH02, 03MC, also cricket in PH02. His daughter Marjorie, 10, also known as The Mere Kid, is saved from diphtheria by Welch's mile run in 02WM.

Brinsley **Mereweather,** New York literary agent for Bill Hardy in PP67.

Merolchazzar, King of Oom in 21CG, is courting the Princess of the Outer Isles.

Theodore **Merrett** of Seymour's is one of Wrykyn's least deserving inmates, a notorious outsider in 05IA. Would-be competitor of Locksley Lines Supplying Trust, Ltd.—which he betrays to Mr. Appleby—and an enemy of Linton's in 05CL. In 06DS, aged 16½, he cheats on a French exam to win a prize so that his father will buy him a banjo.

Merridew is the under-butler at Blandings Castle in SN15.

Miss **Merridew** works at Fuller & Benjamin's in 19SF, where she exchanges Rosie's spring frock.

Amelia **Merridew**, a tall, slim girl, unsuccessfully courted by Vincent Jopp in 21HA to be the fourth of the long line of Mrs. Jopps.

Dwight **Messmore**, Ambrose Gussett's rival for Evangeline Tewkesbury in 51UF.

'Mgoopi **'Mgwumpi**, chief of the Lesser 'Mgowpi who impressed Clarice Fitch with his manly qualities while she was crossing Africa on foot sometime prior to the action of 36AG.

Mr. **Michael**, member of The Barrel in NG07, wrote an operetta that ran two days.

Aubrey **Mickley**, title character of 11EA, enters Wrykyn within a month of his fifteenth birthday, sent by his maternal uncle George over his mother's objections. A little fat brute who looks as if he is bursting out of his clothes, he is set to fag for Jack Pearse at West's.

J.B. **Midgeley** is steward to Messrs. Hignett & Mortimer on the White Star Liner *Atlantic* in TM22.

Arthur **Mifflin**, leading juvenile in the Marvis Bay production of *Fate's Footballs* in 10DW; a long slender youth with green eyes, jet-black hair, and a passionate fondness for the sound of his own voice. His first big New York role is the burglar in *Love the Cracksman*, whose success he enjoys in IJ10. A member of the Strollers' Club, was at school and Cambridge with Jimmy Pitt.

Basil **Milbank**, playboy and ladies' man in WH14, an old flame of Ruth Bannister.

Mill, an unpopular prefect in Seymour's, Wrykyn in GB04 and 05AB.

Alexandra or Sandy **Miller** grew up in a small Illinois town and was put through secretarial college by her rich uncle Alexander. Small, pretty, vivacious secretary to Monty Bodkin at Llewellyn City at the beginning of PG72, takes job as secretary to Grayce Llewellyn and becomes engaged to Bodkin. Friend of Ivor Llewellyn in BA73.

Jeff or Geoffrey G. **Miller**, suitor of Anne Benedick in MB42. Played rugby for his university and England, now a new barrister who would rather write thrillers. A finely-built, athletic young man with straw-colored hair, lives in a third floor front apartment at Halsey Chambers, Mayfair. Wins the love of Anne Benedick when Dolly Molloy knocks him out with a stone tobacco-jar.

Johnson **Miller** is the deaf dance-director of *The Rose of America* in LW20.

Millicent is underhousemaid at Walsingford Hall in SM37.

Miss **Milliken** is Sir Mallaby Marlowe's elderly and respectable stenographer in TM22.

Henry Wallace **Mills**, title character of 16TL, a voracious reader in his middle thirties, paying-cashier at a New York bank. Marries Minnie Hill and tries to learn to dance to please her.

Phyllis **Mills**, daughter of the late Jane Mills and stepdaughter of Aubrey Upjohn in HR60, where she is wooed by Willie Cream. A well-stacked young featherweight, nice but goofy—talks baby talk. Has a dachshund named Poppet.

Sarah **Mills**, disqualified winner of Girls' Egg and Spoon Race in 22PT/IJ23.

Margaret **Milson**, fiancée of Archibald Mealing in 10AB; svelte figure, brown hair, large blue eyes.

Stuyvesant **Milson**, brother to Margaret in 10AB, accumulates gambling debts.

Milton, of Seymour's, Wrykyn in GB04, as good a forward as the school possesses. Wins his colours after the M.C.C. match in 05LP; a prefect of strict habits at Wrykyn in 05PP.

Colonel **Milvery**, master of Millbourne Hall in 13ST, employer of Thomas Kitchener.

Mrs. **Minchley**, cook to Mrs. O'Brien in LC07.

Mitchell, a young gentleman of rich but honest parents, former Wrykyn boy who lives with his father on the outskirts of town in WF07; friend of Stanning.

Jerry **Mitchell**, a battered veteran pugilist, Peter Pett's private physical instructor in PJ17.

The **Mixer** is a terrier of mixed ancestry, the narrator and title character in 15TM and 15MS.

Archibald Tracy **Moffam** (pron. Moom, rhymes with Bluffinghame), English war veteran living in New York, title character of IA21. Fought as a second lieutenant in France, where he met the Sausage Chappie (outside St. Mihiel) and Wilson Hymack (near Armentières). Marries Lucille Brewster in 20MH/IA21, works as an artist's model for James B. Wheeler in 21SE/IA21.

Lucille Brewster **Moffam**, daughter of New York hotel man Daniel Brewster, sister of Yale man Bill Brewster, marries Archie Moffam in 20MH/IA21. Small and slender, with a little animated face set in a cloud of dark hair.

Adelaide Brewster **Moggs**, famous champion of Womanhood in 15AA, refuses to take the name of her husband, Aubrey Rockmetteller Devine.

William, known as the **Moke**, butler-bootboy at Merevale's, St Austin's, in PH02 and 03HS.

Dolly **Molloy**, née Dora Gunn, known early in her career as Fainting Dolly because she would swoon in the arms of rich-looking strangers and pick their pockets when they stooped to render assistance. Confederate-wife to Soapy in SS25, MN28, MB42, IB61, PG72. A young woman of stylish appearance and a certain rather bold and challenging beauty; brassy golden hair and beautiful but intimidating hazel eyes, not the sort that go with a meek and contrite heart. A shop-lifter of unique gifts. Just married to Soapy in SS25. In MB42 she knocks out Jeff Miller with a stone tobacco-jar, resulting in his engagement to Anne Benedick. Shortly before the action of IB61 she has been serving a sentence in Holloway gaol for shoplifting.

Thos G. "Soapy" **Molloy**, oil-stock swindler in SS25, MN28, MB42, IB61, PG72. A fine, handsome, open-faced person in the early forties, with grizzled hair that sweeps in a wave off a massive forehead; resembles an American senator of the better sort. A deceptive associate of Chimp Twist, whom he frequently entangles in his schemes and inevitably swindles. A graduate of Sing-Sing; alias Thomas G. Gunn (Dolly's father) in SS25, where he is just married to Dolly.

Jack **Monk**, a disagreeable boy at Leicester's, Beckford College in PU03, wears scent and has oily manners. Slack mouth, shifty eye, olive complexion, a bully and a bad lot, leads a conspiracy against Gethryn.

Mr. **Montague** sells the Windsor Theatre to Roland Bleke in MM14.

Mr. **Montague-Todd**, recalled in 22BC as a former employer of Jeeves, well-known financier in the second year of his sentence.

Montgomery, a member of the Sixth Form in 01PP, finds Reynolds' poem and adds a couplet of his own to submit in the mandatory poetry competition. Shares a study at Prater's with Smith in 02TT, where they are robbed by the beak's cat Captain Kettle.

Ann Margaret **Moon**, only child of Mr. & Mrs. Thomas L. Moon of New York City, engaged to Lord Biskerton in BM31.

Elmer M. **Moon** lives below J.B. Wheeler in 21SE/IA21; brains of a bond-robbery, sought by police.

Gwendolen **Moon**, author of *Autumn Leaves, 'Twas on an English June,* and other works, contributes a poem, "Solitude," to *The Mayfair Gazette* in 26IC, where she becomes engaged to Sippy Sipperley.

Josephine **Moon** (Mrs. Thomas L. Moon of New York), sister of T. Paterson Frisby in BM31, mother of Ann Margaret Moon.

Sebastian **Moon**, little brother of Gwendolen, is brought in to incite Thos Gregson to violence in 29JL; a latter-day Fauntleroy with golden curls, apt to express himself with a breezy candor.

Moore is a St Austin's cricketer in 01AF.

Eddy **Moore** from Dunsterville, Canada, stock speculator in 11TD, friend of Joe Rendal and Mary Hill.

Eileen "Dinty" **Moore**, secretary to Joe Lehman at Lehmac Productions in BW52; a Moore from County Kerry. In love with Barmy Fotheringay-Phipps.

Jerry **Moore** lives in a house just outside Reigate on money inherited from his father; a bit deaf in one ear, with straw-colored hair. Big, slow, quiet, and simple, likes to put in his days pottering around his garden (cf. Lord Emsworth). Friend of "Gentleman" Bailey, courts Jane Tuxton in 10BA.

Daphne Dolores **Morehead,** a frightfully expensive novelist who has sold a serial novel to Aunt Dahlia for *Milady's Boudoir* in JF54. A pipertino, with hair the color of ripe wheat, eyes of cornflower blue, tiptilted nose, and a figure as full of curves as a scenic highway. Cf. Florence Craye, whom she succeeds in the affections of Stilton Cheesewright.

Bill **Morehouse,** patrolman summoned to Adela Shannon Cork's house in OR51.

Lady Florence **Moresby,** sister to Lord Emsworth, an angular woman of erect bearing estranged from her husband Kevin in SB77. Her first husband was the late American millionaire J.B. Underwood, whose estate she controls as trustee for her stepdaughter Vicky Underwood.

Sir Joseph **Moresby,** uncle of Roland Attwater, metropolitan magistrate at the Bosher Street police-court in 24SS.

Kevin **Moresby,** a handsome but impoverished playwright, estranged husband of Lord Emsworth's sister Florence in SB77.

Lucy **Moresby,** adopted daughter of Roland Attwater's aunt Emily, has been in love with Roland for years in 24SS.

Mr. **Morgan** is one of the math masters at Wrykyn in GB04.

Officer **Morgan** of the Market Blandings police force in BG65, brother-in-arms to Constable Evans.

Moriarty, a middle-weight boxer at Wrykyn in GB04.

Mr. **Morley-Davenport,** a weak batsman, is Thomas Muddock's unsuccessful opponent in the Parliamentary election at Stapleton in 06AB.

Morrell is an Eckleton student living in Mulholland's in HK05.

Morris is butler to the Romneys in 09AC.

Morrison[1], a member of the Sixth Form at St Austin's in 01PP, turns in one of the identical poems for the mandatory poetry contest. Has his eye on the form prize in 03SA.

Morrison[2], rowdiest fag in Ward's house, the rowdiest house in St Austin's College, in PH02.

Morrison[3], Montagu Watson's secretary in 05AH.

Della **Morrison,** daughter of Mr. & Mrs. Richard Morrison of New York, secretary to Westley, Martin & Co. in London until her father inherits a large fortune in PB12. Engaged to

Tom Spiller, a bill-clerk in New York.

Richard **Morrison**, father of Della in PB12, newly heir to a large fortune, New Yorker in England who engages Lord Arthur Hayling as his social "barker" and rents Norworth (pron. "Nooth") Court, a large country house in Hampshire; misses baseball.

Mrs. Richard **Morrison**, mother of Della in PB12, reluctantly enters London society to promote her daughter.

Rupert **Morrison**[1] occupies Bill Bates' apartment at The Albany while trying to write a novel in 10MU.

Rupert **Morrison**[2], landlord at the Beetle & Wedge in CT58, licensed to sell ales, wines and spirits in Dovetail Hammer.

Bream **Mortimer**, son of Henry, a title character in TM22: tall and thin with small, bright eyes and a sharply curving nose, looks like a parrot; one of Billie Bennett's suitors.

Henry **Mortimer**, father of Bream, rents Windles with J. Rufus Bennett in TM22.

Legs **Mortimer** doesn't play golf. Practical joker and life of parties who makes the fatal mistake of teeing up a soap ball for Evangeline Brackett on the 18th tee in the Ladies' Medal competition. Title character of 35FL.

Reginald **Mortimer**, son of Philip, is recommended for a job with the firm of Van Nugget, Diamond, & Mynes in 01AF.

Augustus or Gussie **Mortlake**, trustee of Bond's bank in DB68, a gaby; tall but inclining to stoutness, in his late thirties; member of the Wallingford cricket team.

Major **Moseby** is a deaf member of the golf club in 21SG.

Constable **Mould**, one of the slowest-witted men in Rudge in MN28; eyes like two brown puddles filmed over with scum.

Rollo **Mountford**, wealthy youth with horrid swimmy eyes engaged to Phyllis before she eloped with Mike Jackson: "a man with a name like that was made for suffering" —Phyllis, in LP23.

Ted Beckford, Lord **Mountry**, elder brother of Augustus Beckford; a blond, pink-faced fair-moustached young man of about 28, thick-set and solemn; at Oxford with Peter Burns, courts Cynthia Drassilis in LN13.

M'Todd shares a study at Seymour's, Wrykyn with M. Barry in

Mr. Mulliner entertains the Gin-and-Ginger and

assorted company at the Anglers Rest

GB04.

Thomas **Muddock**, a tall hatchet-faced man running against Morley-Davenport in the Stapleton Parliamentary election in 06AB, father of Alice Catherine Maud.

Mr. **Mulholland** is the master who looks after the music at Eckleton in HK05.

John **Müller** of Schaffhausen brings news of the Austrian Emperor's death in WT04.

Capt. **Muller**, a big, silent retired sea-captain, shared Capt. Gunner's room at the Excelsior Boarding-House in 14DE.

Frederick **Mullett**, valet, cook, and man-of-all-work to George Finch in SB27. Reformed inside burglar, marries Fanny Welsh.

Mavis **Mulligan**, Grayce Llewellyn's daughter by Western movie hero Orlando Mulligan; a super panther or panther plus in PG72, in love with Jimmy Ponder.

Mr. **Mulliner**, habitué of the Angler's Rest, drinker of hot Scotch and lemon, raconteur of 42 stories (see *The World of Mr. Mulliner* in collections).

Adrian **Mulliner**, nephew of the sage of Angler's Rest, dyspeptic detective in love with Lady Millicent Shipton-Bellinger in 31SW, was at Oxford; member of Widgery & Boon, Investigators, of Albemarle St. Dark and thin, with an air of inscrutable melancholy due to his dyspepsia. Concludes in 59DN that Sherlock Holmes is also Professor Moriarty.

Alfred **Mulliner**, twin brother of George[3], a nephew. Professional conjuror under the name of The Great Alfredo in 67GA. Cf. Alfred Lattaker in 12RR.

Angela **Mulliner**, née Purdue, marries Wilfred in 26SL; Augustine's Aunt Angela in 26MB, sends him a supply of Buck-U-Uppo Grade B. Lives at The Gables, Lesser Lossingham, Salop.

Anselm **Mulliner**, younger son of Rupert; curate of the parish of Rising Mattock in Hampshire, suitor of Myrtle Jellaby in 37AG.

Archibald **Mulliner**, nephew of the Angler's Rest raconteur, a Drone of exceptional pinheadedness, son of Lady Wilhelmina and Sir Sholto Mulliner. Celebrated in 28RW and 31KQ for his imitation of a hen laying an egg. Superannuated from Eton, falls in love with Aurelia Cammarleigh in 28RW and wins her hand; still engaged to Aurelia in 35AM and 35CM. Has a fling with Socialism in 35AM, keeps faith with the Code of the Mulliners (an engagement cannot be broken off by the male contracting party) in 35CM.

Augustine **Mulliner**, nephew of the Angler's Rest raconteur, at one time a pale young curate, assistant to the vicar at Lower Brisket-in-the-midden. Flaxen hair, weak blue eyes, with the general demeanor of a saintly but timid codfish. Transformed by Mulliner's Buck-U-Uppo (Grade "B") in 26MB. His story resumes in 27BM, six months after he has become the Bishop's secretary; wins vicarage at Steeple Mummery, Hants, when his younger brother confesses to painting Fatty Hemel's statue. Married to Jane Brandon in 30GN and vicar at Walsingford-below-Chiveney-on-Thames.

Augustus **Mulliner**, a nephew, courts Hermione Brimble in 47RA.

Brancepeth **Mulliner**, another nephew, portrait painter, suitor of Muriel Bromborough in 36BT.

Bulstrode **Mulliner**, a nephew, son of Joseph Mulliner, affianced to Mabelle Ridgeway, gets a job writing screenplay for *Scented Sinners* in 33CA.

Cedric **Mulliner**, a cousin; neat, prim, fussy, precise, one of London's leading snobs, established authority on the subject of dress in 29SC.

Charlotte **Mulliner**, a niece; gentle, dreamy, wistful author of Vignettes in Verse for London's higher-browed but less prosperous periodicals in 29UB.

Clarence **Mulliner**, cousin of the Sage of Angler's Rest, professional photographer in 27RB.

Cyril **Mulliner**, nephew of the storyteller, interior decorator in 32SS. Fragile and delicate, addicted to mystery novels.

Edward **Mulliner**, a cousin, late father of Lancelot in 32SW.

Egbert **Mulliner**[1], a nephew, assistant editor of *The Weekly Booklover* in 30BS, where he woos Evangeline Pembury.

Egbert **Mulliner**[2], a cousin, nephew of Serena Mulliner, has a weight problem in 70AC.

Eustace **Mulliner**, a nephew, attached to the British Embassy in Switzerland after muffing his courtship of Marcella Tyrrwhitt in 32OH.

Ferdinand **Mulliner**, younger son of Angela and Wilfred Mulliner in 56SL.

Frederick **Mulliner**, nephew of the storyteller, formerly under the charge of Nurse Wilks in 27PD.

George **Mulliner**[1], stuttering nephew of the famous raconteur in 26TA. Lives at Chatsworth, East Wobsley; in love with Susan Blake, shares her love of crossword puzzles.

George **Mulliner**[2], brother of Frederick in 27PD, physician to Nurse Wilks.

George **Mulliner**[3], twin brother of Alfred, son of the brother of the sage of the bar parlour of the Angler's Rest, writer of additional dialogue for Hollywood's Colossal-Exquisite in 67GA. Cf. George Lattaker in 12RR.

Ignatius **Mulliner**, another nephew, portrait-painter who tries to give up smoking in 29GU.

Jane Brandon **Mulliner**, wife of Augustine, is suffering from mumps in 30GN. See also Jane Brandon.

John San Francisco Earthquake **Mulliner**, son of William Mulliner in 27SW.

Joseph **Mulliner**, the storyteller's brother, father of Bulstrode.

Lancelot **Mulliner** of 32SW and 32CC is the son of Edward above; orphaned at an early age, artist with a studio in Bott St., Chelsea whose life style is threatened by Theodore Mulliner's cat Webster. Engaged to Gladys Bingley.

Lancelot Bassington **Mulliner**, 24, nephew of the raconteur in 27CD, depends upon his uncle Jeremiah Briggs and unsuccessfully courts Angela Biddlecombe.

Mervyn **Mulliner**, son of a cousin of Mr. Mulliner and related to the Earl of Blotsam (as maternal nephew), vainly courts Clarice Mallaby in 31KQ.

Montrose **Mulliner**, a distant cousin of Mr. Mulliner, assistant director for the Perfecto-Zizzbaum Motion Picture Corp. who wins the hand of Rosalie Beamish in 32MB.

Mordred **Mulliner**, nephew, poet of the modern fearless school who throws cigarettes in wastebaskets in 34FW.

Osbert **Mulliner**, another nephew of the Angler's Rest patriarch, title character of 28OO. Collects jade (his club is the United Jade Collectors), courts Mabel Petherick-Soames. Lives on South Audley Street.

Percival **Mulliner**, elder son of Angela and Wilfred Mulliner in 26SL.

Reginald **Mulliner**, a nephew, son of the storyteller's late brother, lives in Lower Smattering-on-the-Wissel, Worcestershire, and courts Amanda Biffen in 52BB.

Rupert **Mulliner**, cousin, father of Anselm Mulliner in 37AG.

Sacheverell **Mulliner**, a nervous, mild, and timid nephew who does tricks with a string and woos Muriel Branksome in 31VP.

Serena **Mulliner**, extraordinarily rich aunt of Egbert Mulliner[2] in 70AC, one of the stoutest women in the W.1 postal district of London.

Theodore **Mulliner** is the rich uncle and guardian of the artist Lancelot Mulliner in 32SW and 32CC; he is dean of Bolsover and owner of a strait-laced cat named Webster. Elevated to bishop, leaves Webster in charge of Lancelot on assuming his episcopal duties at his see of Bongo-Bongo in west Africa. Entertained by Lady Widdrington on his return in 32CC.

Theophilus **Mulliner**, mentioned as Bishop of Bognor in 47RA, was a childhood friend of Mrs. Willoughby Gudgeon.

Wilfred **Mulliner**, brother of the raconteur, inventor of Mulliner's Magic Marvels (Raven Gypsy Face Cream, Snow of the Mountains Lotion, and many other preparations) in 26SL. A member of the Senior Test Tubes in St James'. Pseud. Straker the valet in 26SL. Well-known analytical chemist in 30GN, famed for his invention of Mulliner's Buck-U-Uppo, a tonic which comes in two grades, the second designed primarily to encourage elephants in India to conduct themselves with an easy nonchalance during tiger hunts. See also 26MB, 27BM.

Lady Wilhelmina **Mulliner**, relict of the late Sholto Mulliner, M.V.O., mother of Archibald who appears to go potty in 35CM.

William **Mulliner**, the storyteller's uncle, father of John San

Francisco Earthquake Mulliner in 27SW.

Wilmot **Mulliner**, distant connection of the storyteller at the Angler's Rest, a Nodder for Mr. Schnellenhamer, wins the love of Mabel Potter in 33NO; in 33JO, he goes on an orange juice diet.

Spike **Mullins**, a Bowery boy with a shock of red hair, burglar befriended by Jimmy Pitt in IJ10.

Mulready, butler to Sir Reginald Witherspoon in 30TC.

Mike **Mulroon** runs a gymnasium on 16th Street in New York. The toughest of the middle-weight boxers of his day, he is Kid Brady's manager in 05BL, 05BB, 06BW, and 06BF.

Jimmy **Mundy** is a revivalist and moral reformer preaching in New York in 16AS.

Sgt. E.B. **Murchison**, detective assigned by Scotland Yard as driver and bodyguard to Sir James Piper in SB77. In love with Marilyn Poole.

Jane **Murchison**, an old friend of Lucille Brewster Moffam in IA21, a tall female with teeth.

Mr. **Murdoch** the glazier in 15CH is Matthew Bennett's companion at draughts on Mondays, Wednesdays, and Fridays.

Murgatroyd[1], butler at ffinch Hall in 26SL, a huge, sinister man with a cast in one eye and an evil light in the other.

Murgatroyd[2], stableman at Langley End in IW31.

Murgatroyd[3] buttled at Brinkley before Pomeroy, as recalled by Bertie Wooster's Aunt Agatha in CW38, where he is described as stoutish, with a face like a more than usually respectable archbishop; pinched a fish slice, put it up the spout and squandered the proceeds at the dog races.

Mr. **Murgatroyd** is a director for Perfecto-Zizzbaum in 33NO.

Murgatroyd's are a Bond Street jeweler who re-set Julia Ukridge's diamond brooch in 26LB.

The **Murgatroyds** are giving a dance near Easby, Shropshire, in 16JT.

Ed. **Murgatroyd**, Chicago bootlegger, is engaged to Genevieve Bootle in 33CA.

Edward Jimpson **Murgatroyd**, gloomy Harley St. physician, warns Tipton Plimsoll about his health in FM47. Called on in AA74 to cure Bertie Wooster of the spots on his chest. Played wing three at Haileybury as a boy; now a gloomy old buster with sad brooding eyes, bushy eyebrows, and long whiskers; looks like a frog.

George Francis Augustus Delamere **Murgatroyd**, fifth Earl of Ippleton, member of the Athenaeum and father of Mabel Murgatroyd in 65BB.

George Winstanley **Murgatroyd**, a Cambridge graduate and tutor to Squire Bloomenstein's son Oscar, is a leading contender in the Lawn Tennis championship at Wambledon in 29PW. In ten years of playing, he has never got his first serve over the net.

Mabel **Murgatroyd**, a red-haired girl of singular beauty with a dimple on the side of the chin, former gambling associate of Bingo Little. Oofy Prosser is entangled with her in 40WS and barely escapes. A ban-the-bomb demonstrator in 65BB, daughter of George Francis Augustus Delamere, fifth Earl of Ippleton.

P.C. **Murgatroyd** is the police officer who arrests Hugo Carmody outside Mario's in FP29.

Angela **Murphrey**, violin student at the Royal College of Music, engaged to Bill Hollister early in SF57.

Claude **Murphy**, constable at Market Blandings in SS61.

Joe **Murphy**, Fleet Street drinker hired to get Biff Christopher drunk and arrested in BM64.

Spike **Murphy**, office boy for the John B. Pynsent Export & Import Company in SS25, high kicking champion managed by Sam Shotter.

Tommy **Murphy**, child film star in LG36, Joey Cooley's predecessor as Idol of American Motherhood.

Col. **Musgrave** is invoked in 22AA/IJ23 by Sidney Hemmingway (Soapy Sid) as having cashed a bad cheque which must be covered.

Jane **Muspratt**, fiancée of Harry Hawk in LC06.

Myrtle is the barmaid at the Bull's Head, High Street, Ashenden Oakshott, Hants. in UD48.

N

Neville-Smith[1] was at Spence's, where he bowled for the Wrykyn eleven and was a close ally of Jackson[3]; at Cambridge in 05DE, he puts together a village cricket team at Bray Lench to play against Chalfont St Peters. Captain and founder of the Bray Lench 15 in 06FM, recruits Jack Williams to play for his team.

Neville-Smith[2], a day-boy, is thoroughly representative of the average Wrykynian in MK09.

Fillmore **Nicholas**, 25, well-fed brother of Sally in AS22, expelled from Harvard, where he knew Reggie Cracknell. Assistant stage manager of *The Primrose Way*, later producer of same as Fillmore Enterprises, Ltd. Marries Gladys Winch.

Sally **Nicholas**, 21, title character of AS22, daughter of the late Ezekiel Nicholas, sister of Fillmore. A small, trim wisp of a girl with the tiniest hands and feet and bright hazel eyes. Wooed and won by Ginger Kemp.

Gerald **Nichols**, youngest member of the eminent law firm of Nichols, Nichols, Nichols & Nichols of Lincoln's Inn Fields in UM16, knew Bill Dawlish at Cambridge. Junior member of Nichols, Erridge, Trubshaw & Nichols, friend of Joe Pickering in BA73.

Mr. **Nickerson**, Ukridge's landlord at Sheep's Cray in 23UD. A man of medium height, almost completely surrounded by whiskers. Looks like one of the less amiable prophets of the Old Testament about to interview the captive monarch of the Amalekites.

Herbert **Nixon**, odd-job man at the English house being rented by Lora Delane Porter in 15PW, is fired when he returns from an evening's revels, divests himself of his upper garments, and stands for twenty minutes before the front door, daring the Kaiser to come out and have his head knocked off.

Norbury-Smith, a rich stockbroker who looks like a movie star in CT58, was at school with Johnny Pearce.

Minna **Norcross**, known for her roles in *Painted Sinners* and *As a Man Sows*, is recognized by John McGee in 50MM when he retrieves her dropped bag in the lobby of the Hotel Delehay.

Minna **Nordstrom**: see Vera Prebble.

Norris, captain of cricket at Beckford College in PU03, is head of Jephson's there and in 04BB.

Peggy **Norton**, trim little chorus-girl in 11IA who lives in Alcala and is nice to Rutherford Maxwell.

Eunice **Nugent**, an intense and kind of spiritual poetess, marries Archie Ferguson in 15CA.

O

Freddy **Oaker**, a Drone in TY34 who writes tales of true love for the weeklies under the name of Alicia Seymour.

Dr. **Oakes** is the school physician at Wrykyn in GB04.

Elliot **Oakes**, pseud. James Burton, young detective employed by the Paul Snyder Detective Agency, assigned to solve murder of Capt. John Gunner in 14DE. Lean and tense, with dark eyes and thin-lipped mouth.

Jane Scobell **Oakley**, aunt of Benjamin Scobell in PA12, daughter of a Vermont farmer, widow of a New York millionaire named Redgrave and a Pittsburgh millionaire named Alexander Baynes Oakley. Lives in a small cottage on Staten Island and dabbles in philanthropy in PA12.

Oakshott[1], butler to Bertie's uncle Willoughby at Easeby, Shropshire, in 16JT.

Oakshott[2], one of those stout, impressive, ecclesiastical butlers, buttles for Julia Ukridge at the Cedars in 35CB, 47SS.

Bill **Oakshott**, master of Ashenden Manor, Ashenden Oakshott, Hants. Boyhood friend of Pongo Twistleton and neighbor of Pongo's Uncle Fred, the Earl of Ickenham; nephew of Sir

Aylmer Bostock and in love with his daughter Hermione in UD48. A large youth of open, ingenuous and sunburned countenance, a human tomato.

Constable Eustace **Oates**, peace officer at Totleigh-in-the-Wold, attacked by Stiffy Byng's Scottie Bartholomew in CW38, where Stinker Pinker steals his helmet; arrests Bertie in SU63.

Issac **O'Brien**, bookmaker in 23LA: see Izzy Previn.

O'Connell is the red-haired Aldertonian who picks a fight with Jimmy Stewart in LS08.

Jane **Oddy**, a coquette in 10WD.

Spike **O'Dowd** loses his pie-eating championship to Washy McCall in 20WM/IA21.

Officer **O'Gorman** is the Bowery police officer who befriends Kid Brady in 05BL.

Genevieve **O'Grady**, employed by the Mammoth Stores for $5.50 a week, flings herself off the side of a ferryboat into the whirling waters of the Hudson river in 15AA, where she is rescued by the husband of Adelaide Brewster Moggs.

Donough **O'Hara** of Castle Taterfields, County Clare, a lightweight boxer at Wrykyn, tars the statue of Sir Eustace Briggs and loses Dick Trevor's gold bat in GB04. An inhabitant of Dexter's in 04JE and 05DE, a member of the Wrykyn eleven. Resembles Jackson[3] in the matter of wildness, has a marvelous way of getting out of scrapes and for making useful suggestions in the crises of others. Tests and approves Sheen's boxing in WF07.

Old Bodders: see Peasemarch.

The **Old Stepper**: see Charles Percy Cuthbertson.

The **Oldest Member**, clubhouse raconteur of golfing stories in 19WW, 19OG, 20RS, 20SH, 20MT, 21UC, 21HA, 21SG, 21LH, 22MP, 23CF, 23AR, 23HG, 24JG, 24RF, 25PR, 25HS, 26KI, 35FL, 36AG, 36LL, 40SM, 48EX, 48TH, 49RR, 50FC, 51UF, 56JB. Has not played golf since the rubber-cored ball superseded the gutty. Often referees finals of the golf championship.

Jane **Oliphant** is Frederick Mulliner's quarrelsome fiancée in 27PD.

The Oldest Member

Timothy **O'Neill**, house detective at the Hotel Cosmopolis in 20AS/IA21.

Senator Ambrose **Opal**, the great Dry legislator in HW32, a man of medium height and more than medium girth, father of Jane.

Jane **Opal**, the senator's daughter, engaged to Blair Eggleston at the beginning of HW32.

M. **d'Orby**, President of the Republic of Mervo in PA12 and PB12. A large, stout statesman with more than the average Mervian instinct for slumber.

Miss **Osbaldistone**, manly young female cubist painter from downstairs in 24JG, has run out of cigarettes and cocaine.

Maggie **O'Toole**, renamed Celestine by her employer Mrs. Pett, maid in PJ17, courted by Jerry Mitchell.

Otto the Sausage, eminent member of the Frith St. Gang in 10MI.

Long **Otto**, lieutenant of Bat Jarvis in the Groome Street Gang in PA12 and PJ15.

Prince **Otto** of Saxe-Pfennig, a German invader in SW09 and 15MI.

Otway is one of the first fifteen halves at Wrykyn in GB04.

Mr. **Outwood**, Mike Jackson's house master at Sedleigh in MK09 and W.J. Stone's in 10SW, is interested in the ruined priories and abbeys of England; head of the Archaeological Society.

George **Ovens**, landlord of the Emsworth Arms, Market Blandings, who serves a home-brewed beer notorious for its potency in UF39 (where it is characterized as a liquid Polyanna), PW52, SS61, and SB77.

General **Owoki** commands the Japanese army invading New York in 15MI.

P

Jane **Packer** hits her ball into the river near the seventh hole and wins the heart of William Bates in 24RF, the first of a triad of stories told by the Oldest Member about her, William Bates, and Rodney Spelvin. In 24JG she is Bates' restless wife, and falls a second time under the spell of Rodney Spelvin. In 25PR, seven years married, she tries to save her sister-in-law Anastatia Bates from the unseemly advances of Rodney. Mother of Braid Vardon Bates.

Painter of Dexter's is an ally of Jackson at Wrykyn in WF07.

Otis **Painter**, brother of Sally in UD48; proprietor of Meriday House, publisher of Sir Aylmer Bostock's memoirs. A stout young man with a pink nose, horn-rimmed spectacles, and short side-whiskers; has just become a Communist.

Sally **Painter**, daughter of an impecunious artist named George Painter, sister of Otis. A sculptress with a little bit of money left her by an aunt in Kansas City; lives in Budge Street, Chelsea. In love with Pongo Twistleton in UD48.

Cooley **Paradene**, uncle to Bill West in BC24, owner of the Paradene Pulp & Paper Company and collector of old books; lives in Westbury, L.I. Small and slight, with a red, clean-shaven face, stiff white hair, and rimless pincenez. Other relatives include brother Otis, brother-in-law Jasper Daly, niece Evelyn Paradene-Kirby, nephew Cooley John Paradene.

Cooley John **Paradene**, son of Otis Paradene in BC24; a glistening child who has the appearance of having been recently boiled.

Henry **Paradene** of Ashby Hall, Ashby Paradene, Sussex, descendant of Beau Paradene, who built Ashby Hall towards the end of the 18th century. Once an actor of juvenile roles, in his fifties in PP67.

Otis **Paradene**, brother of Cooley and father of Cooley John in BC24.

Evelyn **Paradene-Kirby**, niece of Cooley Paradene in BC24, cousin of Bill West. A stout and voluminous woman in the early forties with eyes like blue poached eggs; still talks baby-talk. Married to a man who is always starting new literary reviews.

Parker[1] is the Headmaster's butler at St Austin's in PH02, 03MC.

Parker[2] is Pillingshot's friend at St Austin's in 03HP.

Parker[3] is Mrs. Drassilis' butler in LN13.

Parker[4], Osbert Mulliner's man in 28OO.

Parker[5] is butler to Lady Beatrice Bracken in HW32.

Claude **Parker**, husband of Connie in 35UF. A tall, drooping, middle-aged bird with a soup-strainer moustache.

Connie **Parker**, stern, thin, middle-aged mother of Julia, wife of Claude, sister of Laura Roddis in 35UF.

Francis **Parker**, agent for slumlord Stewart Waring in PJ15.

Herbert **Parker**, Daniel Brewster's English valet in 20MH and 20DF/IA21, a grave, lean individual, dismissed when found wearing one of his employer's shirts.

Julia **Parker**, daughter of Connie Parker in 35UF; about nineteen and a pippin, in love with Wilberforce Robinson.

Mabel **Parker** works in the glove department at Harridge's Stores in 57WT; courted simultaneously by Barmy Barminster, Barmy's uncle Andrew Galloway, and Barmy's valet Wilson. Cf. Marguerite Parker in 11AS.

Marguerite **Parker**, chorus girl at the Duke of Cornwall's Theatre in 11AS. Small and slight, with an impudent nose and a mass of brown hair. Comes from Market Bumpstead. Simultaneously courted by Rollo Finch, his rich uncle Andrew Galloway, and Rollo's valet James Wilson. The valet wins. Cf. Mabel Parker in 57WT.

Martin **Parker**, black-moustached agent for slumlord Benjamin Scobell in PA12. Cf. Francis Parker in PJ15.

Parkinson is the impeccable butler of the Windleband establishment in MM14.

Mr. **Parminter**, curate at Much Middlefold and its best bowler, nearly got his blue at Cambridge; *hors de combat* with a sprained wrist in 07PC.

George **Parsloe**, golfing opponent of Ferdinand Dibble in 23HG.

Sir Gregory **Parsloe-Parsloe**, J.P., seventh baronet of Matchingham Hall, Much Matchingham, Shropshire, phone Matchingham 8-30. Uncle of Monty Bodkin, cousin of Monica Simmons. Came into his title when a cousin died. Lives three miles from Lord Emsworth, his rival in the matter of pigs, pumpkins, and other things agricultural in 24CP, 27PH,

28CG, FP29, SL29, HW33, PW52, SS61. A large (6' 1"), elderly (in the middle fifties), self-indulgent bachelor of portly habit who resembles a florid buck of the old Regency days. Known in school as Tubby. In 1894 or '97 (Galahad Threepwood suspects) he filled Gally's dog Towser up with steak and onions in the back room of the Black Footman just before the Big Rat contest so that his own terrier Banjo should win. In FP29 Gally and Lord Emsworth recall that he stole Lord Burper's false teeth and pawned them at a shop in the Edgware Road in about '96. Owner of a pig named Pride of Matchingham, in 28CG and FP29 hires away Emsworth's pig-man George Cyril Wellbeloved; in HW33 wants to be Unionist candidate in the Bridgeford & Shifley Parliamentary Division of Shropshire. Briefly engaged to Gloria Salt in PW52, where he agrees to marry Sebastian Beach's niece Maudie Stubbs. Husband of Maudie and father of Tubby in SS61.

Mrs. Julia Burdett **Parslow**, author of the "Moments with Budding Girlhood" page in *Peaceful Moments* in PA12, *Cosy Moments* in PJ15.

Albert **Parsons**, another of Sally Preston's suitors in 13ST, a trained boxer.

Thomas **Parsons**, Soho police constable in 10RH.

Willie **Partridge**, son of the late inventor Dwight Partridge in PJ17, trying to complete his father's development of Partridgite, a new explosive which will eventually revolutionize war. Nephew of Nesta Ford Pett.

R.P. de **Parys**, fat and bulgy-eyed theatrical writer in MM14, is associated with Bromham Rhodes, Billy Verepoint, and the Windsor Theatre in MM14.

Fred **Patzel**, hog-calling champion of the Western States, taught his art to James Belford some time before the action of 27PH.

Col. Sir Francis **Pashley-Drake**, uncle of Aubrey Bassinger in 29UB, red-faced former big-game hunter, an almost circular man with eyes like prawns; a guest of Sir Alexander Bassinger at Bludleigh Court, where he is treating his lumbago. In 67GC he lives in Bittleton, Sussex and is the uncle of Gladys

Wetherby (her mother's brother) and executor of her estate. Author of *My Life with Rod and Gun.*

Jane **Passenger**, captain of the England Hockey team on its way to America in LB35; a stalwart young woman with a face like a Mickey Mouse.

Alexander **Paterson**, proprietor of the Paterson Dyeing & Refining Co., finds a treasurer for his firm via an ordeal by golf in 19OG.

Mabel **Patmore** flirts with the bowls-playing Purvis in 24RF.

Patricia is Beatrice Chavender's Peke at Claines Hall in QS40.

J. de V. **Patterne**, cousin to Tommy Armstrong in LS08, is at Alderton College about five miles from Marleigh School. A long, languid youth, dressed with rather more care than the average run of Aldertonians.

Sam **Patterson** writes a novelette, three short stories, and ten thousand words of a serial for one of the all-fiction magazines under different names every month. Ghost-writes *The Children's Book of American Birds* for Muriel Singer in 16AC.

Fred **Patzel**, hog calling champion of the Western States in 27PH.

Payne of Dacre's, St Austin's, bucks up to win a place in the First Fifteen at St Austin's in 02HP. Shares a study with Bowden.

Miss **Payne** is the matron at Wain's in MK09.

George **Peabody**, superior golfer in 36AG.

Joe **Peabody**, American author of soap operas in 58UK, marries Clarissa Boote.

Otis J. **Peabody**, oil millionaire and member of the Collectors Club in PP67, collects old English warming pans.

Ralph **Peabody**, Grace Chugwater's fiancé in SW09.

Mrs. Waddesleigh **Peagrim**, Otis Pilkington's Aunt Olive in LW20.

Adrian **Peake**, an extraordinarily good-looking youth, slender and rather fragile of appearance, engaged to the Princess von und zu Dwornitzchek and Jane Abbott in SM37. A graduate of Oxford, lives on what he can pick up.

Jonathan Twistleton **Pearce**, godson of Lord Ickenham in CT58, master of Hammer Hall, Dovetail Hammer, Berks. where he takes in paying guests. Author of detective novels, incl. *Inspector Jervis at Bay.* Engaged to Bunny Farringdon.

Jack Pearse, 17, a Wrykyn boy in West's house in 11EA, is the son of a Shropshire gamekeeper whose employer is Aubrey Mickley's uncle George. High up in Engineering Sixth, a useful bowler and an energetic forward. Aubrey is set to fag for him.

Peasemarch, known as Old Bodders, fifth Earl of Bodsham in 31FA and 39BI, father of Mavis and old friend of Rev. Aubrey Upjohn.

Albert Eustace Peasemarch, ubiquitous steward on the R.M.S. *Atlantic* in LB35, a round bald man of 46. A veteran of the Home Guards, where he served with the Earl of Ickenham, who years later got him a job buttling for Beefy Bastable. Trained by Fred's butler Coggs. Has inherited a house near Ickenham. Short in stature and brains, in love with Phoebe Wisdom in CT58.

Mavis Peasemarch, only daughter of the fifth Earl of Bodsham, briefly engaged to Freddie Widgeon in 31FA. In 39BI she has a young brother, Wilfred, a student at St Asaph's, and again gives Freddie the raspberry.

Aileen Peavey, a.k.a. Smooth Lizzie, swindler and published poetess in whose poems fairies' tear-drops make the dew, guest of Lady Constance at Blandings and confederate of Eddie Cootes in LP23.

Peter Peckham, the Bishop, is George Rigby's uncle in 05RR, displeased to find an array of Dr. Bohn's *English Translations of the Classics* in Rigby's study at Wrykyn.

Saul Pedder, an energetic Radical candidate for Mayor of Wrykyn in WF07.

One-Round Peebles is Battling Billson's boxing adversary in 35CB.

Hermione Pegler (Mrs. Winthrop Pegler) of Park Avenue and Newport, a handsome, severe woman with elaborately waved hair and plucked iron-grey eyebrows, like an elderly Gibson girl with something on her mind, aunt of Chester and Mavis Todd in FL56, keen on arranging the marriage of Mavis to Freddie Carpenter. First married to a Mr. Vokes, then to the

Marquis de Maufrigneuse (she was his second wife), thirdly to L.J. Quackenbush.

Cyril **Pemberton**, plug-ugly employed by Daphne Dolby to enforce her betrothal to Sir Jaklyn Warner in BA73.

Evangeline **Pembury**, author of *Parted Ways*, wooed by Egbert Mulliner in 30BS.

Gwladys **Pendlebury**, an artist in 29SA who paints a portrait of Bertie later used in soup advertisements, drives a red Widgeon Seven at high speed.

Horace **Pendlebury-Davenport**, a wealthy Drone living at 52 Bloxham Mansions, Park Lane in UF39, where he is engaged to Valerie Twistleton. Still engaged to Valerie in 50SP, where he successfully defends his Drones Darts championship and wins a tidy sum for Bingo Little. A young man of great height but lacking in the width of shoulder which makes height impressive, wears tortoise-shell-rimmed spectacles. Nephew to Alaric, Duke of Dunstable, the son of his late brother. His mother is a Hilsbury-Hepworth, from whom he inherits the large, fawn-like eyes that distinguish that family. In JF54 he is a former Drone and last year's winner of the Darts sweep, now married to Valerie Twistleton, at whose suggestion he has resigned his Drones membership.

Ernest **Pennefather**, cab-driver client of Jeff Miller in MB42, assaulted by Orlo Tarvin.

George William **Pennefather** is a young, disgruntled golfer in the beginning of 22MP.

George **Pennicut**, portly English man-of-all-work to Kirk Winfield in WH14.

Robert Dwight **Penway**, artist and illustrator with a drinking problem, friend of Kirk Winfield hired to teach him the artist's craft in WH14.

Mrs. **Penworthy**, tobacconist's wife, mothers' sack race contender in 22PT/IJ23.

Reggie **Pepper**, a Bertie Wooster prototype in 11AT, 11HF, 12RR, 12DO, 13DC, 15CA, and 15TC, is nephew of the late Edward Pepper of Pepper, Wells, & Co., the colliery people. Heir through his uncle to a sizable chunk of bullion, he has never worked. Was at Oxford with Freddie Meadowes and

Bill Schoolbred. Helps Bobbie Cardew remember his wife's birthday in 11AT. Helps Freddie Meadowes win back the affections of Angela West in 11HF. His valet in 12RR, where he rallies round old George Lattaker, is Harold Voules. In 15CA, where he helps Archie Ferguson conceal his cartoonist's art from Eunice Nugent, his man is named Wilberforce. A despised friend of Florence in 12DO, he helps disentangle her brother Percy from an engagement to the unsuitable Dorothea Darrell, with the result that Dorothea becomes Florence's stepmother. Once engaged to Elizabeth Schoolbred, to oblige whom he destroys the wrong Venus, i.e. Clarence Yeardsley's "Jocund Spring," in 13DC (cf. Bertie Wooster in 59JM). Gets the mitten from Ann Selby in 15TC, the last of the seven Reggie Pepper stories, where he helps save Harold Bodkin's marriage.

Rev. Arthur James Perceval, M.A., headmaster of St Austin's in 01PP and PH02 (where his name is given as Herbert Perceval). Known to the school as the old 'un. His niece Dorothy is the girl with the bicycle in 03MC.

Percy[1] is the obnoxious brother of the late Amelia Bodkin in 15TC.

Percy[2] is one of two swans living at Mulberry Grove, Valley Fields in BM31; his colleague is names Egbert.

Percy[3] is the name of Mrs. Widdrington's cat who is soundly thrashed by the cat Webster in 32CC.

Percy[4], a pimpled boy with a rather supercilious manner, cleans the knives and boots at Ashenden Manor in UD48.

Percy[5] is the boy who cleans the knives & boots at Blandings in SS61.

Percy[6], Aunt Dahlia's cousin, has been to Sir Roderick Glossop's clinic for repairs in 65JG. Got the idea he was being followed about by little men with black beards. Thinks alcohol is a food.

Percy[7] is the office boy at Scrope, Ashby & Pemberton in GB70.

Perkins[1] is Master of the Upper Fourth in PH02.

Perkins[2] is a police constable in NG07.

Perkins[3], a golfer who plays for high stakes in 25HS.

Mrs. **Perkins** is the cook at Chuffnell Hall in TY34.

George **Perkins**[1], a sixteen-handicap youth paired with Marcella Bingley in 20RS.

George **Perkins**[2], employed by bookie Joe Sprockett, lives at 10 Marina Crescent, Bramley, and marries a substantial blonde in 39BI.

Norah **Perkins**, girl friend of Sidney Price in NG07.

Perks is butler to Col. Stewart at Gorton Hall in LS08.

Perkyn, a junior at Jephson's, Beckford College, is bitten by a centipede in 04BB.

Wilmot or Motty, Lord **Pershore**, son of Lady Malvern and Bertie's unbidden guest in 16JU; about 23, tall and thin and meek-looking, with yellow hair plastered down and parted in the middle and a chin that gives up the struggle about half-way down.

Peteiro, an Indian half-caste in Ripton's first fifteen, is defeated by R.D. Sheen for the public schools Light Weight boxing title at Aldershot in WF07.

Peter, 10, only child of a wealthy English family living in the country, son of Helen; adopts the Mixer in 15MS.

Aline **Peters**, only daughter of J. Preston Peters; a small, pretty, good-natured looking girl of about 20 in SN15. Engaged to Freddie Threepwood, courted by George Emerson.

Horace **Peters**, Maud's brother in 10WD.

J. Preston **Peters**, dyspeptic American millionaire in SN15, father of Aline Peters. A little, truculent looking man with thick grey eyebrows and a leaden-colored face. Fanatical scarab collector, forced by his dyspepsia to subsist on a diet of nuts and grasses.

Jno. **Peters**, clerk for the law firm of Marlowe, Thorpe, Prescott, Winslow & Appelby, carries a large pistol in TM22.

Maud **Peters**, manicurist at the Hotel Belvoir in 10WD. The center of her world is Arthur Welsh, the hotel barber.

Aubrey **Petheram**, 24, is editor of *Squibs* in MM14.

Mabel **Petherick-Soames**, wooed and won by Osbert Mulliner in 28OO.

Major General Sir Masterman **Petherick-Soames**, Mabel's uncle in 28OO. Once horsewhipped Capt. J.G. Walkinshaw on the steps of the Drones Club for trifling with the affections of his niece Hester; similarly rebuked Rupert Blenkinsop-Bustard on the steps of the Junior Bird Fanciers for trifling with the affections of his niece Gertrude. Prepared to administer like treatment to Osbert Mulliner on the steps of the United Jade Fanciers for trifling with the affections of his niece Mabel.

Pauline **Petite**, movie star admired by Freddie Threepwood in 26LE.

Nesta Ford **Pett**: see Mrs. Elmer Ford.

Peter **Pett**, the well-known financier of Riverside Drive, New York, whose residence resembles a cathedral, a suburban villa, a hotel, and a Chinese pagoda. A little, thin, grey-haired man, son of a book collector, two years married to Nesta Ford in PJ17.

Mrs. **Pettigrew** of the golf-club has lost her purse and recovers it in 25PR.

Hank **Philbrick**, Canadian friend of S.F. Ukridge in 23US.

Jno. B. **Philbrick**, Manager of the Leave-It-To-Us Correspondence School in 31VP.

Philippe, bartender at the Hotel Splendide, Roville-Sur-Mer in FL56.

Phillipps is the Romney chauffeur in 09AC.

Rev. Edwin T. **Philpott** or Philpotts, cadaverous-looking man with pale blue eyes and melancholy face, writes "Moments of Meditation" for *Peaceful Moments* in PA12, *Cosy Moments* in PJ15.

Barmy **Phipps**, a Drone in 36MT whose cousin Egbert from Harrow is a dead shot with a catapult. See also MS49, where we learn of his annual cross-talk act at the Drones with Pongo Twistleton, and CT58.

Lady Diana **Phipps**, relict of the late Rollo Phipps, a big game hunter killed by a lion years ago; Lord Emsworth's tenth sister in SB77, the only one friendly to Galahad.

George **Phipps**, butler at Rumpling Hall in 36BT.

James **Phipps**, butler to Mrs. Adela Shannon Cork in OR51; ex-safeblower and alumnus of Sing-Sing who changed careers as the result of a religious conversion.

Judson **Phipps**, son of the late Mortimer Phipps, the Suspender King; brother of Julia Cheever. Young American plutocrat with a pleasant, vacant face, horn-rimmed glasses, and large nose, becomes engaged to Elaine Jepp of the ensemble of the Alvin Theatre in 66LF.

W.G. **Phipps**, friend of C.F. Spencer at Dencroft's, Eckleton, acts as his conscience and peacemaker in 08GU.

Dudley **Pickering**, manufacturer of Pickering Automobiles, a rich middle-aged middle westerner inclined to stoutness, in love with Claire Fenwick in UM16.

Harold **Pickering**, partner in a publishing house, in love with Troon Rockett in 40SM. Takes golf lessons from Agnes Flack and becomes a scratch man; accidentally engaged to Agnes in Sidney McMurdo's absence.

Joe **Pickering**, playwright, author of *Cousin Angela* in BA73, gives up job in a solicitor's office to take employment with Ivor Llewellyn to prevent him from marrying for a sixth time; falls in love with Sally Fitch.

Mother **Pickett** owns the Excelsior Boarding-House, Southampton, and solves the murder of Capt. Gunner in 14DE.

Mrs. Mary Jane **Piggott**, cook at Towcester Abbey in RJ53, named after the cook-housekeeper or companion of PGW's aunt, Louisa Deane (see N.T.P. Murphy, *In Search of Blandings*, p. 70).

Arabella **Pikelet**, hideous infant daughter of Charles in 39SB.

Charles "Charley Always Pays" **Pikelet**, turf accountant for Bingo Little in 39SB, 54OB, and 65SS. Father of Arabella.

Emma **Pilbeam**, Mrs. Vanderley's maid in 12RR, breaks her engagement to Harold Voules as the result of a misunderstanding.

Percy Frobisher **Pilbeam**, son of William Albert Pilbeam, cousin of Gwendoline Gibbs; early in his career a journalist, publisher, and editor specializing in sleazy journalism in BC24 and SS25; a nasty-looking reptilian squirt of about 23 with narrow eyes, badly shaped mouth, pimples, sideburns, small repellent moustache, and hair marcelled in ridges, looks like something unpleasant out of an early Evelyn Waugh novel. Member of the Junior Constitutional Club. Was assistant editor of *Pyke's*

Home Companion, in which he was advice columnist Aunt Ysobel. Sub-editor of *Society Spice* under Roderick Pyke in BC24, editor in SS25; no longer an editor in FP29, where he sends Sue Brown flowers; manages the Argus Enquiry Agency (cable address Pilgus, Piccy, London), continuing in this business in HW33, SF57, and BM64. Keen motorcyclist in HW33, engaged by Sir Gregory Parsloe to steal Galahad's memoirs. Hired in SF57 by Roscoe Bunyan to steal letters promising marriage to Elaine Dawn (Emma Billson) and a contract with A. Keggs respecting the employment of Bill Hollister. Hired by former employer Lord Tilbury in BM64 to prevent Biff Christopher from receiving his inheritance.

William Albert **Pilbeam**, father of Percy and uncle of Gwendoline Gibbs, waiter at Barribault's Hotel in BM64; a teetotaler, lives in Valley Fields.

Frederick **Pilcher**, artist in 27TP.

Otis **Pilkington**, amateur playwright, a long, thin young man with tortoise-shell glasses, nephew of Mrs. Waddesleigh Peagrim in LW20. Wrote book and lyrics of *The Rose of America*.

Jane **Pillenger**, private secretary and typist to Mr. Meggs in 14ST. A wary spinster of austere views, uncertain age, and a deep-rooted suspicion of men. Formerly secretary to an Indiana novelist.

Pillingshot misses a mid-term Livy examination in order to go with the St Austin's team and score at Windybury in 03HP; fags for J.G. Scott at St Austin's in 10PD. Scott's ex-fag in 11PP, where he is nonetheless prevailed upon to assume duty as editor of a scurrilous rag called *The Rapier*, for which Beale blacks his eye. Has a fixed policy of never preparing his Livy.

Lucius **Pim**, wavy-haired rival of Bertie for the love of Gwladys Pendlebury in 29SA.

Arlene **Pinckney**, beautiful, strenuous, and athletic daughter of Arnold Pinckney in 66LF; golfer, cousin of Joe Cardinal.

Arnold **Pinckney**, head of Pinckney's Stores, director of the New Asiatic Bank, and trustee on Joe Cardinal's estate in 66LF. Father of Arlene Pinckney. Big wheel in the

Anti-Tobacco League. Engaged to Julia Phipps Cheever in 66LF.

Leila J. **Pinckney,** squashily sentimental novelist in 25HC, wrote 40 novels and 240 short stories—9,140,000 words of glutinous sentimentality—in twenty years at Honeysuckle Cottage. Aunt of James Rodman. Favorite author of Mabel Potter in BA73; author of *Scent o' the Blossom* and *Heather o' the Hills.*

Lady **Pinfold,** relict of the late Sir Ramsworthy Pinfold and stout, elderly mother of Dora Pinfold, old friend of Lord Blicester in 36MT.

Dora **Pinfold,** only daughter of the late Sir Ramsworthy Pinfold and Lady Pinfold, selected as a suitable wife for Freddie Widgeon by his uncle Lord Blicester in 36MT and loved at first sight by Freddie himself, with the usual results.

Prince **Ping Pong Pang,** Chinese invader in SW09.

Rev. Harold P. "Stinker" **Pinker,** Oxford friend of Bertie, attended Magdalen College where he boxed and played Rugby football; later played Rugby for England. Curate at Totleigh-in-the-Wold and engaged to Stiffy Byng in CW38 and SU63, which makes him an adjunct member of the Totleigh Towers gang. A large, lumbering, Newfoundland puppy of a chap who is graceful only on the football field, he upsets furniture whenever he moves about a room. Steals Constable Eustace Oates' helmet for Stiffy in CW38. Major Plank gives him a vicarage in Hockley-cum-Meston in SU63 in order to obtain his services as a prop forward on the local Rugby team (the new vicarage allows him to marry Stiffy). Still giving satisfaction on Major Plank's team in AA74.

Jimmy **Pinkerton,** playwright friend of Reggie Pepper and Freddie Meadowes in 11HF.

Brenda **Piper,** Sir James' formidable sister in SB77.

Sir James **Piper,** England's Chancellor of the Exchequer, was a member of the Pelican Club and the Gardenia Club before entering politics; now in the Athenaeum. In love with Lady Diana Phipps in SB77.

Pirbright is Celia Todd's Pekingese in 48TH.

Angela **Pirbright,** tennis player engaged to golfer Walter Judson in 56JB.

Claude Cattermole **Pirbright**: see Potter-Pirbright.

Cora or Corky **Pirbright**, sister of Claude, a lissom girl of medium height with eyes and hair of browny hazel, giving the general effect of an angel who eats lots of yeast. Was in Bertie's dancing class, where she induced him to bung a mouldy orange at their instructress. Now a Hollywood actress, using the stage name Cora Starr. In love with Esmond Haddock in MS49.

James **Pirbright** is George Cyril Wellbeloved's successor as keeper of the Empress of Blandings in FP29 and HW33. Tall, thin, even scraggier than Lord Emsworth.

Rev. Sidney **Pirbright**, uncle of Cora and Claude in MS49, vicar at King's Deverill, Hants. A tall, drooping man, looking as if he was stuffed in a hurry by an incompetent taxidermist.

James Willoughby **Pitt**, title character of IJ10, went to school and Cambridge with Arthur Mifflin. Inherited $500,000 from a fellow who had been in love with his late mother before her marriage. Studied law at the 'Varsity but never kept it up. An amateur boxer, has worked as an actor, waiter, newspaper man, jeweller. Medium height, with the broad, deep chest, square jaw, piercing brown eyes and good nature of a bull terrier. Wins the hand of Molly McEachern. Mentioned as a friend of John Maude in PB12.

Major "Barmy" **Plank**, landed proprietor at Hockley-cum-Meston, Gloucestershire, invests a vicarage in Stinker Pinker to obtain a prop forward for the local Rugby football team in SU63, where he accuses Bertie of trying to chisel him out of five quid. Friend of Pop Cook and patient of onetime schoolmate Jimpy Murgatroyd in AA74. An elderly one-time explorer with a square empire-building face, much tanned. Suffers from malaria, picked up in equatorial Africa, which affects his memory. Not to be confused with Major Brabazon-Plank, q.v.

Rhoda **Platt** of Wistaria Lodge, Kitchener Road, East Dulwich, waitress at The Buffers, object of Uncle George Wooster's sentimental attentions in 30IS.

Edward **Plimmer**, ugly police constable with a beat on Battersea Park Road in 15RU, falls in love with Ellen Brown.

148

Miss **Plimsoll**, aunt of Tipton Plimsoll, owns six Pekes in 50BS.

Eustace H. **Plimsoll**, the Laburnums, Alleyn Road, West Dulwich, Bertie's alias in the Vine St. Police station when arrested for attempting to steal a policeman's helmet on Boat-Race Night, as remembered in RH34.

Horace **Plimsoll**, family lawyer to the Havershots and friend of Reggie in LG36.

Tipton **Plimsoll**, heir via his late uncle Chester Tipton to a large fortune in shares of an American supermarket chain, Tipton's Stores. A Drone, long and thin like a string bean, with a beaky nose and horn-rimmed glasses, many times engaged: to Doris Jimpson, Angela Thurloe, Vanessa Wainwright, Barbara Bessemer, Clarice Burbank, Marcia Ferris, and finally, in FM47 and BG65, to Veronica Wedge. The wedding is celebrated in 50BS on Long Island, attended by Veronica's uncle Lord Emsworth.

Ernest Faraday **Plinlimmon**, a smallish man with spectacles, looks like the second vice-president of something. An average adjustor, devout and skilful golfer with a handicap of four. Wins the love of Clarice Fitch in 36AG.

Edwin **Plummer**, Millie's brother in DD19, in love with Maud Marsh and before that with Alice Faraday. Sings badly.

Millie **Plummer**, small and young and fluffy admirer of George Bevan's show tunes in DD19; sister of Edwin.

Everard, Lord **Plumpton**, cricket enthusiast and uncle to Conky Biddle in 51HT.

Plunkett, disliked Mutual Friend of Dallas and Vaughan who shares their study in PH02. Prefect of Ward's house, St Austin's, wears spectacles and reads Herodotus in Greek for pleasure. Caught trespassing on Sir Alfred Venner's land with tobacco and smoking accessories.

Herbert **Pobsley**, a talking golfer in 21SG.

Robert **Podmarsh**, once the scourge of his club, a teller of humorous stories now prospering among the M'Pongo, who have assigned him a special hut and seven wives in 15DP.

Rollo **Podmarsh**, 27, tall, and well-knit, the only son of his widowed mother, awakened in 23AR. A hardened golfer in 50FC known to have finished a round though he thought he had been poisoned because he had a chance of breaking 100 for the first time.

General **Poineau**, commander of the 115-man army of Mervo and leader of its Royalist Party in PA12, PB12.

Vanessa **Polk**, kind to Lady Constance Keeble on the boat from New York during one of her attacks of neuralgia, poses as the daughter of financial emperor J.B. Polk, by whom she is employed as confidential secretary. Actually daughter of former valet G.P. Polk of Norfolk county, an emigrant to America, and a onetime Blandings parlour-maid. Very sound on pigs, marries Willie Trout in PB69.

Pollen is butler to the Abbots at Walsingford Hall in SM37.

Rev. Alistair **Pond-Pond**, vicar of Rudge-in-the-Vale in MN28.

Jimmy **Ponder**, suitor of Mavis Mulligan in PG72. Crawling with money, partner in a big jewellery firm. Small clipped moustache. Victim at Cannes of Soapy Molloy and his Silver River shares.

Ponsonby[1], boy in the Upper Fifth at St Austin's who carries a message from Mr. Yorke to Mellish's room in 02BL.

Ponsonby[2], butler to Harold and Hilda Bodkin in 15TC.

Marilyn **Poole**, maid to Lady Diana Phipps, courted by Sgt. Murchison in SB77.

Augustus or Aubrey **Popgood**, senior publishing partner of Cyril Grooly, q.v.

Popjoy, police constable at Lower Smattering-on-the-Wissel in 52BB.

Graf von **Poppenheim**, Prince Otto's aide-de-camp in SW09.

Arthur **Popworth**, proprietor of the Dovetail Hammer station cab in CT58.

Lora Delane **Porter**, for years in the forefront of America's Feminist movement, is working on a book called *Woman in the New Era* in 15PW and is renting a house in England for the summer. Her disciple is Sybil Bannister, wife of her nephew Hailey. In WH14 she is a gimlet-eyed crank on eugenics and germs, authoress of *The Dawn of Better Things*, *Principles of Selection*, and *What of Tomorrow?* Relict of a newspaper man named Porter, aunt of Ruth Bannister in WH14.

Orlo J. **Porter**, 27, was on the same staircase at Oxford with Bertie; he was a prominent figure at the Union, where he made fiery far-to-the-left speeches; now employed by the London & Home Counties Insurance Co. and active in political demonstrations. Well-nourished, irritable, red-headed, a Communist and birdwatcher, in love with Vanessa Cook in AA74. Her father is trustee of his large estate inherited from his uncle Joe, Cook's partner in a big provision company.

Sir Chester **Portwood**, actor-manager at the Leicester Theatre in LW20. Produces Wally Mason's disastrous play *Tried by Fire*.

Gwendoline **Poskitt**, courted by W. Byng in 36LL, daughter of Joseph.

Joseph **Poskitt**, Gwendoline's father in 36LL, member of a foursome known at the golf-club as the Wrecking Crew; his muscle-bound style has made him known as the First Grave Digger; owns a dog named Alfred.

Postlethwaite, of the Upper Fourth at Wrykyn in 05PP, takes Chapple's place in the spare room of Seymour's house.

Miss **Postlethwaite**, courteous and efficient barmaid at the Angler's Rest in the Mulliner stories, e.g. 26SL, 28RW, 28OO, 29SC, 30BS, 31SW, 32MB, 33RM, 33CA, 34FW, 36BT, 37AG, 47RA. Prominent first-nighter at the Bijou Dream.

Claude "Mustard" **Pott**, private investigator in UF39, father of Polly, lives at 6 Wilbraham Place, Sloane Square. A stout, round, bald, pursy little man of about 50 with two chins and a waddle. Former actor, club manager, and bookie who still loves to organize (and win) betting games. Lord Ickenham suspects him of being a defrocked butler.

Edwin **Pott**, a little gnome of a man well stricken in years with no roof to his mouth, pig man at Blandings in FM47. Retires into private life after winning a football pool.

Polly **Pott**, daughter of Claude, engaged to Ricky Gilpin in UF39.

Mrs. **Potter**, cook employed by Col. Francis Pashley-Drake, keeps him fat in 67GC; will not work for anyone who smokes.

Albert **Potter**, a mechanic in the motor works around the corner from the Coppins in MM14, is courting Muriel Coppin and holds a low opinion of Roland Bleke.

Sgt. Claude **Potter** of Scotland Yard is brother-in-law to Supt. Jessop of the Wallingford constabulary in DB68.

Edwin **Potter**, Muriel Bromborough's fiancé in the beginning of 36BT. Son of Sir Preston Potter.

George **Potter**, vegetarian and teetotaler, is Walter Judson's opponent in the final of the President's Cup (min. handicap 18) in 56JB. Engaged to Mabel Case.

Harold **Potter**, 28, represents the awful majesty of the law in Ashenden Oakshott in UD48. Affianced to Elsie Bean, housemaid at Ashenden Manor.

John Hamilton **Potter**, founder and proprietor of the New York publishing house J.H. Potter, Inc., guest of Lady Wickham in 26PT.

Mabel **Potter**, private secretary of Mr. Schnellenhamer, expert imitator of the call of the cuckoo, wooed by Wilmot Mulliner in 33NO, his fiancée in 33JO. Reappears as secretary to theatrical manager Edgar Sampson in BA73, friend of Sally Fish.

Mervyn **Potter**, dipsomaniac and world-famous star of the silver screen, plays male lead in *Sacrifice* in BW52.

Sir Preston **Potter**, Bart., of Wapleigh Towers, Norfolk, owner of a moustache named Love in Idleness in 36BT.

William **Potter**, Egbert Mulliner's physician in 70AC.

Claude Cattermole "Catsmeat" **Potter-Pirbright**, son of a writer of theater music and a New York actress named Elsie Cattermole; brother of Cora Pirbright. Was at Rev. Upjohn's prep school with Bertie, where the Rev. Aubrey described him as "brilliant but unsound." Now an actor who plays "Freddie" roles in Society comedies (the lighthearted friend of the hero carrying the second love interest). Graduate of Oxford and a Drone, distinguished for his imitations of Beatrice Lillie, and for once having hit the game pie six times with six consecutive rolls from the far window of the Drones' dining room, as recalled in CW38. Cited in UF39 as a snappy dresser, the modern Brummel. Engaged to Gertrude Winkworth in MS49. Leaving for Hollywood in JF54; specializes in juvenile roles in 65JG and 65SS, using the stage name Claude Cattermole. Recalled in MO71 as having told Bertie a disgusting (but otherwise unspecified) anecdote at the Drones.

Cora **Potter-Pirbright**: see Cora Pirbright.

Rev. Sidney **Potter-Pirbright**: see Rev. Sidney Pirbright.

Mr. **Pottinger** is co-producer with a Mr. Abeles of *Ask Dad* in 29BG.

Freddie and Eustace **Potts** are remembered by Galahad in BG65 and elsewhere because on the Riviera their French chef picked up a dead hedgehog from the road on the way to the market to buy a chicken. He pocketed the money and served up the hedgehog *en casserole*. Eustace the teetotaler died; Freddie, who had lived mostly on whiskey since childhood, showed no ill effects whatsoever.

Loretta Stickney **Pound**, J. Wendell Stickney's stout sister in PP67, his elder by three years. Well known lecturer and publicist, owns a Pomeranian dog she is crazy about. Rules her brother, made him hire his English valet Clarkson.

Mr. **Prater** is a house-master at St Austin's in 02BL, owns a larcenous cat named Captain Kettle in 02TT; also mentioned in 03MC.

Ellabelle **Prebble**, Dudley Finch's wholesome, sweet-natured Australian fiancée in 40DI, is the niece of his godfather's brother's second wife.

Julia **Prebble**, dark horse candidate for the Ladies' Vase in 48TH.

Vera **Prebble**, Jacob Z. Schnellenhamer's stage-struck parlour-maid in 33RM, takes the stage name Minna Nordstrom.

Dahlia **Prenderby**, daughter of Sir Mortimer and Lady Prenderby, courted by Freddy Widgeon in 34GB, soon forgotten in 36MT.

Lady **Prenderby**, one of those tall, rangy, Queen Elizabeth sort of women with tight lips and cold, blanc-mange-y eyes, wife of Sir Mortimer and mother of Dahlia in 34GB.

Sir Mortimer **Prenderby**, master of Matcham Scratchings, Oxfordshire, father of Dahlia in 34GB.

Prendergast, a short, broad young man with a fair moustache, captain of the Lower Borlock cricket team in MK09.

Prescott is the hardest tackler in St Austin's in 03MC. Thirteen stone ten, all muscle, captain of Dacre's fifteen.

John **Prescott**, Elizabeth Boyd's neighbor at Brookport, L.I. in UM16.

Mabel **Prescott** collects subscriptions for the Temple of the New Dawn, Sister Lora Lulla Stott's temperance organization. Looks like a vicar's daughter who plays hockey. Eggy Mannering falls in love with her in LG36.

Pauline **Preston**, chorus-girl at the Frivolities in 20AS/IA21.

Sally **Preston**, a pretty, small and trim girl in 13ST, bored with Millbourne, where she is staying with her Aunt Jane. Daughter of an austere ex-butler who lets lodgings in Ebury Street and preaches on Sundays in Hyde Park. Loves movies, promises to marry Tom Kitchener, Ted Pringle, Joe Blossom, and Albert Parsons.

Izzy **Previn**, alias Issac O'Brien, stout, dark, beady-eyed bookie with large ears who enters a bookmaking partnership with S.F. Ukridge in 23LA at 3 Blue Street, St. James's, telegraphic address "Ikobee, London." Decamps with cash in 23EB.

Jean **Priaulx**, title character of 12MC, aspiring painter who falls in love with Marion Henderson; engaged as private secretary to M. Paul Sartines.

Jules **Priaulx**, rich uncle of Jean above, proprietor of the Hotel Jules Priaulx in 12MC.

Jane **Priestley**, former Nanny of Sally Fitch, lives in Valley Fields: very tall, very thin, very stony about the eyes, bears a distinct resemblance to Lady Macbeth. Next-door neighbor to Amelia Bingham in BA73.

Bella **Price**, sister of Lord Droitwich's butler Slingsby in IW31, was nurse to Lord Droitwich. Married to a barber in Mott Street, Knightsbridge, she exchanged her own baby for the heir to the Earldom of Droitwich, thus becoming the actual mother of Anthony Claude Wilbraham Bryce, Lord Droitwich, instead of the Cockney barber Syd Price. Has a jumpy heart, for which she takes too much brandy; highly superstitious.

Cuthbert **Price**, pig man at Blandings in PB69.

Mabel **Price** of Balbriggan, Peabody Road, Clapham Common, courted by S.F. Ukridge in 23NW.

Sidney **Price**, one of the narrators of NG07, agrees to act as "nom de ploom" for James Orlebar Cloyster's Society dialogues for a 10% share of the fee. Lives at The Hollyhocks, Belmont Park Road, Brixton, and works for the Moon Assurance Company. His girl friend is Norah Perkins.

Sydney Lancelot **Price**, a Cockney Socialist with a small and rather horrible moustache, runs Price's Hygienic Toilet Salon in Mott Street, Knightsbridge in IW31. Born in India the son of John, fourth Earl of Droitwich, with the name Anthony Claude Wilbraham Bryce, he was sent back to England on the death of his mother to be nursed by the sister of Slingsby, the family butler at Langley End (Bella Price), who exchanged him for her own son, who grew up to be Lord Droitwich. Has a scar from a burn on his arm which proves his actual identity. Employer of Polly Brown.

Pringle, age seventeen and a half, is a resident at the School-house in Beckford College in PU03; one of the school's eleven, has advice for everybody, but is a good batsman. Copies a poem on the death of Dido out of a book in his uncle's library and gives it to Lorimer to use as his prize poem entry.

Professor **Pringle** of Cambridge, father of Heloise Pringle; a thinnish, baldish, dyspeptic-looking man with an eye like a haddock, Bertie's unwitting host in 25WO.

Mrs. **Pringle**, mother of Heloise in 25WO, was a Miss Blatherwick; her elder sister married Sir Roderick Glossop. Her aspect is that of one who had bad news round about the year 1900 and never really got over it.

Heloise **Pringle**, daughter of Prof. & Mrs. Pringle of Cambridge, resembles her cousin Honoria Glossop. Takes a bead on Bertie in 25WO thinking he is Sippy Sipperley, and tries to persuade him to avoid the company of B. Wooster. Her voice, like her cousin's, sounds like a lion tamer making some authoritative announcement to one of the troupe.

Miss Jane **Pringle**, 86, Prof. Pringle's aunt in 25WO, has poor hearing but good eyesight and a wonderful memory.

Ted **Pringle** is one of Sally Preston's suitors in 13ST.

The **Pro**, a small, bearded gardener of King Merolchazzar with bushy eyebrows and a face like a walnut. Captured by one of His Majesty's invincible admirals on a raid at S'andrews. Gowf instructor to the King in 21CG.

Sam **Proctor**, the Tennessee Bear Cat, is a pugilist who dines at the East Side Delmonico's and boxes Freddie Bingham after eating a large meal in 13JW.

Prof. **Prosser**, pseud. Edith Butler, lit'ery gent, Regius Professor boarding with the Dormans in Shropshire, engaged to Vera Delane in 11PO. Large and black-bearded, author of some half dozen works on sociology.

Alexander Charles "Oofy" **Prosser**, the Drones' stout and pimpled tame millionaire in 31KQ, 33LS, 37AW, 39SB, UF39, 40WS, 48FO, 50SP, 54LA, 54OB, 58FL, IB61, SU63, BG65. Referred to in BM31 as Oofy Simpson. His father was Prosser's Pep Pills. His uncles include Hildebrand, who has an apoplectic stroke in 1947, and Stanley, who dies of cirrhosis of the liver in 1949. Horace Prosser turns out to be a distant relative, but no uncle. Lives in Bloxham Mansions, Park Lane. Wears sidewhiskers, silk underwear, and shoes by Lobb. Notwithstanding his vast wealth, he is constantly involved in chancy schemes to make more money. Sends strawberries to Clarice Mallaby in 31KQ; gives Pongo Twistleton 100 to 8 that Adolphus Stiffham will never marry Geraldine Spettisbury in 33LS (he loses). Barely escapes proposing to a girl in 39SB. Godfather to Algernon Aubrey Little in 40WS, where he is entangled with Mabel Murgatroyd. Married in IB61 to Myrtle Shoesmith, whose jewelry he has insured for double its value; still recently married in BG65, where his wife wants to buy a country house. "In the 1890's a prosser was one who borrowed money or was mean with it. 'Oof' was slang for money and 'an oofy bird' was someone with plenty of it."—N.T.P. Murphy, *In Search of Blandings*, p. 27.

Horace **Prosser**, an enormously fat relative of Oofy, has just returned from many years in the Argentine in 58FL.

Myrtle Shoesmith **Prosser**, Oofy's wife in IB61, a young woman of considerable but extremely severe beauty; has had her jewelry stolen by Dolly Molloy.

Ted **Prosser**, one of Annabell Sprockett-Sprockett's seven suitors in 34FW.

Charlton **Prout**, sleek, stout young secretary of the Pen & Ink Club in 23US; author of *Grey Myrtles*.

Rupert (or Ronald) Eustace **Psmith**, schoolboy and young man in MK09, PC10, PJ15, LP23. Very tall, very thin, with a solemn face and immaculate clothes; wears a monocle. Was at Eton, and in the cricket XI, before coming to Sedleigh. Son of the Smith who used to own Corfby Hall, Lower Bedford, near Much Middlefold, Shropshire. Decides to add a silent P to his family name while buying a penny butterscotch from a machine in Paddington Station while on his way to Sedleigh for the first time in MK09: "It seemed to me that there were so many Smiths in the world that a little variety might well be introduced." Embraces Socialism on his arrival at Sedleigh: "You work for the equal distribution of property, and start by collaring all you can and sitting on it." Shares a study at Outwood's with Mike Jackson in MK09. Educated expensively until his father dies, leaving only debts; supports himself for a time working in his uncle's fish business. Member of the Drones and the Senior Conservative Club in PC10, but remains a practical Socialist of sorts: "Others are content to talk about the Redistribution of Property. I go out and do it." Addresses people as "Comrade." Enters and leaves employ of the New Asiatic Bank in PC10. Visiting America with Mike Jackson in PJ15 after their first year at Cambridge together, becomes sub-editor of *Cosy Moments* in New York under Billy Windsor. Named Ronald in LP23 to avoid confusion with Rupert Baxter, whom he succeeds as Lord Emsworth's secretary, and successfully courts Eve Halliday. According to PGW based on Rupert D'Oyly Carte, son of the impresario. "Years ago a cousin of mine told me that he was at Winchester with a long, thin, solemn, immaculately dressed boy who used to wear an eyeglass and talk kindly, but not patronisingly, to the head

157

Psmith

master. The character, Psmith, who has appeared in several of my books, was based on my idea of that youth, whom I never met."—PGW, "How I Write My Books" in *What I Think* (London: George Newnes, 1926). See also PGW's preface to *The World of Psmith* (London: Barrie & Jenkins, 1974).

Mr. **Pugh**, a wizened little man, one of a deputation of four gamblers to John Maude, Prince of Mervo, in PB12.

Mrs. **Pulteney-Banks** is Lady Widdrington's shawl-draped mother in 32CC. Believes cats are cleverer than we think.

Mrs. Alice **Punter**, cook of Lord Shortlands at Beevor Castle in SF48, sought as wife by Lord Shortlands and his butler Mervyn Spink. Long-lost fiancée of Augustus Robb.

Diana **Punter**, statuesque niece of Nelson Cork's godmother in 33AH, courted by N. Cork, hitches up instead to Percy Wimbolt. Has an Uncle George who suddenly left England in 1920 without stopping to pack up, and a brother Cyril who was warned off the turf in 1924.

Angela **Purdue**, wholesome, sunburned fiancée of Wilfred Mulliner and heiress of the Purdue millions in 26SL.

Purkis, chauffeur to the Steptoe household in QS40.

Henry Cuthbert **Purkiss**, proprietor of *Wee Tots*, hires Bingo Little to edit his magazine in 37BP and continues as Bingo's employer in 39ER, 40WS, 50SP (where his initials are P.P.), 54LA, 54OB, 65BB, 65SS.

Julia **Purkiss**, wife of Henry in 37BP, 39ER, 40WS, 54OB. Owns a Peke; lifelong friend of Rosie Banks.

Purvis is Aunt Agatha's butler in 26JI.

Annabel **Purvis**, conjuror's assistant for the Great Boloni, later Sir Aylmer Bastable's nurse in 37RD; affianced to Freddie Fitch-Fitch.

Lancelot **Purvis** comes from Ostoria, Ohio and works as a barber at the Hotel Cosmopolis in New York. A veteran of the War, where he looked after horses in the rear of the American Expeditionary Force lines. In love with May Gleason in 20GF. Cf. Arthur Welsh in 10WD.

P.K. **Purvis**, winner of the Market Snodsbury Grammar School Prize for spelling and dictation in RH34; about three feet six inches in his squeaking shoes, with a pink face and sandy hair.

Slingsby **Purvis**, of Purvis's Liquid Dinner Glue, is courting Angela in 27CD.

Kate Amelia **Putnam**, a thin, colorless featherweight with horn-rimmed spectacles and an air of quiet respectability; social secretary to Mrs. Gedge in HW32, employed by the James B. Flaherty Detective Agency of New York.

Clarence van **Puyster** (a Greek god) lives with his parents at the north end of Washington Square in 10PP and falls in love with Isabel Rackstraw. Pitches for the Giants under the pseudonym Brown. Cf. Clarence Tresillian in 12GK.

Vansuyther van **Puyster**, father of Clarence in 10PP; silver-haired, not given to thinking, descendant of an original van Puyster who acquired a square mile or so in the heart of Manhattan for ten dollars cash and a quarter interest in a pedler's outfit. Has just about enough brain to make a jay-bird fly crooked, and no more.

George **Pybus**, friend of Montrose Mulliner in 32MB, works in the Press Department of the Perfecto-Zizzbaum Motion Picture Company.

Sir George Alexander (Stinker) **Pyke**: see Lord Tilbury.

Laura **Pyke**, Rosie Banks' school friend, is a food crank in 30JO.

Roderick **Pyke**, o.s. of the late Lucy Maynard and Sir George Alexander Pyke, Lord Tilbury. A graduate of Oxford, published a book on the prose of Walter Pater at his own expense. A tall, thin young man with large brown eyes and chestnut hair swept flowingly over the forehead, lives at #7 Lidderdale Mansions, Sloane Square. Nominal and unwilling editor of *Society Spice* in BC24, wants to marry Flick Sheridan.

Homer **Pyle**, eminent corporation lawyer with Pyle, Wisbeach & Hollister in GB70, brother of Bernadette Clayborne. Amateur poet with large, round face and horn-rimmed spectacles, member of P.E.N.

Vera **Pym**, barmaid at the Rose and Crown in Loose Chippings and fiancée of Chibnall in QS40.

John B. **Pynsent**, import-export merchant and uncle of Sam Shotter in SS25.

Q

Queenie: see Queenie Silversmith.

Solly **Quhayne**, son of Abraham Cohen, rising young music-hall and vaudeville agent in SW09 and 15MI.

Dante Gabriel **Quintin**, an artist who lives next door to the Littles in 40WS.

R

Daniel **Rackstraw**, a tainted millionaire and father of Isabel in 10PP, is a little, gray, dried-up man, a baseball nut and collector of baseball memorabilia. Puts up his Neal Ball glove against Jacob Dodson's Hans Wagner bat that the Giants will beat the Tigers in a private game at his country estate. A multi-millionaire City man and Radical politician in 12GK, a soccer fan whose collection of football memorabilia rivals that of Jacob Dodson. Fan of Houndsditch Wednesday.

Isabel **Rackstraw**, slim, radiant (a peach in 10PP, an angel in 12GK) daughter of Daniel Rackstraw, sought in marriage by Clarence van Puyster in 10PP, by the Hon. Clarence Tresillian in 12GK.

Mortimer **Rackstraw**, the Great Boloni, conjuror and one-time fiancé of Annabel Purvis in 37RD.

Raikes[1], cricketer at Appelby's, Wrykyn in MK09.

Raikes[2], New York character actor and member of the Strollers' Club in IJ10.

Lord **Rainsby**, "Dog-Face," son of the Earl of Datchet and a chorus girl. Half-crazed cousin of Claude & Eustace Wooster, keeps cats in 22SR/IJ23.

Raisuli, head of a band of Moroccan Brigands invading

England in SW09.

Ram is a new boy from Calcutta at Marleigh School in LS08. Small, round, and dark-skinned with gold-rimmed spectacles, he is the boys' favorite orator.

Rand-Brown of Seymour's is a weak football player at Wrykyn in GB04.

Randall, the curate at Bray Lench in 06FM, is an old Trinity man.

Reginald "Ruthless" **Rankin**, a small, weedy, and ugly resident of Seymour's at Wrykyn in 05RR and 05AB, weighs seven stone three. His green eyes wear a chronic look of suspicion and secretiveness. His hobby is revenge. Fags for Rigby, on whose shelves he puts an array of Dr. Bohn's *English Translations of the Classics* for his uncle the Bishop to see. His adversary in 05AB is Shoeblossom Leather-Twigg.

Mrs. **Rastall-Retford**, a massive lady with prominent forehead and some half-dozen chins, ill-tempered dieter attended by Eve Hendrie in 11BS.

Mr. **Rastrick**, father of Gussie and sometime guest of the Romneys in 09AC, was at school with Mr. Romney and owns a private school near London. A tall man of commanding aspect, with large, penetrating eyes and a pointed beard.

Augustus or Gussie **Rastrick**, about fifteen, is Mr. Rastrick's short, fat, and furtive son in 09AC. A good slow bowler but inexperienced with cigars.

Lefty **Rawson**, seaman on the *May Moon* in 07BT.

Ted **Ray**, friend of Rollo Podmarsh in 23AR.

Geoffrey **Raymond**, nephew and heir of the late Wilbur Raymond of 11a Belgrave Square. Spreading suitor of Maud Marsh, whom he loses to George Bevan in DD19.

Peter **Rayner**, Mrs. Elphinstone's brother, courts Eve Hendrie in 11BS.

Reade of Philpott's house, member of the St Austin's fifteen, dislocates a collar-bone in 02HP; Barrett's studymate in PH02.

Reece keeps wicket for the Beckford College eleven in PU03; wierd, silent individual in the Sixth.

Freda **Reece**, chorus girl and friend of Bailey Bannister in

WH14.

Reeve-Smith, Cambridge friend of John Maude in PB12.

Reginald is not spending the weekend with Wilkinson Bodfish in 15SP.

Spider **Reilly,** head of the Three Points gang in PA12.

Joe **Rendal** from Dunsterville, Canada, successful New York stock broker who employs Mary Hill in 11TD.

Thomas **Renford** is Milton's fag at Seymour's, Wrykyn in GB04; answers the roll for Shoeblossom in 05AB. Still a younger boy at Seymour's in WF07.

J. Brabazon **Renshaw,** editor of *Peaceful Moments*, a journal of the home owned by Benjamin Scobell in PA12. Cf. J. Fillken Wilberfloss in PJ15.

Jack **Repetto,** black-jack-toting member of the Three Points Gang in PA12 (where he is an albino) and PJ15.

Reuben, title character of 10LM, is John Barton's bulldog, beloved of Aline Ellison and dreaded by Bertie Fendall.

Reynolds of the Remove is in the infirmary at St Austin's in 01PP, where he writes a prize poem for Smith[1].

Sylvia **Reynolds** owns a destructive pug named Tommy who is shot in 01WP.

Col. **Reynolds,** V.C., shoots daughter Sylvia's pug in 01WP.

Bromham **Rhodes,** fat and bulgy-eyed theatrical writer in MM14, is associated with R.P. de Paris, Billy Verepoint, and the Windsor Theatre in MM14.

Henry Pifield **Rice,** detective employed at Stafford's International Investigation Bureau in the Strand, courts Alice Weston in 15BB; lives in a boarding-house on Guildford Street.

Edith **Riddell,** the Aunt Edith of the Joan Romney stories (05WP, 06PI, 07PC, 08LG, 09AC), lives on Sloan Street in London. Her son William is at New College, Oxford in 08LG.

William B. **Riddell,** cousin to Joan Romney and son of her Aunt Edith, is at New College, Oxford and gets a century against William Batkins in 08LG.

Ridgway, valet to Bill West in BC24.

Mabelle **Ridgway,** affianced to Bulstrode Mulliner in 33CA.

Abe **Riesbitter**, vaudeville agent, a fat man with about fifty-seven chins, gets Gussie a job singing in 15EY.

Rigby, a placid Six Former in Seymour's house at Wrykyn in 05RR (where Ruthless Reginald Rankin is his fag), is head of the house in WF07. His uncle is Bishop Peter Peckham.

Millicent **Rigby**, Lord Tilbury's secretary, recently disengaged from Archie Gilpin in SS61.

Riggs, butler to Lady Dora Garland at Wiltshire House, Grosvernor Square in PW52.

Oliver **Ring** of New York is head of Ring's Come-One Come-All Up-to-date Stores in 05IA, opening a branch at Wrykyn.

Ferdie "the Fly" **Ripley**, small, wizened cat burglar and factotum for Horace Appleby at Restharrow in DB68.

Ripton, in the Lower Third at St Austin's, is robbed by Prater's cat Captain Kettle.

Toddy van **Riter** of New York, friend of Judson Coker in BC24, did not found the Fifth Avenue Silks.

Jack **Roach**, tall, stringy waiter who gives the impression of having no spine. Sandy hair, weak eyes set close together, red stubble on chin, not in the lily class. Narrator of 10BA, friend of Gentleman Bailey and onetime fellow-guest of Jerry Moore.

Augustus **Robb**, ex-burglar, hired by G. Ellery Cobbold as his son Stanwood's butler in SF48. Retired from burgling after being saved at a revival meeting. A large, spreading man with a bald forehead, small eyes, extensive ears and a pasty face.

Mr. **Robbins** of Robbins, Robbins, Robbins, & Robbins, Solicitors and Commissioners for Oaths, a tall, thin man of ripe years, lawyer to T.P. Frisby in BM31. Phone Chancery 09632.

Roberts[1], the Keiths' chauffeur in 10GA and 10LM, is a wooden-faced man who wears a permanent air of melancholy.

Roberts[2] is butler to Cooley Paradene in BC24.

Inspector **Roberts**, Scotland Yard detective who probes the mystery of the stolen pots in PH02.

Mr. **Robertson**, housemaster at Beckford College in PU03. A long silent man with grizzled hair, keeps best order of any master in the school; also the most popular of the staff.

Robinson[1] is a member of Outwood's cricket team at Sedleigh in MK09. Crony of fellow Outwoodian W.J. Stone in 10SW.

Robinson[2] is the coatroom waiter at the Drones in 33AH.

Jno. **Robinson**, proprietor of the Market Blandings station cab in HW33, PW52, SS61, BG65, PB69, SB77. Called Ed. Robinson in UF39.

Reginald **Robinson**, Tony Graham's fag at Merevale's in PH03, thirteen years old, a runner.

Wilberforce **Robinson**, engaged to Julia Parker in 35UF, is an assistant in a jellied eel shop.

Kirk **Rockaway** of Oakland, San Francisco (*sic*), author of juvenile fiction in 65SS. One of the fattest men that ever broke a try-your-weight machine. A Rosie Banks romance fan, in love with Myrtle Beenstock.

John **Rockett**, twice British Amateur Champion, three times runner-up in the Open in 40SM. Named Walter in British edn.

Troon **Rockett**, daughter of John, a scratch golfer courted by Harold Pickering in 40SM. Named Marion in British edn.

Bream **Rockmetteller**, a colleague of Freddie Threepwood's at Donaldson's in 66LF.

Isabel **Rockmetteller**, title character of 16AS, aunt of Rockmetteller Todd; a large, solid, moneyed female from Illinois.

Mrs. Balderstone **Rockmettler**, fat American owner of fat cat Alexander in 12MC.

Mr. **Roddis** of The Cedars is a large, red-faced man in 35UF.

James **Rodman**, distant cousin of the Mulliner who holds forth at Angler's Rest, is a writer of sensational mystery stories in 25HC; legatee of Leila J. Pinckney, he produces three novels and eighteen short stories annually.

Herbert, Lord **Roegate**, is the young man intended by Lady Constance to marry her niece Jane in 36CW. PGW rented Rogate Lodge, Sussex, in the summer of 1928. Cf. Lord Hunstanton.

Rösselmann is the local priest in WT04.

Rogers is chauffeur at Belpher castle in DD19.

Farmer **Rollitt** lends his pasture for a country cricket match in 05TD on condition his eldest son Ted be put in to bowl first.

Ted **Rollitt** is put in to bowl first in 05TD.

Rollo is Lord Pershore's bull terrier in 16JU, won in a raffle.

Linda **Rome** keeps house for her uncle, Lord Tilbury at The Oaks, Wimbledon Common in BM64. Attractive, good-humored, sensible, works for Leonard Gish of Gish Galleries. Marries Biff Christopher.

Bob **Romney**, Joan Romney's brother, is a freshman at Magdalen in 05WP and in his second year in 06PI, where he gets his Blue in soccer. In 08LG he has a friend named Townend. He is away on a cricket tour with the Authentics in 09AC.

Joan **Romney**, 16 or 17, manipulative narrator of 05WP, 06PI, 07PC, 08LG, and 09AC, lives in Much Middlefold with her father Sir William and her brother Bob. Wants to spend the winter in London in 05WP. She has an Aunt Edith, a muddling Aunt Flora, and an Aunt Elizabeth, who is perfectly awful. In 06PI she winters on Sloane Street with her father and intervenes with T.B. Hook to get brother Bob on the Oxford footer team. Recruits Alan Gethryn (a distant cousin) from Beckford to bowl for Much Middlefold in 07PC; in 08LG she patches up a rift between her maid Saunders and William Batkins. Delays the end of a cricket match in 09AC so that the villagers will defeat her father's team and keep their right-of-way across her father's field.

Sir William **Romney**, father of Bob and Joan in the Joan Romney stories, hates London and plays cricket for Much Middlefold. Their butler Morris refers to him as the colonel in 09AC.

Freddie L. **Rooke** fagged for Derek Underhill at Winchester. Now a Drone living at the Albany, wears an eyeglass. Woos and wins Nell Bryant in LW20.

Rosie, fiancée of George Mellon in 19SF, sells tickets at a movie palace.

W.K. **Ross**, of The Elms, one of 19 suitors who send Sylvia Reynolds nineteen new pugs in 01WP.

Mr. **Rossiter**, head of the Postage Department at the New Asiatic Bank in PC10.

Cyprian **Rossiter**, one of Hermione's brothers in 29GU: pale and thin, writes art-criticism for the weekly papers. Face like a camel; whiskers; says "one senses"; has nasty, dry snigger; fruitarian; recites poetry; bony hands; heavy smoker.

George Plimsoll **Rossiter**, Hermione's other brother in 29GU; pink and stout, does no work of any kind; face like a pig, pimples, a confirmed sponger, says "What ho!", slaps backs, eats too much, tells funny stories, clammy hands, heavy smoker.

Herbert J. **Rossiter** of 3 Scantlebury Square, Kensington, father of Hermione in 29GU.

Hermione **Rossiter**, sister of Cyprian and George, daughter of Herbert, courted by Ignatius Mulliner in 29GU.

Jno. **Rossiter**, purveyor of Provisions, Groceries, and Home-Made Jams in Blandings Parva in 28EG.

Martin **Rossiter**, shooting guest at the Keiths' in 10GA.

Marvin **Rossiter**, engaged to Elsa Keith in PA12 and PB12.

Charlotte Corday **Rowbotham**, daughter of a revolutionary in 22CB/IJ23; all eyes and teeth, a woman of billowy curves and leftist sentiments loved by Bingo Little and Comrade Butt, gives Bingo the raspberry when he has a bad day at Goodwood.

Lord **Rowcester**: see W.E.B.O. Belfry.

Miss **Roxborough** is a professional dancer at Geisenheimer's in 15AG.

Royce of the Junior School at Wrykyn is a member of Day's team in 05SC.

Wilmot **Royce**, mother of Felicia Blakeney in 23CF, author of *Sewers of the Soul*, *Grey Mildew*, and *The Stench of Life*.

Rudd is prefect of the School House at St. Austin's in 11PP. A member of the Gym six and Secretary of Football, a solid, grave youth who always looks a little mournful.

Lord **Rumbelow**, patient with a complicated case at Droitgate Spa in 37RD, member of a club called the Twelve Jolly Stretcher-Cases.

Johnny **Runcible** is a member of Bachelors Anonymous in BA73.

L.P. **Runkle** of Runkle's Enterprises, extremely stout with a large pink face and a panama hat with a pink ribbon, a big financier who visits the Travers household in MO71 in hopes of selling T.P. Travers an old silver porringer for his collection. Onetime employer of Tuppy Glossop's late father, from whose invention of a headache cure (Runkle's Magic Midgets) he has profited enormously.

Lady **Runnymede**, a proud old aristocrat in 12GK.

Ruthven of Donaldson's is one of Wrykyn's least deserving inmates; he rags Trevor's study and is caught with the gold bat in GB04; still a notorious outsider in 05IA.

Desmond **Ryan**, bell boy at the Astor Hotel in PA12.

S

Bobbie **St Clair**, chorus-girl at the Frivolities in 20AS/IA21.

E.J. **Saintsbury** lobs for the Incogniti against the Wrykyn 11 in 05LP.

Gloria **Salt**, betrothed to Sir Gregory Parsloe and then to Jerry Vail in PW52; tall and slim, the last word in langorous elegance, her dark beauty makes her look like a serpent of the old Nile.

Peter **Salt**, a persevering middleweight, is Kid Brady's taciturn trainer and sparring partner in 05BB, 06BW, and 06BF.

Mr. **Saltzburg**, music-director of *The Rose of America* in LW20, an unsuccessful writer of musical comedy.

Salvatore, a dark, sinister-looking waiter at the grill-room in the Hotel Cosmopolis in 20DF/IA21; a strong, ambidextrous talker, dissatisfied with his working conditions.

Bernie **Sampson**, fixer or dramatic doctor in BW52, a sallow young man with an air of dessicated sophistication.

"Sammy" **Sampson**, Mr. Downing's bull terrier, is painted red in MK09.

Sanderson, the nervous batsman for the Weary Willies Cricket Club in 05LB, is a beautiful bat but has an impossible set of nerves.

Meier of **Sarnen** is a sheepowner in WT04.

Saunders[1], the narrator's maid, confidante, and informant in the four Joan Romney stories, is courted by Billy Simpson and Harry Biggs in 05WP. In 06PI she makes Billy Simpson let Joan Romney's father hit his bowling about in the match with the Cave men. In 08LG her first name is given as Ellen; she has a lovers' quarrel with William Batkins which is patched up by her mistress.

Saunders[2], the cricket pro who coaches the Jackson boys in MK09, bowls for the Marylebone Cricket Club.

Saunders[3], butler at Dreever Castle in IJ10.

John, the **Sausage Chappie** in 20AS/IA21, is an amnesiac war veteran who gave Archie Moffam a bit of sausage outside St Mihiel during the War. Remembers he was born in Springfield, Ohio, and was an actor before the war.

Howard **Saxby**, literary agent, senior member of Howard Saxby & Sons, father of Howard Saxby Jr. A long, thin old gentlemen in his middle seventies, the leading gargoyle of the Demosthenes Club. Fishy-eyed and absent-minded, knits to keep himself from smoking. Agent for Beefy Bastable's *Cocktail Time* in CT58. Leila Yorke's literary agent in IB61.

Mr. **Scarborough**, a blond young man with a small moustache and pure BBC diction, makes deliveries for the Cohen Brothers in BM64.

Jacob Z. **Schnellenhamer** is President of the Perfecto-Zizzbaum Motion Picture Corporation in 32MB, 33NO, 33JO, 33RM, 33CA, head of Colossal-Exquisite in 67GA.

Mrs. **Scholfield** is a sister of Bertie in 22BC, returning from India with her three little girls. He contemplates giving up his flat and taking a house where they can all live with him. He changes his mind.

Bill **Schoolbred**, Elizabeth's brother in 13DC, was at Oxford with Reggie Pepper, hates paintings.

Elizabeth **Schoolbred** (misprinted Shoolbred in 11HF), once engaged to Reggie Pepper, comes from an old Worcestershire family with pots of money. Tall and splendid, pretty as a picture, married to painter Clarence Yeardsley in 13DC.

James or John R. **Schoonmaker** of Park Avenue, New York and The Dunes, Westhampton, L.I., friend (and later husband) of Lady Constance Keeble, father of Myra in FP29 (where Galahad remembers his name as Johnny) and SS61. An All-American footballer in his youth, now a large and impressive monarch of finance in his late fifties, with a massive head and handsome face interrupted about halfway up by tortoise-shell-rimmed spectacles. An old friend of Lord Ickenham, who admires his mint juleps: they creep up to you like a baby sister and slide their little hands into yours, and the next thing you know the judge is telling you to pay the clerk of the court fifty dollars.

Myra **Schoonmaker**, daughter of prec. in FP29, where she is favored by Lady Julia and Lady Constance as a suitable match for Ronnie Fish. Described there as a tall girl, like something left over by Dana Gibson. In SS61 she is a pretty girl of the small, slim, slender type, in love with Cuthbert Bailey.

Schwartz, a stout saloon-keeper, Matthew Bennett's draughts-companion on Tuesdays, Thursdays, and Saturdays in 15CH.

Schwed is cited as a successful litigant against Meredith in BW52, and is one of J. Sheringham Adair's fictitious detectives in IB61. Cf. Peter Schwed, PGW's publisher at Simon & Schuster.

Benjamin **Scobell**, a nasty little financier in PA12 and PB12 with lean body and vulturine face, greedy mouth, liquid green eyes, and sallow complexion. Stepfather of Betty Silver, brother of Marion. Owns a villa on Mervo, where he opens a casino and imports John Maude to assume his late father's role as Prince of Mervo; in PA12 he also owns slums on Broster St., New York, and is nephew of Jane Oakley.

Marion **Scobell**, sister of Benjamin and manager of his household in PA12 and PB12; a tall deliberate, negative woman in PA12, in PB12 a confirmed reader of the more sentimental class of fiction.

Rodney **Scollop**, powerful young surrealist and friend of Lancelot Mulliner in 32SW.

J.G. Scott, biggest hitter at St Austin's in 01AF, 02OT, and 03HP, is Pillingshot's prefect in 10PD. In 11PP he prevails on his ex-fag, Pillingshot, to edit a scurrilous anti-Henry's rag called *The Rapier* until Rudd persuades him he would rather play on the School fifteen. Lives in the School-house.

Crispin Lancelot Gawain **Scrope**, older brother of Willoughby Scrope and master of Mellingham Hall, Mellingham-in-the-Vale, Hants. in GB70. An elderly man with thinning hair, watery blue eyes and a drooping moustache; takes in paying guests to make ends meet.

Willoughby or Bill **Scrope**, younger brother of Crispin and Jerry West's uncle and trustee in GB70. A large, prosperous-looking man, senior partner of Scrope, Ashby, & Pemberton, Attys, Bedford Row. Once engaged to Flora Faye.

Seabury, son of Lady Chuffnell by an earlier marriage, cousin of Chuffy Chuffnell in TY34. Smallish, freckled kid with aeroplane ears, about third in Bertie's rogue's gallery of repulsive small boys: not quite so bad as Aunt Agatha's son Thos. or Mr. Blumenfield's Junior, but well ahead of Sebastian Moon, Aunt Dahlia's Bonzo, and the field.

Squiffy, Lord **Seacliff** was at school with Archie Moffam; has a drinking problem in 20DO/IA21; left in Archie's charge by his uncle, General Mannister.

Ann **Selby**, Hilda Bodkin's sister, gives Reggie Pepper the mitten in 15TC.

Maj. Christopher **Selby** is Jill Mariner's uncle in LW20. A tall, soldierly man of 49 who raised Jill since she was fourteen, loses her fortune in the crash and goes to New York to raise her a new one.

Reginald **Sellers**, commercial artist in 10MU, acquaintance of Annette Brougham; long, offensive, patronizing.

Rev. Aubrey **Sellick**, writer of tales for the young, editor of *Tiny Tots* in HW33.

Selwicke is G.B. Ellison's inseparable friend in 05LP. A Sixth Former and house prefect at Donaldson's, he becomes Ellison's rival for the last place on the Wrykyn 11.

Seppi the cowboy, an ancestor of Buffalo Bill, is wounded by Friesshardt in WT04.

Seppings, Aunt Dahlia's butler at Brinkley Court in RH34, CW38, JF54, HR60, MO71.

Arnold of **Sewa**, Swiss envoy to Hermann Gessler in WT04.

Mr. **Seymour** is in charge of football and a house-master at Wrykyn in GB04, 05PP, WF07 and MK09, where he is master of the lower Fifth.

Mr. Reginald **Seymour**, pseud. Walter Walsh, substitutes for mathematics master Rev Septimus Brown at St Austin's in 01AU. Author of a play called *The Way of the World*. A poor mathematician but a good master, was a Cambridge Rugger blue.

Percy **Shanklyn**, elegant, sleek, perpetually resting English actor who lives by his wits in WH14; suave but unpleasant.

Kay **Shannon**, niece of Wilhelmina Shannon and Adela Shannon Cork in OR51. Loves Joe Davenport.

Wilhelmina "Bill" **Shannon**, sister of Adela Shannon Cork; title character of OR51. A breezy, hearty, genial woman in the early forties, built on generous lines: rugged face, high cheekbones, masterful chin relieved by large, humorous eyes of a bright blue. Everybody likes her, even in Hollywood, where nobody likes anybody. Member of the New York jury that convicted James Phipps. Working on the memoirs of her sister Adela. In matrimonial pursuit of Smedley Cork.

Miss **Sharples**, efficient secretary to G.E. Cobbold in SF48

J.B. **Sharples** plays cricket for the Weary Willies in 05LB.

Dr. Theodore **Shaw** is the pseudonym of a gambler trying to neutralize Kid Brady in 06BF, posing as a Boston oculist and amateur photographer.

Shawyer is bidden to tea at Prater's in 02TT.

Isabel **Shearne**, mother of Thomas in 08GU.

J.K. **Shearne**, father of T.B.A. Shearne in 08GU.

P.W. **Shearne**, eldest brother of T.B.A. Shearne, has just entered Sandhurst in 08GU.

Thomas Beauchamp Algernon **Shearne**, the youngest of the Shearnes in 08GU, enters Eckleton and lives in Blackburn's. Pleasant, with a rather meek cast of countenance, pink cheeks and golden hair.

R.D. **Sheen**, a sixth former in Seymour's at Wrykyn in WF07; no athlete but a good scholar (he wins the Gotford scholarship), and plays the piano well. Hates to offend; learns to box from Mr. Joe Bevan and wins the public schools Light

Weight boxing title at Aldershot.

Mr. **Shepperson**, man with double-jointed hips, inhabitant of Clarissa Cork's clean-living colony at Shipley Hall in MB42.

Mr. **Sheppherd**, Audrey's father in 11PO, looks like a heavy father out of a three-volume novel. Manner inclined to bleakness.

Audrey **Sheppherd** loves Owen Bentley in 11PO.

Mrs. **Sheridan**: see Audrey Blake.

Felicia or Flick **Sheridan**, daughter of the late Jack Sheridan, killed with his wife in a railway accident; niece of Sinclair Hammond in BC24. 21, slim, fair-haired, blue-eyed, with a boyish figure, wooed and won by Bill West.

Roscoe **Sheriff**, a press-agent to Lady Wetherby in UM16, has made her keep a snake and Eustace, a monkey; apostle of Energy and acquaintance of James B. Wheeler at the Pen-and-Ink Club in 20DO/IA21.

Mr. **Shields**, housemaster at Wrykyn in 05SC and MK09, the most inconspicuous master of the staff.

Lady Millicent **Shipton-Bellinger**, younger daughter of the fifth Earl of Brangbolton, living at 18A, Upper Brook Street, falls in love with Adrian Mulliner in 31SW.

Reginald Alexander Montacute James Bramfylde Tregennis **Shipton-Bellinger,** fifth Earl of Brangbolton, Lady Millicent's father in 31SW.

Shoeblossom, student at Locksley in 05CL.

Gerald **Shoesmith**, 27, nephew of solicitor John Shoesmith, read law at Cambridge but never ate his dinners. A large young man with reddish hair, editor of *Society Spice* in BM64. Lives at 3 Halsey Chambers, Halsey Court, Mayfair. In love with Kay Christopher.

John **Shoesmith** of Shoesmith, Shoesmith, Shoesmith and so on of Lincoln's Inn Fields, well-known solicitor and father of Myrtle Shoesmith in MB42, IB61, BM64. Oofy Prosser's solicitor in IB61, has hired Freddie Widgeon as a favor to Oofy. Member, Demosthenes Club. Looks like a cassowary.

Myrtle **Shoesmith**, only daughter of the well-known solicitor, briefly engaged to a reluctant Jeff Miller in MB42, wife of Oofy Prosser in IB61 (see also Myrtle Prosser).

Elizabeth **Shoolbred**: see Elizabeth Schoolbred.

Lord **Shortlands**: see C.P.J.D. Cobbold.

Sam Pynsent **Shotter**, title character of SS25, son of the late Anthony Shotter and nephew of John B. Pynsent. A graduate of Wrykyn with Claude Bates and J. Willoughby Braddock, played football in school. In love with Kay Derrick.

Clarence "Skipper" **Shute**, American pugilist in 10WD, boxing champion by virtue of his defeat of Joseph Edwardes, the English champ. Pays attention to Maud Peters.

Constable **Sibley** of Bray Lench arrests Jack Williams for disorderly conduct in 06FM.

Lord **Sidcup**, old-silver hound and expert on jewelry, recently dead in JF54 and succeeded in his title by Roderick Spode, q.v.

Sigsbee, member of the Sybarites' Club in 10AB, Cape Pleasant golfer and friend of McCay and Archibald Mealing.

Betty **Silver**, 24, title character of PA12 and PB12. Friend of Elsa Keith, stepdaughter of Benjamin Scobell. In love with John Maude, in PA12 she writes the Broster Street articles for *Peaceful Moments*; in PB12 Della Morrison takes her on as French interpreter and paid companion.

Billy **Silver** of Kay's is Jimmy's younger brother at Eckleton in HK05.

Jimmy **Silver**, head of Blackburn's in HK05, is head of the Eckleton eleven. His younger brother Billy is at Kay's.

Ed **Silvers**, abandoned husband in 31FA.

Mrs. **Silvers**, wife of the above in 31FA, has left her husband and lives in flat 4A somewhere on 69th St. in New York, where she finds Freddie Widgeon attractive.

Charlie **Silversmith**, Jeeves' sixteen-stone uncle, butler to Esmond Haddock of Deverill Hall. Father of Queenie below.

Queenie **Silversmith**, daughter of prec., parlourmaid at Deverill Hall in MS49, engaged to P.C. Ernest Dobbs.

Vera **Silverton**, actress in 20RH/IA21 cast in a play by George Benham; thrice divorced, owns a bulldog named Percy.

Simms, village blacksmith in 09AC, wins the day for Much Middlefold when he gets a 56 against Mr. Romney's team.

Simmonds, fellow-detective with Henry Pifield Rice at Stafford's International Investigation Bureau in 15BB.

Simmons[1], a floor-waiter at the Hotel Cosmopolis in 20DF/IA21.

Simmons[2], butler to Lady Wickham at Skeldings Hall in 24SS and 25AG.

Mrs. **Simmons**, cook at Ashby Hall in PP67, once jilted by Clarence Binstead.

G.G. **Simmons**, an unpleasant, perky-looking stripling, mostly front teeth and spectacles, winner of the Scripture Knowledge Prize at the Market Snodsbury Grammar School in RH34. In handing out the award, Gussie Fink-Nottle hints at a guilty liaison between Master Simmons' mother and the headmaster.

Monica **Simmons**, pig-girl to the Empress of Blandings in PW52 and BG65. One of six daughters of a rural vicar, all of whom played hockey for Roedean. A cousin of Sir Gregory Parsloe, looks like an all-in wrestler (or a Norse goddess, in the eyes of Wilfred Allsop, who elopes with her in BG65).

Susan **Simmons**, detective sent to Blandings by Wragge's at Baxter's request in LP23, assumes role of parlourmaid.

Ernest **Simms**, 16-stone constable at Mellingham-in-the-Vale in GB70.

Billy **Simpson**, pro cricketer for Sir Edward Cave's team in 05WP, is in love with Joan Romney's maid Saunders. In 06PI Saunders makes him let Joan Romney's father hit his bowling about in the match with the Cave men.

Enoch **Simpson** recites "Dangerous Dan McGrew" at the Oddfellows' Hall in the East End in 27JS.

Jane **Simpson**, friend of Mary Kent in 23AR.

Oofy **Simpson** is the richest Drone in BM31.

Mr. **Sims**, president of the Temperance League in 25BD.

Babe **Sinclair**, chorus girl at the Regal in DD19, courted by Spenser Gray.

Muriel **Singer**, chorus girl in *Choose Your Exit*, engaged briefly to Bruce Corcoran in 16AC, marries Alexander Worple.

Oliver Randolph "Sippy" **Sipperley**, friend of Bertie in 16AS, has an aunt Vera in Yorkshire on whose subsidies he is financially dependent. Endeavored to steal an occupied policeman's helmet in Leicester Square one Boat Race Night on Bertie's advice just prior to the action of 25WO and was sentenced to 30 days without the option of a fine for biffing a cop in the stomach. A sometime writer, in 26IC editor of the *Mayfair Gazette*, in love with Gwendolen Moon. Was Gussie Fink-Nottle's fellow student at university. See also 29JL.

Vera **Sipperley** of the Paddock, Beckley-on-the-moor, Yorkshire, aunt and financial supporter of Sippy, wants Sippy to sing at the village concert in 25WO. A large stout female with a reddish face and something of a village autocrat, she is at odds with the local constable, who is Jeeves' cousin.

Mr. **Skidmore**, Roscoe Bunyan's butler at Shipley Hall in SF57.

Skinner[1], a fag at Leicester's, is a sort of juvenile Professor Moriarty at Beckford College in PU03.

Skinner[2]: see Bingley Crocker.

Soup **Slattery**, expert safe-blower in HW32, was a financier before the Depression.

Sleddon, butler to J. Willoughby Braddock in SS25.

Slingsby, chauffeur at Blandings Castle in SN15, succeeded by Voules.

Alexander **Slingsby**, of Slingsby's Superb Soups, a Roman-emperor looking sort of bird, jealous husband of Beatrice in 29SA.

Beatrice Pim **Slingsby**, sister to Lucius Pim and wife of prec. in 29SA.

Ted **Slingsby**, butler at Langley End in IW31, brother of Bella Price and supposed uncle to Syd Price. A man of ample build.

Wilfred **Slingsby**, London manager of the Paradene Pulp & Paper Co. and theatrical investor in BC24. Dark jowls, flashing smile.

Smethurst, Col. Mainwaring-Smith's personal gentleman's gentleman, in love with Rhoda Platt in 30IS.

Adeline **Smethurst**, niece of Mrs. Willoughby Smethurst, courted by Cuthbert Banks in 21UC.

Bertie **Smethurst**, friend of Freddie Chalk-Marshall in IW31.

Rev. J. G. **Smethurst**, onetime headmaster of Harborough

College, a man who chewed bottles and devoured his young, Bishop of Bognor in 31VP.

Mrs. Willoughby **Smethurst**, president of the Wood Hills Literary and Debating Society in 21UC. Aunt of Adeline Smethurst.

Smith[1], a sixth former at St Austin's, intended beneficiary of Reynolds' poem in 01PP. Shares a study at Prater's with Montgomery in 02TT, where they are robbed by Captain Kettle.

Smith[2] is one of the school porters at Wrykyn in GB04.

Smith[3] is a Wrykyn boy living in Day's in WF07.

Smith[4], friend of John Maude in PB12, works for the *News*. Cf. Rupert Smith in PA12, Psmith in PJ15.

Smith[5] is Peter Burns' valet in LN15.

Constable Cyril **Smith** has a glass of Mulliner's Buck-U-Uppo-and-soda in 30GN.

J.B. **Smith**, gone to the Malay States in 34NO.

Rupert **Smith**, former reporter for the New York *News*, was at Harvard with John Maude. Temporary editor of *Peaceful Moments* in PA12. Same role, appearance and mannerisms as Psmith in PJ15.

Dr. Sally **Smith**, title character of DS32, general practitioner, courted by Bill Bannister.

Mr. Somerville **Smith** is substitute fourth form master at Beckford in PU03.

T.C. **Smith** plays cricket for Marvis Bay. One of the lost bowlers of 05LB, abducted by a runaway motor car.

T.T. **Smith** is in some sort of agency business in 34NO.

Smithers, a man of about 50, is the Empress of Blandings' veterinary surgeon in 27PH.

Bud **Smithers** runs a hospital for fat, unhealthy dogs on Long Island to which Ann Chester proposes to send Ogden Ford in PJ17.

Smithy, American burglar working in England for Horace Appleby in DB68, has a long mild face, drooping moustache, and clear honest eyes behind horn-rimmed spectacles.

Smythe, at the top of the form at St Austin's in 03HP, in the same house as Pillingshot, i.e. the school-house.

Jack, Lord **Snettisham**, house guest of Aunt Dahlia in 29JL.

Jane, Lady **Snettisham**, wife to foreg., wagers on the comparative deportment of Thos Gregson and Aunt Dahlia's son Bonzo to win Anatole from Dahlia, her hostess in 29JL.

Snow is the abusive mate of the *May Moon* on which Kid Brady is shanghaied in 07BT.

Paul **Snyder** runs the detective agency on New Oxford St. in Southhampton that employs Elliot Oakes in 14DE. Looks like a comfortable and prosperous stock broker.

Marjorie **Somerset** is an aspiring painter, courted by the narrator of 03CP.

Mabel **Somerset**, cousin of Ladies' Open Golf Champion Mary Somerset in 20SH, herself the Ladies' Open Croquet Champion. A small and rather frail-looking girl with big blue eyes and a cloud of golden hair, marries Mortimer Sturgis.

Lady Monica **Southbourne**, photographic subject of Clarence Mulliner in 27RB.

Dr. **Spelvin**, Lord Wivelscombe's physician in 33LS.

Anastatia **Spelvin**: see Anastatia Bates.

Rodney **Spelvin**, cousin of the actor George, a tall, dark-haired, slim, sickeningly handsome poet who fails to qualify for the hand of Jane Packard in 24RF, the first of three golfing stories told about him by the Oldest Member. In 24JG he is famous as the author of *The Purple Fan*, a romantic novel in the neo-decadent style. In 25PR he is purified by the golfing instruction of Bill Bates' sister Anastatia. Married to Anastatia in 49RR with a son named Timothy; writes mystery thrillers but suffers a relapse into poetry.

Timothy **Spelvin**, child of Rodney and Anastatia in 49RR.

Mr. **Spence**, master of his form as well as of his house, also looks after cricket at Wrykyn in 04JE. A former Cambridge boxer trained by Joe Bevan, looks after cricket and gymnasium at Wrykyn and chooses candidates for the Public Schools boxing competition at Aldershot in WF07; master of the Wrykyn Lower Fifth in MK09, still cricket-master and a graduate of Winchester.

Grayce **Spence**: see Grayce Llewellyn.

Mabel **Spence**, sister of George Spence and Grayce Llewellyn.

A small, dark, pretty Beverly Hills osteopath courted by Reggie Tennyson in LB35.

Spencer[1], Kennedy's fag at Kay's in HK05.

Spencer[2], valet to Looney Coote in 23LA, has broken his leg.

C.F. **Spencer** of Dencroft's fags for Kennedy in 08GU. Told by mother to look after T.B.A. Shearne. Nephew of a Mrs. Davy. Goes seven rounds with Shearne in a field, W.G. Shaw refereeing.

Spenlow is a friend of G. Montgomery Chapple at Wrykyn in 05PP.

George **Spenlow**, the timber wolf, lives next door to Freddy Threepwood on Long Island in 50BS; throws wild parties for blondes in his wife's absence. A stout, pink, globular man in the lumber business who makes Lord Emsworth think of the Empress of Blandings.

Spenser is Aunt Agatha's butler in 22SR/IJ23.

Lionel **Spenser** is office boy at the Argus Enquiry Agency in BM64.

Harold **Sperry**, a Westport, Ct. telephone worker whose drill hits a lead pipe in an epic simile in 11BS.

Geraldine **Spettisbury**, daughter of Ferdinand James Delamere, 6th Earl of Wivelscombe, loves Adolphus Stiffham in 33LS.

Spiking, stationer in the High Street in 05CL.

Spiller[1]'s study at Outwood's is appropriated by Psmith and Mike Jackson in MK09.

Spiller[2] is a stout youth friendly to John Maude in PA12; employed in the offices of Westley, Martin & Co.

Tom **Spiller** is Della Morrison's secret flame in New York in PB12.

Mr. **Spinder**, one of the best-informed men on Indian mythology in England, is Mr. Haviland's temporary replacement as housemaster at Marleigh School in LS08. Small and wiry, with a sharp face, hooked nose, thin lips, steely gray eyes, and gold-rimmed spectacles.

Mervyn **Spink**, butler to Lord Shortlands at Beevor Castle in SF48, wants to marry the cook, Alice Punter, as does his employer. Tall, aristocratic, and elegant, looks more like an earl than a butler. Has a mother living in East Dulwich and a habit of gambling and losing. Formerly employed by G. Ellery Cobbold.

Roderick **Spode** of Totleigh Towers, head of the Black Shorts in CW38, secretly designs ladies' underclothing under the trade name of Eulalie Soeurs, of Bond Street—knowledge of which renders him harmless to Bertie, whom he despises, distrusts, and often threatens with violence. Cf. Sir Oswald Mosley, 1930's leader of the British Union of Fascists. An eloquent public speaker, Spode is founder and head of the Saviours of Britain, a mob of underlings wearing black shorts who shout "Heil, Spode!" or words along those general lines. His idea, if he doesn't get knocked on the head with a bottle in one of the frequent brawls in which his followers indulge, is to make himself Dictator. A club acquaintance of Tom Travers, he becomes seventh Earl of Sidcup on the death of his uncle in JF54, exits Eulalie Soeurs, and some time thereafter disbands the Black Shorts. About eight feet high with a small moustache and the sort of eye that can open an oyster at sixty paces. His aunt, Mrs. Wintergreen, is engaged to Sir Watkyn Bassett in SU63. He himself is engaged to Madeline Bassett in SU63 and MO71, where he suspects Bertie of trying to alienate her affections.

Cora McGuffy **Spottsworth**, dark, subtle, exotic snake with hips, has large, dark, and lustrous eyes like those of some inscrutable priestess of a strange old religion. A widow from Illinois, author of *Furnace of Sin*. Publisher's slogan is "Spottsworth For Blushes." A fine golfer, competes against Agnes Flack in the Women's Singles in 50FC. A woman of socialist views, attracts the amorous attention of Sydney McMurdo.

Rosalinda Banks Bessemer **Spottsworth**, rich American widow in RJ53. Born Rosalinda Banks of Chillicothe, Ohio, her first husband was Clifton Bessemer, the Pulp Paper Magnate, who died in a head-on collision with a beer truck; her second was Alexis B. Spottsworth, sportsman and big-game hunter, killed by a wounded lion. Recent devotee of psychic research, a Rotationist with homes in Pasadena, Carmel, New York, Florida, Maine, and Oregon. Buys Towcester Abbey to move it to California stone by stone. Owns a Peke named Pomona

Roderick Spode

and the undying love of Captain Brabazon-Biggar.

Ebenezer **Sprockett** is a tenant of Lord Emsworth in Blandings Parva in 28EG.

Lulabelle **Sprockett**, heiress of Sprockett's Superfine Sardines, worth $100 million, owns a Peke who interferes with a golf match in 50FC.

Annabell **Sprockett-Sprockett**, only daughter of Sir Murgatroyd and Lady Aurelia Sprockett-Sprockett of Smattering Hall, Lower Smattering-on-the-Wissel, Worcestershire. Object of Mordred Mulliner's fiery wooing in 34FW.

Dora **Spurgeon**, friend of Rosie Banks in 37AW.

Gally **Stale**: see under Puffy Benger.

William **Stanborough**, fellow of infinite jest in LN13, friend of Lord Mountry commissioned to paint a portrait of Ogden Ford for his mother.

Staniforth, butler to Mrs. Willoughby Gudgeon in 47RA.

Stanning, a member of the Wrykyn first fifteen in WF07, lives in Appleby's; a competitor for the Gotford scholarship and lightweight boxer, hates Drummond.

Stanworth, one of those tall, languid youths who seem to take to batting naturally, lives at West's in 11EA. Old for his years, brilliantly clever at Classics, a good dresser. Member of the first eleven and a school prefect. Formerly a day-boy, he became a boarder when his parents took a villa at Nice.

Werner **Staufacher**, Swiss envoy to Hermann Gessler in WT04, has grey hair and is always wondering how to pronounce his name.

Steena is Jane Oakley's Swedish housekeeper in PA12.

Rupert **Steggles** is a member of the reading-party sweating up the Classics under Old Heppenstall in IJ23; a little rat-faced fellow, with shifty eyes and a suspicious nature; makes book on sermons in 22SH, on the school treat races in 22PT, on the rivalry of Bingo Little with Hubert Wingham for the hand of Mary Burgess in 22MT.

Carl **Steinberg**, a concert impresario in 20MK/IA21.

Herr **Steingruber**, German master at Marleigh School in LS08, is extremely short-sighted and speaks a great deal of broken English.

Howard "Mugsy" **Steptoe**, an enormous mass of a man with a squashed nose and ears like the handles of an old Greek vase. Sometime boxer in preliminary bouts on the Pacific coast, an opponent of Wildcat Wix and onetime film actor, now married to Mabel Steptoe and nominal master of Claines Hall in QS40.

Mabel **Steptoe** of Los Angeles, new owner of Claines Hall, a Tudor mansion in Sussex near Loose Chippings, wife of Howard in QS40. Phone Loose Chippings 803.

Miss **Stern**, Jacob Z. Schnellenhamer's secretary in 33CA.

Stevens, Sir George Wooster's man in 22EC/IJ23.

Col. **Stewart** of the Indian Army, father of Jimmy in LS08, commanded the North Surreys on the Indian frontier. Master of Gorton Hall.

Jimmy **Stewart**, son of the Colonel, lives at Gorton Hall when not at Marleigh School, where he shares a study with Tommy Armstrong in LS08.

J. Wendell **Stickney** of Park Avenue, New York, only son of the late G.J. Stickney of Stickney's Dairy Products, brother of Loretta Stickney Pound and distant relative of Henry Paradene in PP67. Lives with his Aunt Kelly and English valet Clarkson in an apartment on the upper end of Park Avenue. A cultured dilettante with tortoise-shell-rimmed spectacles, collects French 18th century paperweights. Member of the Collectors Club.

Kelly **Stickney**, aunt of J. Wendell Stickney and Loretta Stickney Pound, relict of the late Theodore Stickney; lives in her nephew's spare bedroom in PP67. A one-time chorus girl in her middle forties, on the buxom side, resembling a Ziegfeld Follies girl who has been left out in the rain and swollen a little.

Adolphus "Stiffy" **Stiffham**, formerly secretary to Lord Wivelscombe, makes a bundle in a crap game in New York and returns to marry Geraldine Spettisbury in 33LS.

Joe **Stocker**, Rodney Spelvin's opponent in the Rabbits Umbrella in 49RR. A famous amateur wrestler in his youth, now a musclebound golfer.

Percy, Lord **Stockheath**, nephew of Lord Emsworth in SN15, cousin to Algernon Wooster. Involved recently in a breach-of-promise case with a barmaid named Miss Chester.

Lord **Stockleigh**, remembered as Keggs[1]'s former employer in 10GA, father of Angelica and Bertie Fendall there and in 10LM.

Dwight **Stoker**, juvenile son of American millionaire J. Washburn Stoker in TY34.

Eileen **Stoker** of Beverly Hills, Universally Beloved Hollywood Star, engaged to Stanwood Cobbold in SF48.

Emerald **Stoker**, younger daughter of American millionaire J. Washburn Stoker and friend of Bertie: "There was a sort of motherliness about her which I found restful." Looks like a Pekingese, takes office in SU63 as cook at Totleigh Towers after losing a turf investment at Kempton Park, elopes with Gussie Fink-Nottle.

J. Washburn **Stoker**, second cousin of the late eccentric George Stoker, from whom he has inherited $50 million in TY34; father of Pauline, Emerald, and Dwight.

Oswald **Stoker**, novelist, stepson of Mrs. Willoughby Gudgeon in 47RA.

Pauline **Stoker**, Emerald's elder sister, a beauty so radiant that strong men whistle after her in the street. Daughter of J. Washburn Stoker, was engaged to Bertie for a period of about 48 hours in New York shortly before the action of TY34, where she is involved with Chuffy Chuffnell. Unquestionably an eyeful, she has the grave defect of being one of those girls who want you to come and swim a mile before breakfast and rout you out when you are trying to snatch a wink of sleep after lunch for a merry five sets of tennis. Escapes from her father's yacht by swimming in TY34 and takes refuge in Bertie's cottage, where he finds her shortly after midnight wearing his heliotrope pyjamas. In SU63 she is married to Lord Chuffnell.

Stokes[1], sometime farmhand and casual laborer around St Austin's, steals the prize cups from the Pavilion in PH03.

Stokes[2], Thomas' fellow footman at Blandings in LP23, HW33, and BG65; a serious-looking man with a bald forehead.

Maj. Percy **Stokes** of the Salvation Army is Jane Bramble's brother in 13KI, opposed to pugilism.

W.J. Stone is in the Outwood's cricket team at Sedleigh in MK09. Collard, the school sergeant, catches him smoking in 10SW.

Clare Throckmorton **Stooge**, authoress of *A Strong Man's Kiss* in 32SW.

Stopford resigns his captaincy of the St. Austin's first fifteen to try for a scholarship at Cambridge in 11PP.

Percy Brimble, Bishop of **Stortford**, known in his school days as Boko, drinks Buck-U-Uppo in 27BM and 30GN; the same portly churchman is guest at a garden-party given by Sir Alexander Bassinger at Bludleigh Court in 29UB.

Priscilla, the Lady Bishopess of **Stortford**, a woman of ample and majestic build, of whom it was once remarked that all she needed was a steering-wheel and a couple of machine-guns and you could move her up into any Front Line and no questions asked. Transformed by Buck-U-Uppo in 30GN.

Sister Lora Luella **Stott**, temperance and clean-living evangelist, head of the Temple of the New Dawn in LG36.

Duane **Stottlemeyer**, shiny young man employed in GB70 by Guildenstern's Stores, Madison Avenue, New York; writes songs of protest.

Horace **Stout**, Julia Ukridge's ex-butler in 67US, sacked in connection with the robbery of antique furniture from The Cedars; brother of Percy Stout.

Percy **Stout**, bookie, brother to Horace and his partner in a shortlived antique furniture business in 67US.

Strachan plays back for the Wrykyn 15 in 05LP but is delayed at home with scarlet fever. Succeeds to the captaincy of the Wrykyn 11 after Mike Jackson leaves in MK09.

Hilda **Stretchley-Budd** is a neighbor of the Travers/Brinkley Court ménage in RH34.

Mr. **Strudwick** is master of the fourth form at Beckford in PU03.

Prudence **Stryker**, American chorus-girl in London, sometime companion of Wilfred Slingsby in BC24. Big, dark, and Spanish-looking, with black hair, large flashing eyes, and violent temper.

Buffy **Struggles** is remembered by Galahad in BG65 and elsewhere because someone lured him into a temperance lecture illustrated with colored slides showing the liver of the drinker of alcohol. He ordered ten pounds of tea, swore off alcohol, and was dead two weeks later, run over by a hansom cab in Piccadilly, his system so weakened by tea that he was unable to dodge the vehicle.

Mrs. Bella **Stubbs**, 33, sister of Constable Potter in UD48, mother of George Basil Percival Stubbs, 9 mo.

Maudie Beach **Stubbs**, niece of Blandings Castle butler Sebastian Beach, formerly a barmaid at the Criterion in London under the nom de guerre Maudie Montrose. Widow of Cedric Stubbs, proprietor of Digby's Day & Night Detectives. Once affianced to Sir Gregory Parsloe, reunited with him in PW52 and his wife in SS61.

May **Stubbs**, from East Gilead, Idaho, once engaged to George Finch, tells fortunes in SB27 as Madame Eulalie and wins the otherwise rational heart of J. Hamilton Beamish.

Sturgis, Lester Carmody's butler at Rudge Hall in MN28, a flatfooted little man of advanced years with snowy hair.

Denman **Sturgis**, the eminent private investigator, a tall, thin man with an eye like a gimlet, undertakes to find the man who assaulted his Serene Highness the Prince of Saxburg-Liegnitz in 12RR. Proprietor of the International Detective Agency in PJ17, where he is a gaunt, hungry-looking man of about 50 and assigns Miss Trimble the task of protecting the Partridgite in Mrs. Pett's mansion.

Mortimer **Sturgis** takes up golf in 20MT at the age of 38 but gives up his engagement to Betty Weston because he hasn't the time to combine golf with courtship. Marries Ladies Open Croquet Champion Mabel Somerset in 20SH.

Stuttering Sam poses as a curate in 25BD.

The **Subadar**, east-of-Suez associate of Capt. Brabazon-Biggar in RJ53.

Susan, maid at Windles in TM22.

Sutton, thrice-married actor at the Majestic Theatre in New York and member of the Strollers' Club in IJ10.

Oscar **Swenson**, waterfront boatman who dives in to retrieve the scattered money in TM22.

Reginald John Peter **Swithin**: see Havershot.

J.J. **Swodger**, Old Boy from Wrykyn, has received the Ruritanian Order of the Silver Trowel (with crossed pickaxes) in 23LA.

Swordfish: see Sir Roderick Glossop.

Beau "Hobo" **Sycamore**, a one-time schoolmate of Captain Brabazon-Biggar, now a bum in Shanghai (RJ53).

T

George **Tanner**, nephew of Sir Godfrey in 14CI and now in his thirties, keeps a private school in Kent, started on money lent him by his uncle.

Sir Godfrey **Tanner**, K.C.M.G., retired Colonial governor in 14CI, fires manservant Jevons for putting a piece of ice down his neck; later shoots the gardener at his nephew's school with Tom Billing's air gun.

Orlo **Tarvin**, interior decorator and friend of Lionel Green, defendant in an action for assault (Pennefather v. Tarvin) prosecuted by Jeff Miller in MB42. Lionel Green's partner in the interior decorating and antique furniture business (Tarvin & Green) in PP67. A wierd little weedy object in harlequin glasses, Ascot tie, side-whiskers, and beard.

Taylor is Fenn's fag at Kay's, Eckleton in HK05.

Mr. **Teal**, employed by Lord Evenwood as butler at Evenwood Towers in MM14, possesses the cat-like faculty of entering a room perfectly noiselessly. His niece at Aldershot is Maud Chilvers.

Hedwig **Tell**, wife of William Tell, daughter of Walter Fürst in WT04.

Walter **Tell**, son of William and Hedwig Tell, puts the apple on his head in WT04.

William **Tell**, best shot with the crossbow in all Switzerland and a great hunter in WT04;

Mr. **Templar** teaches Livy at Wrykyn in 05RR, is lieutenant of the Wrykyn corps in 05DE.

Celia **Tennant** cures her fiancé's mania for talking in 21SG by hitting him in the head with her niblick.

Ambrose **Tennyson**, older brother of Reggie and cousin of Gertrude Butterwick in LB35, minor novelist of the heartiness-and-beer class, engaged to Lottie Blossom. Large and muscular, with keen eyes, a strong chin, high color, and hands like hams. Worked for the Admiralty, resigned to write scripts in Hollywood for Superba-Llewellyn.

Reggie **Tennyson**, a Drone, cousin to Gertrude Butterwick and Ambrose's younger brother. Was at Eton and Oxford with Monty Bodkin; has a rich uncle John. Slim and long-legged, falls in love with Mabel Spence in LB35.

Evangeline **Tewkesbury**, a girl of radiant beauty, tennis player wooed by Ambrose Gussett in 51UF.

Miss Martha **Tewkesbury**, Evangeline's aunt in 51UF.

Digby **Thistleton**, a former employer of Jeeves, financier and creator of Hair-O, now Lord Bridgworth in 16AC.

Thomas[1] is Lord Emsworth's footman in FP29 (his colleague is James). His colleague is Stokes in LP23, where he entertains tender feelings for the new parlourmaid Susan, who is actually the detective Susan Simmons; see also HW33, FM47, BG65.

Thomas[2], another footman, works at Lady Wickham's Skeldings Hall in 24SS, 25AG.

Lloyd **Thomas** of Llunindnno is Battling Billson's boxing adversary in 23EB.

Mr. John **Thompson**, master of the Sixth at St Austin's in PH02, accuses Jim Thomson of stealing the cups.

Allen **Thomson**, Tony Graham's cousin in PH02, son of a Wiltshire baronet and a splendid boxer. Brother of Jim Thomson.

Jim **Thomson**, Allen's brother, house prefect at Merevale's, shares a study with Tony Graham; accused by Mr. Thompson of stealing the cups in PH02. Plays centre with MacArthur in 03MC.

Thorne is head gardener at Blandings in SN15. Named after the gardener at Cheney Court, Box in Wiltshire, where PGW spent much of his childhood (see N.T.P. Murphy, *In Search of Blandings*, pp. 37-42).

Lady Charlotte **Threepwood**, one of the ten sisters of Clarence and Galahad Threepwood, mentioned as the mother of Jane in 36CW. No married name is given.

Clarence **Threepwood**, ninth Earl of Emsworth, amiable and boneheaded peer, appears first in SN15; a long, lean, bald-headed, stringy man of about sixty with a reedy tenor voice, a widower for 25 years. Called Fathead at Eton in the '60s. Cleanshaven except in 26LE, where he grows a beard. Ruler of Blandings Castle, one of the oldest inhabited houses in England, and owner of a black Berkshire sow named Empress of Blandings in 27PH, 28CG, 31GG, HW33, UF39, FM47, PW52, SS61, BG65, PB69, SB77. In SN15 he has a sister, Lady Ann Warblington, presumably a widow, who is chatelaine of Blandings. In later stories a different sister, Lady Constance Keeble, rules at Blandings Castle, succeeded in this role by another sister, Lady Hermione Wedge, in FM47 and BG65. His other autocratic sisters are variously mentioned as Lady Charlotte (Jane's mother in 36CW), Lady Julia Fish, Lady Dora Garland, Lady Georgiana, Marchioness of Alcester, Lady Jane (deceased—he is trustee of Jane's daughter Angela in 27PH), and Lady Florence Moresby. Lady Diana Phipps is the only sister who does not chew broken bottles. An uncle Harold is mentioned in FM47, another uncle—his mother's brother, named Alistair—in 28CG. Trustee of his nephew, Ronnie Fish, in HW33. Comes from a long-lived family: his father was killed in the hunting-field at 77; his uncle Robert lived till nearly 90; his cousin Claude was nearly 84 when he broke his neck trying to jump a five-barred gate. Hates and fears all secretaries including The Efficient Baxter, whom his sister Connie is always thrusting upon him as secretary, and the relatively harmless Sandy Callender, forced on him by Hermione in BG65 when she takes over from Constance as chatelaine of Blandings castle. A backwoods peer to end all backwoods peers, dines at the Senior Conservative Club, of which he is a country member, when in London (which he hates). His elder son is George,

Lord Emsworth and the Empress of Blandings

Lord Bosham, his younger son Freddie. In 24CP he acquires a telescope, his main preoccupation being not yet a sow but a pumpkin. The love of his life, the Empress of Blandings, first appears in 27PH. Visiting Long Island for a niece's wedding to Tipton Plimsoll in 50BS, he undertakes to sell richly bound encyclopedias of Sport and sells a gross of them to Freddie's neighbor George Spenlow, who mistakes him for a private detective. Just back from New York in BG65, where he attended sister Constance's wedding to James R. Schoonmaker. Fond of morning dips in his lake. Nature has equipped him with a mind so admirably constructed for withstanding the disagreeableness of life that, if an unpleasant thought enters it, it passes out again a moment later.

Lady Constance **Threepwood**; see Constance Keeble. In PB69 she is Constance Schoonmaker, wife of a New York millionaire.

Daredevil Dick **Threepwood**'s marriage to an actress is remembered in HW33.

Lady Dora **Threepwood**, one of the ten sisters of Clarence and Galahad Threepwood. Never leaves London except to go to fashionable resorts on the Riviera and in Spain (PB69). See Dora Garland.

The Hon. Freddie **Threepwood**, second son of Lord Emsworth, brother of George[1], Lord Bosham; heavy and loutish-looking in SN15 but slender in FM47, distinguished by a long and vacant face. Went to Eton, was expelled for breaking out at night and roaming the streets of Windsor in a false moustache; sent down from Oxford for pouring ink from a second-story window on the Junior Dean of his College. Failed to pass into the Army after two years at an expensive London crammer's. Engaged to Aline Peters in SN15. Proposes to Eve Halliday early and often in LP23; marries Aggie Donaldson in 24CP; has gone to Long Island City to sell Donaldson's Dog Biscuits for his wife's father, as recalled in 26LE, 31GG, UF39, SS61, etc. Eight months married in 26LE, where his wife leaves him for a short time because she thinks he has been unfaithful. In 28CG, 31GG, FM47, 66SW, 66LF and SB77 he is temporarily back in England promoting

Donaldson's Dog Joy, and has given up his black-rimmed monocle because it reminded his colleagues at Donaldson's of something in a musical comedy. In 50BS he has been with Donaldson's Inc. for three years and is long since transformed from the vacant-faced younger son of an English Lord to a go-getter for Donaldson's Dog Joy, impatient with his father's boneheaded manner. His collection of mystery thrillers, bequeathed to Beach when he left for Long Island City, is said in BG65 to be the finest in Shropshire. A member of the Drones in 66LF; has sent friend Howard Chesney to visit Blandings in PB69. Revisits England, and Blandings Castle, in SB77.

The Hon. Galahad **Threepwood**, the only genuinely distinguished Threepwood, Lady Constance Keeble's "deplorable brother" in many stories and novels. Younger brother of Clarence, Lord Emsworth; all but one of his ten sisters regard him as a waster, Lady Diana Phipps in SB77 being the exception. When not on missions of mercy at Blandings Castle, lives in Duke St., St. James or at Berkeley Mansions, London W. 1, 4th floor, on a younger son's allowance. Author of scandal-ridden memoirs from the nineties, which he is writing in FP29. A member of the old Pelican Club in his youth, he once wanted to marry Dolly Henderson, to prevent which his family shipped him off to South Africa. Arrested so often in his prime that he got to know most of the policemen in the West End of London by their first names; has in fact known more policemen by their first names than any man in London. Seems never to have gone to bed till he was fifty. His age is given as 57 in HW33, the middle fifties in FM47, but in BG65 he is in the early fifties. His niece Millicent remarks "it really is an extraordinary thing that anyone who has had as good a time as he has can be so amazingly healthy." A short, trim, dapper little cock-sparrow of a man, of the type one associates in one's mind with checked suits, tight trousers, white bowler hats, pink carnations, and race glasses bumping against the left hip. Wears a black-rimmed monocle. Friend and kindred spirit of Frederick Twistleton, Earl of Ickenham, in UF39. See also PW52,

The Hon. Galahad Threepwood

66SW, PB69.

George **Threepwood**[1], Lord Bosham, elder son and heir of Clarence, Earl of Emsworth, brother of Freddie, nephew to Constance Keeble; husband of Cicely Donaldson in UF39, father of James and George[2] in 36CW (in SN15 he is mentioned as having three sons). Not renowned for intelligence, once bought a gold brick from a man in the street; gives his wallet to a stranger named Claude Pott in UF39.

George **Threepwood**[2], Lord Emsworth's grandson, son of Clarence's elder son George, Lord Bosham, is a small boy of twelve with ginger or auburn hair and freckles. Has an air gun with which the Efficient Baxter (his tutor) is shot repeatedly in 36CW. In SS61 he makes movies with a camera given him by his grandfather.

Hermione **Threepwood**; see Hermione Wedge.

Lady Julia **Threepwood**, one of ten sisters of Clarence and Galahad. See Julia Fish. Like her sisters Dora and Charlotte in PB69, never leaves London except to go to fashionable resorts on the Riviera and in Spain.

Millicent **Threepwood**, daughter of a Lancelot Threepwood, Lord Emsworth's niece, cousin to Ronnie Fish: a tall, fair girl with soft blue eyes and a face like the Soul's Awakening, courted by Hugo Carmody in FP29.

Tibbit of the Junior School is a member of Day's team at Wrykyn in 05SC.

Lord **Tidmouth**: see Squiffy Bixby.

Tilbury is Merrett's rival for the despised French prize at Wrykyn in 06DS.

George Alexander "Stinker" Pyke, First Viscount (but only a Baron in BM64) **Tilbury**, younger brother of American millionaire Edmund Biffen Pyke. Founder-proprietor of the Mammoth Publishing Co., of Tilbury House, Tilbury St., London, publishers of the *Daily Record*, *Tiny Tots*, *Pyke's Weekly*, *The Sabbath Hour*, *Home Gossip*, and *Society Spice*. Short, square, stumpy, Napoleonic of aspect and about 25 pounds overweight, inclined to come out in spots when he eats lobster. Brother of Frances Hammond. Widower of Lucy Maynard and father of Roderick in BC24, employer of Sam

Shotter in SS25, Ronnie Fish in FP29, Monty Bodkin in HW33. Lives at The Oaks, Wimbledon Common, where his niece Linda Rome keeps house for him in BM64. Has a country place in Buckinghamshire where he keeps pigs, including the prized Buckingham Big Boy. Makes arrangements for the theft of the Empress of Blandings to his Buckinghamshire piggery in SS61. Always eager to add to his huge fortune, hires Percy Pilbeam to trick Biff Christopher out of brother Edmund Pyke's estate in BM64, where he courts Pilbeam's cousin Gwendoline Gibbs.

Mrs. **Tinkler-Moulke**, owner of a Pomeranian in TY34, lives in flat C6 at Berkeley Mansions, directly below Bertie and his banjolele.

Alf **Todd**, Billson's boxing adversary at the Universal Sporting Club in 23RB.

Celia **Todd** marries Smallwood Bessemer at the beginning of 48TH.

Chester **Todd**, brother of Mavis Todd, with whom he controls Clear Spring sparkling table water in FL56. Nephew of Hermione Pegler, husband of violinist Jane Parker, friend of Freddie Carpenter.

James **Todd**, friend of Peter Willard and his rival for the hand of Grace Forrester in 19WW.

Sir Jasper **Todd** of Wissel Hall, retired financier; uncle and guardian to Amanda Biffen in 52BB.

Mavis **Todd**, sister of Chester Todd, becomes Freddie Carpenter's fiancée in FL56. Her uncle George was Snake Todd, the '30s football star.

Rockmetteller "Rocky" **Todd**, sluggard poet in 16AS, nephew, namesake, and dependent of Isabel Rockmetteller of Illinois; in 16JU he is a friend of Bertie's who lives all alone in the wilds of Long Island.

Clarence "Hash" **Todhunter**, a long, lean man of repellent aspect in the early 30s, former cook on the tramp steamer *Araminta*, cooks for Sam Shotter at Mon Repos in SS25.

Tomlin lives in the School House at Wrykyn in WF07.

Miss **Tomlinson**, handsome but strong-minded schoolmistress of a girls' school near Brighton whom Jeeves induces to invite Bertie to address the young ladies in 22BC.

Tommy, Sylvia Reynolds' foppish pug in 01WP, destroys carnation plants, for which he is shot dead by Sylvia's papa.

Tootles, infant borrowed to restore a broken romance in 11HF and 26FF.

Lancelot, Lord **Topham,** guest of Adela Shannon Cork in OR51, one of the richest men in England, constantly short of cash and temporarily out of favor with his girl friend Toots Fauntleroy.

Lady Adela **Topping,** eldest daughter of Lord Shortlands in SF48. See Adela Cobbold.

Desborough **Topping,** philatelist, husband of Lady Topping in SF48: a small, slight, pince-nezed man in the middle forties, was at college with Ellery Cobbold.

Lord **Towcester:** see William Egerton Ossingham Belfry.

Mr. **Townend,** friend of Bob Romney in 08LG, is too busy playing cricket to get on with his painting. A long, pleasant-looking young man with a large smile and unbrushed hair.

Rev. **Travers** is the new curate at Much Middlefold in 09AC.

Angela **Travers** is Dahlia's daughter, cousin to Bertie in 29JS, where she has been neglected by Tuppy Glossop; betrothed to Tuppy in 30TC, RH34, and MO71. Believes she was attacked by a shark while aquaplaning at Cannes just prior to the action of RH34. Her last name is never given: she may be Dahlia's daughter by her first husband, who is never named.

Bonzo **Travers,** son of Dahlia in 29JL, young pest pitted against his cousin Thos Gregson. See also HR60, where he is in school somewhere.

Dahlia **Travers,** wife of Thomas; see Dahlia Wooster.

George **Travers,** another uncle of Bertie's in 25CR, lives in Harrowsgate; presumably a brother of Thomas.

Thomas Portarlington **Travers,** of Brinkley Court, Brinkley-cum-Snodsfield-in-the-Marsh, Worcestershire (sometimes given as Brinkley Manor, Market Snodsbury), London address 47 Charles St. Second husband of Aunt Dahlia in 25CR, 29JS, RH34, CW38, JF54, 59JM, HR60, SU63, MO71, AA74. Married Dahlia the year Bluebottle won the Cambridgeshire.

Aunt Dahlia Travers

A bit of a squirt with greyish hair and a face like a walnut, he made a pile of money out in the East, but in so doing put his digestion on the blink. In 25CR, he won't live in the country; Anatole is hired as chef to mollify his digestion and disposition. Nervous about burglars, with a delusion that everybody known even slightly to the police is lurking in the garden, waiting for a chance to break into the house. Rich as creosote and eloquent on the subject of income tax and supertax, he is a kindly old bimbo but dislikes most of his houseguests and thinks most of his circle fatheaded asses. His four-year sponsorship of Aunt Dahlia's publication *Milady's Boudoir*, which he calls *Milady's Nightshirt*, supposedly ends with its sale to L.G. Trotter in JF54, but in 59JM he is still footing the bill for it. His collection of old silver has become one of the finest in England in HR60.

Aubrey Trefusis: see Aubrey Bassinger.

Evangeline **Trelawny**, Col. Wyvern's fifteen-year-old cook in RJ53.

Trent is prefect in Evans' house in 10PD.

Josephine **Trent**, sister of Kate and Terry in FL56, a strikingly pretty girl courted by Henry Weems.

Kate **Trent**, older sister of Jo and Terry, with whom she owns a chicken and bee farm on Tuttle's Lane in Bensonburg, L.I. in FL56 (cf. Elizabeth Boyd in UM16). Daughter of playwright Edgar Trent; looks at you like a Duchess looking at a potato bug.

Teresa **Trent**, sister of Kate and Jo, masquerades as Jo's maid Fellowes during the first part of their vacation in France. Marries Jefferson Auguste, Comte d'Escrignon in FL56.

Dick **Trentham** is head of Prater's house at St Austin's in 02TT; his sister is Mrs. James Williamson.

The Hon. Clarence **Tresillian** (a Greek god) lives with his parents in Belgrave Square; a great soccer goalie, plays for Houndsditch Wednesday under the name of Jones. In love with Isabel Rackstraw in 12GK.

Lady **Tresillian**, wife of the Earl of Runnymede, mother of Clarence and Lord Staines, daughter of a Chicago millionaire named Trotter in 12GK. There are few things more horrible than a Chicago voice raised in excitement or anguish.

Lord **Tresillian**, Earl of Runnymede, father of Clarence and Lord Staines in 12GK, member of the House of Lords and the Bachelor's Club.

Roland **Trevis**, composer of music for *The Rose of America* in LW20, wears long black hair. His sister Angela is fifteen, frivolous, and freckled.

Dick **Trevor**, head of Donaldson's, Wrykyn, a school prefect, member of the cricket 11, and captain of the first fifteen in 04RS and 05LP, is official holder of the gold bat in GB04. He shares a study with Clowes in 04RS and MK09. In WF07 he is on the Oxford A team in a visiting match against the Wrykyn first fifteen.

Miss **Trimble**, detective employed by Sturgis in PJ17, a stumpy, square-shouldered woman with thick eyebrows, a wandering right eye, stubby, aggressive nose, forbidding mouth, and socialist views.

Daisy **Trimble** of the Gaiety married well (a friend of Bertie Mannering-Phipps) and turned herself into an aristocrat, as remembered in 15EY.

Lord Teddy **Trimble** is Paul Bond's social agent in England in 06TP.

Amanda or Amelia **Trivett**, guest at Manhooset, fought over by Rollo Bingham and Otis Jukes in 21LH.

George **Trotter**, second Baron Holbeton, engaged to Sally Fairmile in QS40. Son of the co-founder of food purveyors Duff & Trotter.

Percy **Trotter**, first Lord Holbeton, late father of George in QS40.

Lemuel Gengulphus **Trotter**, husband of Emily and Percy Gorringe's stepfather, a dyspeptic little man with a face like a weasel who owns a lot of papers in Liverpool; a friend of Bertie's Aunt Agatha, buys *Milady's Boudoir* from Aunt Dahlia in JF54.

Emily "Ma" **Trotter**, wife of Lemuel, mother of Percy Gorringe in JF54. A burly heavyweight with a beaked nose, Mrs. Alderman Blenkinsop's social rival in Liverpool.

Ephraim **Trout** of Trout, Wapshott & Edelstein, attorney and old friend of Ivor Llewellyn, member of Bachelors Anonymous in BA73, falls in love with Amelia Bingham.

Wilbur J. **Trout,** American playboy, inherited millions from his father, a big businessman in California; has been often married and divorced. A sentimental man with ginger hair and a broken nose. Once engaged to Vanessa Polk, whom he marries in PB69.

Eustace **Trumper,** a shrimplike member of Clarissa Cork's colony in MB42, her fawning suitor.

B.B. **Tucker,** Gents' Hosier & Bespoke Shirt Maker, of Bedford St., Strand, creditor of Bingo Little in 37BP.

Rev. Joseph **Tucker,** Vicar of Badgwick, a scratch starter in 22SH.

George **Tupper,** Old Tuppy, onetime Wrykyn schoolmate of S.F. Ukridge and James Corcoran, was head of the school in his last year. Used to write sentimental poetry for the school magazine; now the sort of man who is always starting subscription lists and getting up memorials and presentations. An earnest man with a pulpy heart, takes other people's troubles very seriously. Successful member of the Foreign Office in the Ukridge stories (e.g. 23UD, 23NW, 47SS). Frequently touched by Ukridge for loans.

Prof. **Tupper-Smith** is a neighbor and friend of Lora Delane Porter in 15PW, one-time guest of Hailey and Sybil Bannister in New York.

Lana **Tuttle,** an immigrant from the Bottleton East section of London, is cook to Mr. & Mrs. Freddie Threepwood on Long Island in 66LF.

Dick **Tuxton,** uncle of Jane in 10BA, owns a parrot which is roughly treated by Jerry Moore.

Jane **Tuxton,** courted by Jerry Moore in 10BA; brown, slim, wiry-looking girl with eyes the color of Scotch whiskey.

Ralph **Tuxton,** Jane's brother in 10BA, a bank clerk and a dude.

Mrs. **Twemlow** is housekeeper at Blandings Castle in SN15 and 26LE. Has the same appearance of imminent apoplexy and the same air of belonging to some dignified and haughty branch of the vegetable kingdom as Beach, the butler.

Stanhope **Twine**, fiscally crippled sculptor in SF57, lives at Peacehaven next door to Lord Uffenham; engaged for a time to Jane Benedick.

Archibald **Twirling**, a builder specializing in bungalows in 29PW, is a leading contender for the Lawn Tennis championship at Wambledon. All his tennis strokes are lobs, and he cannot return a backhand.

Alexander "Chimp" **Twist**, unsuccessful crook, alias private investigator J. Sheringham Adair (Tilbury Detective Agency) with an office opposite Lord Tilbury's in SS25. In MN28 he is Dr. Alexander Twist, proprietor of Healthward Ho, Worcestershire, dedicated to the reconditioning of overfed gentry. Again posing as J. Sheringham Adair and headquartered at the Halsey Buildings, Mayfair, in MB42, IB61, and in PG72, where Grayce Llewellyn hires him to look after her pearls and Pop Llewellyn's diet. A small, weedy man with a waxed moustache and the face of an untrustworthy monkey. Formerly a Chicagoan, now frequently associated with Soapy and Dolly Molloy in schemes which involve burglary and end unprofitably for all three.

Frederick Altamont Cornwallis **Twistleton**, 5th Earl of Ickenham, living at Ickenham Hall, Bishop's Ickenham, Hants. Valerie and Pongo Twistleton-Twistleton's Uncle Fred in 35UF, UF39, UD48, CT58, and SS61. Known in school as Barmy; for years a younger son, spent twenty of those years in the U.S.: punched cows in Arizona, jerked soda, did a bit of newspaper work, prospected in the Mojave Desert. A sort of elderly Psmith, now sixty if a day and married to an American, Jane, who threatens to skin him with a blunt knife if he strays from Ickenham Hall—particularly to London, which he does whenever her back is turned, and steps high, wide and handsome, acting a youngish 22 (much to Pongo's dismay). By living in the country he generates, as it were, a store of loopiness which expends itself with frightful violence on his rare visits to the center of things. In the late afternoon of his life he retains, together with a juvenile waistline, the bright enthusiasm and fresh, unspoiled outlook of a slightly inebriated undergraduate. A tall, slim, distinguished-looking man with a jaunty moustache and an alert and enterprising eye. Loopy to the tonsils, a longtime friend of Galahad Threepwood (they used to be thrown out of nightclubs together). Inventor of the Ickenham System for speeding the course of true love. Fond of impersonations, which he undertakes whenever his sporting impulse (e.g. in 35UF) or the plight of young lovers seems to require it—"Help is a thing I am always glad to be of."

Gladys **Twistleton**, remembered by Galahad in HW33 as a girl afraid of thunderstorms, would fling her arms around the neck of the nearest man, hugging and kissing him until it was all over. A beautiful girl with large, melting eyes, married a fellow in the Blues called Harringay.

Jane **Twistleton**, née Bastable, Countess of Ickenham, half-sister of Beefy Bastable and wife of Frederick in UF39 and elsewhere, has prudently decided that the evening of her husband's life should be spent exclusively at his rural seat, going so far as to inform him that if he ever tries to sneak up to London she will skin him with a blunt knife. Broke off her engagement to Fred six times before tying the knot.

Lord Marmaduke **Twistleton** has a son at St Austin's in 01AF, where he promises Richard Venables a job as his estate-agent in Scotland after he finishes Oxford. Remembered in 35UF as Lord Ickenham's bewhiskered uncle, owner of Mitching Hill, now a part of south-east London.

Reginald G. "Pongo" **Twistleton-Twistleton**, nephew of Fred Twistleton (Lord Ickenham) in 33LS, 35TF, 35UF, UF39, UD48, RJ53, CT58, SS61. A slender, personable Drone with lemon-colored hair and an attractive face who by the time of UF39 has fallen in love at first sight with a mixed gaggle or assortment of females to the number of about twenty. In 33LS he takes 100 to 8 odds (and a large sum of money) from Oofy Prosser on a bet that Adolphus Stiffham will marry Geraldine Spettisbury. In UF39 he is reading for the bar and driving a Buffy-Porson two-seater which is still going in UD48, where he is still reading for the bar and uncomfortably engaged to Hermione Bostock. Marries Sally Painter in UD48; in MS49 we learn of his annual cross-talk act at the Drones smoker with Barmy Phipps; by CT58 marriage has made him a sober citizen, more uncomfortable than ever with Uncle Fred's exuberant ways. Oxford friend of Bill Bailey in SS61.

Valerie **Twistleton**, sister of Pongo, niece of Frederick Twistleton, Earl of Ickenham; a tall, handsome girl engaged to Horace Pendlebury-Davenport in UF39 and 50SP, his wife in JF54.

Marcella **Tyrrwhitt**, owner of a Peke named Reginald and a canary named William; niece of Major-General George Tyrrwhitt of the Buffs. Courted by Eustace Mulliner in 32OH.

Mrs. John **Tyson** of Rodney, Maine, has been working as a professional dancer at Geisenheimer's in 15AG.

U

George, sixth Viscount **Uffenham**, of Shipley Hall, brother of Beatrice Benedick and guardian of her daughters Anne (in MB42) and Jane (in SF57). In MB42 he is renting Shipley Hall to Clarissa Cork and posing as a butler named Cakebread, hoping he will recover from a head injury and remember where he has hidden the family jewels. In SF57 he is living at Castlewood, Mulberry Grove, Valley Fields, a property owned and shared by his former butler Augustus Keggs. Pear-shaped and bald-domed, with a long upper lip, pointed chin, and rugged brows over huge, unblinking eyes. Member of the Mausoleum Club. Inspired by Max Enke, PGW's fellow-internee in Germany during WWII (see N.T.P. Murphy, *In Search of Blandings*, pp. 118-121).

Julia **Ukridge**, wealthy and popular novelist, aunt of the much-enduring Stanley (sister of his late father) in the Ukridge stories. Lives in Heath House, one of the row of large mansions which face Wimbledon Common. Intermittently takes in her nephew and chucks him out, forces him to dress up in expensive clothes which she buys and he pops. For some reason best known to her own distorted mind it is impossible to induce her to part with a little ready cash. Author of *The Heart of Adelaide* and other rotten novels, keeps Pekingese dogs, collects snuffboxes, and belongs to the Pen & Ink Club. Her house, also called The Cedars, is the staging-point for Stanley's various money-making schemes. Has a cottage at Market Deeping, Sussex, called Journey's End. Goes to Hollywood in 31UH on a one-year contract to write dialogue, cut short when she swats the Main Boss of Colossal-Superfine on the ear. See 23UD, 23FA, 23US, 24UR, 25BL, 25BD, 26LB, 35CB, 47SS, 55TC, 67US.

Millie **Ukridge** is Mrs. S.F. Ukridge in LC06. She has a wealthy Aunt Elizabeth, Lady Lakenheath.

Stanley Featherstonehaugh **Ukridge** (rhymes with Duke-ridge; middle name pronounced as spelled, acc. to Debrett's *Correct Form*), much-enduring, disreputable entrepreneur in LC06 and nineteen Ukridge stories where his schemes generally go awry. Attended school at Wrykyn, where his cronies included James Corcoran and George Tupper. Expelled from Wrykyn for breaking out at night to try his skills at the coconut-shies of the local village fair. First appears in LC06, where he has a wife Millie and a wealthy Aunt Elizabeth (Lady Lakenheath), and attempts to establish a chicken farm with the help of writer friend Jeremy Garnet, his onetime colleague on the staff of a private school. Nephew of author Julia Ukridge, whose Pekingese dogs attend Ukridge's Dog College in 23UD. Other misappropriated belongings of his Aunt Julia include a diamond brooch, which he pops in 26LB. Wears a bright yellow mackintosh, his companion through many discreditable adventures, and a pince-nez held in place by ginger-beer wire. A bachelor except in his first appearance, he used to date Dora Mason during one of his many stays at Wimbledon; he helps her get started in business in 23FA, 23US. Briefly engaged to Mabel Price in 23NW, to Millie Lakenhurst in 24UR, to another Mabel in 25BL. A large man himself, he discovers and manages the boxing career of the even larger Battling Billson in 23DB, 23RB, 23EB, 35CB.

Ukridge

Frequently dependent on George Tupper and James Corcoran for loans, lodging, and articles of clothing. Sleeping-partner in bookmaking firm of Issac O'Brien in 23LA, where he assists the political campaign of former schoolmate B.V. Lawlor. His London residence is Arundel Street, Leicester Square. Said to be PGW's favorite character: "Ukridge is a real character. He was drawn from a friend of mine with whom I used to run about from 1903 onwards. I have not seen him for years, and I suppose he is old and respectable now!"—PGW letter to a Mr. Simmons, 9/27/51. "Ukridge was a friend of W. Townend, the writer of sea-stories, who told me about him."—PGW in "How I Write My Books" (*What I Think*. London: George Newnes, 1926). "Ukridge was drawn originally from what Townend told me about a man named Craxton, and shortly after that I met a man named Westbrook who was very much the same sort of chap."—PGW letter to Perceval Graves dated 9/26/60. He is often identified with Herbert W. Westbrook; cf. also Julian Eversleigh in NG07, co-authored by Westbrook and PGW. Richard Usborne compares him with James Cullingworth in Conan Doyle's *Stark Monro Letters*; in the first two editions of *Goodbye to All That* Robert Graves sees him as a gentle caricature of his brother Perceval Graves (see N.T.P. Murphy, *In Search of Blandings*, pp. 45-48).

Ulric, smith in WT04.

Lady Underhill, strong-willed mother of Sir Derek in LW20, bullies him into breaking off his engagement with Jill Mariner. Has the same long upper lip, thin, firm mouth and prominent chin as her son. Has a brother Edwin.

Sir Derek Underhill, M.P., a strikingly handsome man with a strong, forceful face; dark, lean, and cleanly shaven. Afraid of his mother, Lady Underhill. Breaks off his engagement to Jill Mariner in LW20.

Victoria Underwood, daughter of the late American millionaire J.B. Underwood, stepdaughter of Florence Moresby. Galahad Threepwood's favorite niece, imprisoned at Blandings Castle to prevent communication with Jeff Bennison, with whom she is in love in SB77.

Rev. Aubrey **Upjohn**, M.A., headmaster of St Asaph's school on Mafeking Road, Bramley-on-Sea, where Bertie Wooster once won a prize for Scripture Knowledge. The school is called Malvern House in HR60 and 65JG. An old friend of Lord Bodsham, and former headmaster of Reginald Herring, Catsmeat Potter-Pirbright, and Freddie Widgeon; Freddie inadvertently leaves Bingo Little's baby in his study in 39BI. Retired in HR60, widower of the late Jane Mills and stepfather of Phyllis Mills, he has grown a moustache and hopes to run for Parliament as the Conservative candidate in the Market Snodsbury division. See also MS49.

Vera **Upshaw**, only daughter of the late Charles Upshaw and Dame Flora Faye, the actress. Engaged to Jerry West at the beginning of GB70; writes slim volumes of whimsical essays, e.g. *Morning's at Seven* and *Daffodil Days*.

V

Gerald Anstruther **Vail**, one of the Loamshire Vails, a nephew of Plug Basham, was at Harrow with Orlo Vosper. A writer of thrillers, in love with Penny Donaldson in PW52, where he lives in flat #33, Prince of Wales Mansions, Battersea Park Road, London S.W. Hired as Lord Emsworth's secretary in PW52. Sound on pigs; needs £2000 to set up a health-care establishment.

Penny **Vail** (Mrs. Gerald Vail), formerly Penelope Donaldson (q.v.), sister of Freddie Threepwood's wife in PB69, where she exchanges letters with Beach about news from Blandings and the health-care establishment in which her husband is engaged.

Joan **Valentine**, daughter of a rich man who died suddenly, leaving her without money. Was at school with Aline Peters, has since supported herself by various means; was in the chorus at the Piccadilly Theatre, where she was ardently courted by Freddie Threepwood (whose importunate letters and gifts she ignored). Now writes short stories for *Home*

Gossip, published weekly by the Mammoth Publishing Company. Lives at 7A Arundell St., where her neighbor is Ashe Martin. Tall, about 5' 7", with blue eyes. Something of a feminist, believes a woman can do nearly everything better than a man. Marries Ashe Marson in SN15.

Katherine or Kitchie **Valentine**, American niece of Major Flood-Smith in BM31, at the beginning of which she is engaged to New York actor Merwyn Flock. Her mother is Maj. Flood-Smith's sister, living in Great Neck. Shipboard friend of Ann Moon, falls in love with Lord Biskerton.

Mr. **Van Courtland** is Joe Johnson's manager in 05BL.

Eustiss **Vanderleigh**, a playwright of the Little Theatre school, recently shipped to Hollywood in a crate of twelve in 33JO.

Stella **Vanderley** is on the yacht *Circe* with her mother in 12RR; breaks off her engagement to George Lattiker as the result of a misunderstanding.

Joe J. **Vanringham**, Tubby's brother in SM37, was a sailor on a tramp steamer, a bouncer at some bar in New York, and did a bit of prize-fighting. Breezy and impertinent, sometime odd-job man for J. Mortimer Busby. Playwright, author of *Angel in the House*, which makes fun of his stepmother, Princess von und zu Dwornitzchek. Lean and hard of body; in love with Jane Abbott.

Theodore P. "Tubby" **Vanringham**, stout young American guest at Walsingford Hall in SM37, in love with Prudence Whittaker. Son of the late Franklin Vanringham, brother of Joe, dependent stepson of Princess von und zu Dwornitzchek.

Reggie **Van Tuyl**, friend of Archie in IA21; a long, somnolent youth from a wealthy New York family; has an uncle Edgar who thought he was twins.

Vaughan, student at Ward's house in PH02.

Mary **Vaughan**, visiting Marvis Bay with an aunt in 10DW, pulls George Callender out of the water.

Archibald **Venables**, Richard's brother, is a student at King's College, Cambridge, in 01AF.

Major-General Sir Everard **Venables**, V.C., K.C.M.G., father of Richard and Archibald in 01AF (03HS indicates the existence of a third son, who is not named, the youngest; a daughter,

Dorothy, is Mrs. James Anthony in 01AF).

Richard **Venables**, capt. of school cricket at St Austin's in 01AF, 03HP, 03HS. Plays wing three-quarter on the school fifteen in 03HS, where his younger brother arrives at St Austin's. Promised a job after Oxford as a land agent for Lord Marmaduke Twistleton in Scotland, where he can play for the local cricket club (cf. Mike Jackson).

Venner is Lord Biskerton's manservant in BM31.

Sir Alfred **Venner**, M.P. of Badgwick Hall, neighbor of St Austin's in PH02, hates trespassers and poachers, has many gamekeepers. London address 49A Lancaster Gate.

Billy **Verepoint**, the actress, persuades Roland Bleke to buy the Windsor Theatre in MM14.

Elizabeth **Vickers** is engaged to Fred Bullivant in 11HF.

Vickery of the Wrykyn Upper Fourth owns study three at Appleby's in 04HT; likes scent.

George **Vince**, Ruth Warden's suitor in 12RE, son of Vince's Stores, specializing in children's toys.

Hilda **Vince** models for Kirk Winfield in WH14; engaged to a young gentleman who travels for a hat firm.

Miss Angelica **Vining**, the poetess, a gaunt sort of toothy female, friend of Julia Ukridge and fellow-member of the Pen and Ink Club in 31UH, wants to borrow Julia's diamond brooch in 26LB.

Violet, trim, energetic little person with round blue eyes and a friendly smile, housemaid at Harrow House in 09OS.

Gen. **Vodkakoff**, Russian invader in SW09.

Hildebrand **Vosper**, for eighteen years the Duke of Bootle's butler, acquired by Evangeline Fisher in 25HS, keeps the Fishers up to a Dukely standard in 26KI. A tall, stout, ambassadorial man with pendulous cheeks, curving waistcoat, protruding eyes, and a sequence of rolling chins.

Orlo, Lord **Vosper**, a dull, earnest young man who looks like a screen star and has political ambitions, a member of one of the oldest families in England and plenty of money. Was at Harrow with Jerry Vail. Connie wants him to marry Penelope Donaldson in PW52, but he is unsound on pigs and opposed on those grounds by Lord Emsworth.

Alfred **Voules** is chauffeur at Blandings in FP29, HW33, PW52, SS61, BG65, PB69.

Rev. Gideon **Voules**, replacement clergyman hired to marry George Finch and Molly Waddington in SB27. Face like a horse, eye like a poached egg, white socks.

Harold **Voules** is Reggie Pepper's valet in 12RR; moves as silently as Jeeves but drops and adds h's in Cockney fashion, especially when intoxicated. Briefly engaged to Emma Pilbeam.

Ted **Voules**, police sergeant at Chuffnell Regis, uncle to Constable Dobson in TY34; built rather on the lines of the Albert Hall, round in the middle and not much above.

W

Wace, butler at Sinclair Hammond's Holly House in BC24.

Hypatia **Wace**, niece and ward of Percy, Bishop of Stortford, school friend of Jane Brandon Mulliner; engaged to Ronald Bracy-Gascoigne in 30GN.

Cyril **Waddesley-Davenport** came down from Balliol, Oxford in '26; gorilla for Perfecto-Zizzbaum's *Black Africa* in 32MB.

G.G. **Waddington**, proprietor of Waddington's Ninety-Seven Soups, rich father of Violet in IW31.

Molly **Waddington**, 20, daughter of Sigsbee H. Waddington, has a round face, tiptilted nose, and large eyes. Marries George Finch in SB27.

Sigsbee Horatio **Waddington**, father of Molly in SB27; a red-faced, absent-minded little man with stiff grey hair, a synthetic Westerner who has never been outside New York state. Henpecked and financially dependent on Mrs. Waddington.

Mrs. Sigsbee H. **Waddington**, Molly's stepmother in SB27, relict of the late P. Homer Horlick, the Cheese King, who left her with several million dollars. Bulging and socially ambitious, wants Molly to marry Lord Hunstanton. Looks like Catherine of Russia.

Violet **Waddington**, tall, slender, cool and languid heiress of Waddington's Ninety-Seven Soups, engaged to Lord Droitwich in IW31.

Claude **Wade-Pigott**, neighbor of Henry Paradene in PP67, heir to a large estate. Member of the Stock Exchange and the firm of Bates, Wade-Pigott, & Pollard.

Wagstaff, scoutmaster in SW09.

Mr. **Wain**, house master at Wrykyn, a tall thin man with a serious face partially obscured by a grizzled beard; Wyatt's stepfather in MK09.

Hugo **Walderwick**, owner of umbrella at the Drones which Psmith gives to Eve Halliday in LP23.

Charles Augustus **Walkinshaw** is football secretary at St Austin's in O2HP.

Captain J.G. **Walkinshaw**, horsewhipped on the steps of the Drones Club by Major-General Sir Masterman Petherick-Soames for trifling with the affections of the latter's niece Hester; see 28OO. Unknown relationship to Walkinshaw's Supreme Ointment, recommended by one of Jeeves' aunts some time prior to 16JT. Cf. Douglas Walkinshaw, pseud. of Pongo Twistleton in 35UF.

Mr. **Waller** is Paying Cashier, head of the Cash Department in the New Asiatic Bank in PC10; an avid Socialist orator.

Walter **Walsh**: see Mr Reginald Seymour.

Walton, of Kay's, a large, unpleasant-looking youth at Eckleton in HK05, is a perfect specimen of the public school man at his worst.

Horace **Wanklyn**, eminent novelist in 55TC whose works plumb the passionate heart of Women. A long, thin, stringy man in the early fifties with a long, thin, stringy neck.

Lady Anne **Warblington**, one of Clarence Threepwood's ten sisters, chatelaine of Blandings Castle in SN15 and owner of a Persian cat named Muriel.

Mr. **Ward**, house master at St Austin's College in PH02, has the unpleasant habit of jarring, or speaking so as to make the person to whom he is speaking uncomfortable.

Sergeant **Ward**, aspiring actor in OR51, investigates a suspected burglary at the Carmen Flores place.

Eugene **Warden**, Ruth's idle father in 12RE; an amiable drifter, jaunty and slightly disreputable, lives on remittances.

Ruth **Warden**, daughter of Eugene Warden, secretary-clerk to M. Gandinot and title character of 12RE.

Mrs. **Wardle**, Augustine Mulliner's housekeeper in 26MB.

Marion **Wardour**, showgirl plagued by the rivalrous attentions of Claude & Eustace Wooster in 22EC/IJ23.

Stewart **Waring**, owner of the Pleasant Street tenements and candidate for New York alderman in PJ15.

Sir Jaklyn **Warner**, 7th Baronet and cadger who achieves his ends by looking wistful and pathetic, twice engaged to Sally Fitch, compelled to make good on his betrothal to Daphne Dolby in BA73.

Wassick is Julia Ukridge's new secretary in 24UR.

Rupert **Watchett** is a contender for the club golf championship in 40SM.

Waterall, young New Yorker and baseball fan in 14OT, London correspondent of the New York Chronicle.

Waterbury is the chauffeur at Brinkley Court in RH34.

Jas or Jos **Waterbury**, the greasy bird of 36MT, gin-lover and pianist hired to accompany Freddie Widgeon at the Bottleton East Palace of Varieties. Since Freddie saved him from the pub brawl in 36MT, he comes frequently to the Drones to touch Freddie for small loans. Persuades Oofy Prosser to invest in two massive all-in wrestlers, Porky Jupp and Plug Bosher, in 48FO. In 65JG he is a greasy-headed theatrical agent on Charing Cross Road.

Old **Waterbury**, Sippy Sipperley's onetime head master, unwelcome contributor to the *Mayfair Gazette* in 26IC, e.g. "The Old School Cloisters" and "Some Little-Known Aspects of Tacitus." A large, important-looking bird with penetrating eyes, a Roman nose, and high cheek-bones. Authoritative, looks like a traffic-policeman.

Trixie **Waterbury**, niece to Jas Waterbury in 65JG, about 5'9", bulges in every direction. Plays Fairy Queens in pantomime.

Jane **Waterfield**, a school friend of Felicia Blakeney in 23CF.

Waterford is one of a bad lot of boys at Leicester's house, Beckford College in PU03.

Luella Granville **Waterman**, author of the "Moments in the Nursery" page of *Peaceful Moments* in PA12, *Cosy Moments* in PJ15.

Ramsden **Waters**, a timid man with a weak mouth and as much ferocity and self-assertion as a blanc-mange, a solitary golfer in love with Eunice Bray in 20RS.

Orlo **Watkins**, the Crooning Tenor, Beefy Bingham's rival for Gertrude in 31GG. Wears short but distinct side-whiskers, dislikes and fears all dogs.

Myrtle **Watling** is Cedric Mulliner's secretary in 29SC; one of those calm, strong young women who look steadily out upon the world through spectacles with tortoiseshell rims.

Watson[1] is the ground man of Beckford College in PU03.

Watson[2] is the headmaster's butler at Eckleton in HK05.

Watson[3] is captain of soccer at Oxford in 06PI.

Watson[4] is Lord Tilbury's chauffeur in BM64.

Jane **Watson**, Mortimer Little's gourmet cook of seven years' service in 21JS/IJ23; Jeeves has an "understanding" with her which she breaks off in order to marry her employer; she is Lady Bittlesham, i.e. Mortimer's wife, in 22CB/IJ23.

Montagu **Watson**, novelist tricked in 05AH. Author of *The Soul of Anthony Carrington* (Popgood & Grooly: 6s.) and *Pan Wakes*, lives at Chesterton, two miles from Locksley School. Notorious foe of autograph hunters.

Beatrice **Watterson**, onetime flame of Eustace Mulliner in 32OH.

Muriel **Watterson**, hawklike editress of *Woman's Sphere* and associate of Julia Ukridge in 23FA, belongs to the Pen & Ink Club.

Mr. Everard **Waugh-Bonner**, septuagenarian guest at Walsingford Hall in SM37.

Lady Julia **Waveney**, Dowager Duchess, elderly lady visiting Roville with her paid companion (unnamed), to whom George Balmer proposes in 12TM. A well-known political hostess, former employer of Algie Wetherby's butler Wrench in UM16.

Wayburn is head of the Kay's contingent from Eckleton in the summer camp at Aldershot in HK05.

J.G. Weatherby, lawyer for Lord Droitwich in IW31.

Joss (Jocelyn Parmalee) Weatherby, cheerful, loose-limbed artist-turned-valet in QS40, a Psmith type. Painted Beatrice Chavender's portrait, now illustrates ads for Duff & Trotter; in love with Sally Fairmile.

Duke of **Weatherstonhope** (pron. Wop), owner of an ancient castle at which the story of Sir Agravaine (12SA) was found.

Clarice **Weaver** plays heroine in *The Girl from Brighton* in 15BB; sings badly, acts indifferently, throws her weight about.

Mr. **Webber** is the vet who attends on the Empress of Blandings in HW33.

Webster[1], Theodore Mulliner's austere and censorious cat, succumbs to Drink in 32SW, in his prime under the care of Lancelot Mulliner in 32CC.

Webster[2], Horace Pendlebury-Davenport's man in UF39.

Montagu **Webster**, J. Rufus Bennett's English valet in TM22: Webster has personality. He exudes it. Has an almost superhuman intelligence.

Col. Egbert **Wedge**, husband of Hermione for 24 years and father of Veronica in FM47 and BG65, was in the Shropshire Light Infantry.

Lady Hermione **Wedge** is the only one of the female members of the Emsworth family who is not statuesquely handsome: short and dumpy, looks like a cook of strong character. In residence at Blandings Castle in FM47, she has succeeded her sister Constance as chatelaine of the family manor in BG65. Mother of Veronica, aunt of Wilfred Allsop. No longer at Blandings or on speaking terms with her brother Clarence in PB69.

Veronica "Vee" **Wedge**, 23, only daughter of Col. Egbert and Lady Hermione Wedge of Rutland Gate, London S.W. 7. A tall girl of a radiant blonde loveliness but no more brain than would fit comfortably into an aspirin bottle, she is the dumbest but most beautiful girl registered among the collateral branches of Debrett's Peerage. Once engaged to her cousin Freddie, engaged to Tipton Plimsoll in FM47 and BG65.

Weeks is butler to Master Peter's parents in 15MS.

Teddy **Weeks**, sickeningly handsome actor who takes out accident insurance in 23UA.

Henry **Weems** of Kelly, Dubinsky, Wix, Weems, & Bassinger, attys; a grave, solid young man, wants to marry Jo Trent in FL56.

Fanny **Welch**, pickpocket who marries Frederick Mullett in SB27; retroussé nose and expressive black eyes.

J.G. (for George) **Welch**, a friend of Richard Venables and member of the St Austin's eleven in 01AF, is captain of Merevale's cricket team in 02OT; shares a study at Merevale's with Charteris in PH02 and 03MC, plays wing at footer in 03MC. A good student and excellent all-around athlete, Captain of Cricket in PH02. Runs a fast mile to summon Dr. Adamson for house-master Merevale's daughter in 02WM. See also 03HS.

Mrs. Clara **Wellbeloved**, needy parishoner of the Rev. Sidney Pirbright, visited by his niece Corky in MS49; knows everything about Hollywood, e.g. how many times Artie Shaw has been married.

George Cyril **Wellbeloved**, 29, pigman of Lord Emsworth in 27PH, 28CG, HW33, SS61: Long, lean, red-haired; no feast for the eye, having a sinister squint, a mouth like a halibut and a broken nose acquired during a political discussion at the Goose and Gander in Market Blandings (his views are strongly communistic), and a good deal of mud all over him, but beyond question a force in the piggery when sober. Pigs like him. Hired away by Lord Emsworth's rival Sir Gregory Parsloe-Parsloe in 28CG, back at Blandings again after a period of employment at Matchingham Hall in FP29, but working again for arch-fiend Parsloe in PW52. Retired in BG65, having inherited a public house in Wolverhampton from a relative.

Marlene **Wellbeloved**, niece of George Cyril Wellbeloved, is barmaid at the Emsworth Arms in BG65.

Percy **Wellbeloved** of Shropshire is an old gardener at Towcester Abbey in RJ53.

Mr. Mortimer **Wells**, college friend of Rev. Percival, reviews the St Austin's prize poem entries in 01PP. Reappears in

George Cyril Wellbeloved

PU03 as the priggish judge of the upper Fifth poetry contest at Beckford College. Author of a privately printed volume of poems entitled *The Dark Horse.*

Arthur **Welsh** is a jealous barber at the Hotel Belvoir in 10WD, in love with manicurist Maud Peters.

Angela **West**, estranged fiancée of Freddie Meadowes in 11HF (cf. Elizabeth Vickers in 26FF).

Gerald Godfrey Francis **West**, 27, son of the late Joseph West, manufacturer of chinaware up north, nephew of Crispin and Willoughby Scrope in GB70. An artist specializing in comic cartoons, engaged to Vera Upshaw and in love with Jane Hunnicut.

William Paradene **West**, 26, nephew to Cooley Paradene in BC24, played football at Harvard, now lives on quarterly remittances from his uncle. Goes to London with friend J. Birdsey Coker, lives there at #9, Marmont Mansions, Battersea. Falls in love with Flick Sheridan.

Westaway, secretary of the Hearty Lunchers Cricket Club in 09RR, is stout and sentimental.

Westbrook, master at Mike Jackson's old school King-Hall's in MK09, a good slow bowler. See also Julian Eversleigh.

Andrew **Westley**, brother of the late Maude Westley, John Maude's uncle, guardian, and sometime employer in PA12 and PB12. A capable rather than lovable man, too self-controlled to be quite human. Proprietor of Westley, Martin & Co. in New York (PA12) or London (PB12). Gave nephew John his mother's first name as a surname to erase all memory of his father, the late Prince Charles of Mervo, and (in PB12) brought him up as an Englishman. Dislikes John intensely.

Alice **Weston**, small and quiet, rather pretty, lives at the same boarding-house as Henry Pifield Rice in 15BB. Chorus-girl in *The Girl from Brighton*, has a sister Genevieve who married a commercial traveler.

Betty **Weston**, an ardent, vivid girl with an intense capacity for hero-worship, breaks off her engagement with Mortimer Sturgis in 20MT and marries explorer Eddie Denton.

Algie, Lord **Wetherby**, a dapper, trim little man of about forty, conveys a subtle suggestion of horsiness. Married to Polly in UM16; a painter who has cast himself as a nervous, highly-strung artist.

Gladys **Wetherby**, poetess with the face and figure of the better type of pin-up girl, niece of Col. Francis Pashley-Drake, engaged to Lancelot Bingley in 67GC.

J.G. Wetherby of Polk, Wetherby, Polk, and Polk, family solicitor to the Droitwich clan in IW31.

Pauline or Polly, Countess of **Wetherby**, née Pauline Davis of Carbondale, Illinois, former chorus girl married to Algie Wetherby in UM16. Earns her living performing barefoot "Greek" dances at Reigenheimer's on 42nd Street. Friend of Claire Fenwick.

Julie **Weyder**, daughter of Cornelius Weyder the Copper King, is engaged to Lord Worfield in 06BJ.

James B. **Wheeler** makes a large annual income as an illustrator for the magazines in 21SE and 21WV/IA21; a member of the Pen-and-Ink Club, hires Archie Moffam as a model in 21SE, engaged to Alice Wigmore in 21WV.

Augustus **Whiffle** or (in BG65) **Whipple**, author of *On the Care of the Pig* (Popgood & Grooly, 35s) Lord Emsworth's favorite reading in the Blandings stories. A member of the Athenaeum Club, had an uncle who grew a second set of teeth in his 80th year and used to crack Brazil nuts with them. Once lunched with Galahad at the Athenaeum; occasional adviser to the Minister of Agriculture.

Lord Percy **Whipple**, second son of the Duke of Devizes, nephew of Lady Corstorphine in PJ17.

White[1] shares a study in St Austin's with Kendal, Bradshaw, and the narrator of 02BL.

White[2] is the butler-detective at Sanstead House in 13EC and LN13; a stout but active man of middle age, without that quality of austere aloofness noticeable in other butlers. See Smooth Sam Fisher.

Benjamin **White** is proprietor of *Cosy Moments* in PJ15.

Gladys **Whittaker**, a large, spreading, Junoesque blonde, plays the heroine in *Sacrifice* in BW52; sister of Jack McClure's wife.

Prudence **Whittaker**, secretary to Sir Buckstone Abbott, mooned after by Tubby Vanringham in SM37. Tall, slender, and elegant, with a tiptilted nose and affected accent.

Lady **Wickham** of Skeldings Hall, Hertfordshire, relict of the late Sir Cuthbert Wickham, cousin to Mr. Mulliner, mother of Roberta, old friend of Aunt Agatha. A beaky female built far too closely on the lines of Aunt Agatha for Bertie's comfort; her eye is a combination of gimlet and X-ray, her chin reminiscent of a battleship going into action. Author of popular sentimental novels in 24SS, 25AG, 26PT, 27JY, 29JD, 30JK, HR60, writes under the name George Masterman. A member of the Pen and Ink Club, wants J.H. Potter in 26PT to be the U.S. publisher of her books, which include *Agatha's Vow*, *A Strong Man's Love*, *A Man for A' That*, *Meadowsweet*, and *Fetters of Fate*. She takes a few shots at Dudley Finch in 40DI, but the bullets whistle harmlessly past his ears.

Clementina **Wickham**, Bobbie's young cousin, title character of 30JK: a quiet, saintlike girl of thirteen who fills inkpots at St Monica's with sherbet.

Cuthbert **Wickham**, a vast young man with protruding jaw, rippling muscles, and a dog named Tulip, lives at Bloxham Mansions, Park Lane. He is the son of Bobbie Wickham's Aunt Rhoda. 40DI takes place on the eve of his wedding.

Marcia **Wickham** is Bobbie Wickham's aunt in 28PA.

Rhoda **Wickham**, mother of Cuthbert and aunt of Bobbie in 40DI, owns a house called Balmoral in Wimbledon Common.

Roberta "Bobbie" **Wickham**, daughter of Sir Cuthbert and Lady Wickham of Skeldings Hall, Herts, volatile and frivolous redhead, object of Bertie's attentions in 27JY, 29JD, 30JK; Jeeves strongly disapproves of her. A girl of remarkable beauty, resembling a particularly good-looking schoolboy who has dressed up in his sister's clothes; a spirited but erratic girl with an instinct for mischief, inclined to treat her suitors badly: every fellow who comes in contact with her finds himself sooner or later up to the Adam's apple in some ghastly mess. Drives a scarlet roadster. Courted by Roland Attwater in 24SS, Dudley Finch in 25AG, Clifford Gandle in

26PT, Ambrose Wiffin in 28PA, Reggie Herring in HR60. Dudley Finch discovers to his cost he is still in love with her in 40DI, where her home is in Essex. London headquarters is the residence of her aunt (Marcia?) in Eaton Square, phone Sloane 8090.

Wilfred **Wickham** is Bobbie's cousin, son of her Aunt Marcia in 28PA.

Lord **Wickhammersley** of Twing Hall, Glos., father of Egbert and Cynthia, great friend of Bertie's late father, lends his Hall grounds for the annual village school treat in 22PT, host in 22SH/IJ23.

Lady Cynthia **Wickhammersley**, youngest daughter of foreg. in IJ23 (22PT, 22SH), dashed pretty, lively and attractive girl, but full of ideals: the sort of girl who would want a fellow to carve out a career; successfully courted by James Bates in 22SH/IJ23.

Egbert **Wickhammersley**, younger brother of Cynthia, tutee of Bingo Little in 22SH, 22PT, 22MT (IJ23).

Lady **Widdrington**, widow of the late Sir George Widdrington, C.B.E., daughter of Mrs. Pulteney-Banks. Residing at Widdrington Manor, Bottleby-in-the-Vale, Hants., entertains Theodore Mulliner on his return to England from Bongo-Bongo in 32CC. Owner of a combative cat named Percy.

Frederick Fotheringay **Widgeon**, a Drone in 31FA, 34NO, 34GB, 35TD, 36MT, CW38, 39BI, JM46, 48FO, RJ53, JF54, 58FL, IB61 and 65BB, might have stepped straight out of the advertisement columns of one of the glossier and more expensive magazines, though criticisms have been made from time to time of his intelligence. Went to school at St Asaph's. Dependent on his uncle Rodney Widgeon, Lord Blicester (q.v.). Another uncle in 31FA is a bishop. Girls always like Freddie at first—but he is a constantly unsuccessful suitor. Gets the bird from Mavis Peasemarch in 31FA and again in 39BI. Courts April Carroway in 35TD, where he loses his pants. Other girls with whom he has been in love include Drusilla Wix, Dahlia Prenderby, Vanessa Vokes, Helen Christopher, Dora Pinfold, and Hildegard Watt-Watson. If all the girls he has loved and lost were placed end to end, they would reach halfway down Piccadilly—or further, as some of them were pretty tall. Courts Dora Pinfold in 36MT, where he performs anonymously at Amateur Night in the Bottleton East Palace of Varieties and saves greasy bird Jos Waterbury from a nasty pub brawl. Frequently touched by Waterbury for small loans since then, he becomes involved with Waterbury and Oofy Prosser in a wrestling promotion scheme in 48FO. Once pinched at Hurst Park by his cousin Cyril, a policeman, as recalled in JM46. Bertie's rival in the Drones' Darts Sweep in JF54. Originator of the Fat Uncles sweepstakes at the Drones in 58FL, where his middle name is given as Fortescue. Finally woos and wins Sally Foster in IB61, where Percy Cornelius loans him £3000 to start a coffee plantation in Kenya. Of an innocent and unsuspicious nature, he believes everything he reads in *Time*.

Rodney **Widgeon**: see Lord Blicester.

Ambrose **Wiffin**, a Drone involved with Bobbie Wickham in 28PA.

Alice **Wigmore**, J.B. Wheeler's fiancée in 21WV/IA21, amateur painter, creator of the Wigmore Venus.

J. Fillken **Wilberfloss**, editor-in-chief of *Cosy Moments* in PJ15, a little man with a long neck and large pince-nez who chirrups.

Wilberforce[1] is Reggie Pepper's man in 15CA.

Wilberforce[2] or Willoughby is Myrtle Beenstock's butler in 65SS.

Maudie **Wilberforce**, aunt of Rhoda Platt in 30IS: a woman of billowy curves, formerly Uncle George Wooster's barmaid fiancée who was bought off, reunited with him in 30IS.

Sybil **Wilbur**, daughter of the Robert Wilburs, marries Bailey Bannister in WH14; a tiny, restless creature, lively and effervescent.

Wilhelm, a whacking great Alsatian belonging to Lady Prenderby at Matcham Scratchings in 34GB.

Wilkins is the overgrown youth who cleans the knives and boots of Spinder's house in LS08.

Nurse **Wilks**, former nurse of Frederick Mulliner and of Jane Oliphant, lives at Wee Holme, Marazion Rd, Bingley-on-Sea;

title character of 27PD.

George **Willard**, friend and neighbor of Lord Emsworth in LP23.

Jill **Willard**, daughter of Anthony Willard, an impecunious squire in the west country, nurse in attendance on Mike Bond's aunt Isobel. In love with Mike, in DB68, helps burgle his bank.

Peter **Willard**, golfing friend of James Todd and his rival for the hand of Grace Forrester in 19WW; classified in 22MP as an Unfortunate Incident, Wallace Chesney's partner in the medal competition; also appears in 25PR. Defeated golfing rival of Sir George Copstone in 48EX.

Willett, New York actor who plays bluff fathers in musical comedy, member of the Strollers' club in IJ10.

William[1] is the butler-bootboy at Leicester's house, Beckford College in PU03.

William[2] is the dog who saves James Rodman from marriage in 25HC.

Williams[1] is a prefect at Blackburn's, Eckleton in HK05.

Williams[2] plays for the Sedleigh School fifteen in 10SW.

Jack **Williams**, brother of village carpenter Tom in 06FM, was reserve center three-quarter for England and is recruited by Neville-Smith[1] to play for the Bray Lench fifteen.

Jane Preston **Williams**, Mr. Preston's married sister and Aunt to Sally Preston; formerly parlour-maid at the Rectory, lives in Millbourne, Hampshire; hostess to Sally in 13ST.

Williamson, captain of football at Alderton in LS08, referees the fight behind the gym between Jimmy Stewart and O'Connell.

Mrs. James **Williamson** is Dick Trentham's married sister in 02TT.

Dr. **Willis** declares Jimmy Stewart free of mumps and treats Corporal Sam Burrows' shoulder wound in LS08.

Willoughby: see Wilberforce.

Uncle **Willoughby** of Easeby, Shropshire, Bertie's trustee in 16JT, was at Oxford with Lord Worplesdon and was thrown out of a music-hall with him in 1887. Somewhat on the tabasco side as a young man, now a rather stiff, precise sort of old boy who likes a quiet life. Writes a scandalous autobiography called *Recollections of a Long Life*.

Miss **Willoughby**[1] is Lady Mildred Mant's lady in SN15.

Miss **Willoughby**[2], aunt of the Crumpet who narrates 58UK, has a cottage named Kozy Kot at Marvis Bay in Devonshire.

Mrs. **Willoughby**, cook at Blandings Castle in PB69.

Enid **Willoughby**, Rollo Podmarsh's sister, Lettice's mother in 23AR.

Lettice **Willoughby**, young granddaughter of Rollo Podmarsh's mother, Enid's daughter in 23AR. A good and consistent trencherwoman, particularly rough on the puddings.

Wilson[1] is Julia Ukridge's chauffeur in 47SS.

Wilson[2] is Barmy Barminster's valet in 57WT, where he successfully courts Mabel Parker. Spent boyhood in Lower Smattering. Cf. James Wilson in 11AS.

James **Wilson**, valet to Rollo Finch in 11AS, lived in Market Bumpstead before coming to London, where he completes his courtship of Marguerite Parker.

P. (for Percy) V. **Wilson** is a new boy at Beckford College in PU03; Marriott's aunt's friend's friend's son.

Jack **Wilton**, vacationing at Marvis Bay in 15WH, proposes to Mary Campbell and is refused. Strong man in his village of Bridley-in-the-Wold, invents fiancée Amy who dies in his arms on the day of their wedding.

Percy **Wimbolt**, a Drone, hat owner and suitor of Elizabeth Bottsworth in 33AH. A large, stout, outsize young man with a head like a watermelon. Becomes engaged to Diane Punter.

Percy **Wimbush**, a Drone in 58FL.

Clifford **Wimple** is sinking balls in the lake off the second tee in the beginning of 25PR.

Gladys **Winch**, a square, wholesome, good-humoured looking girl with a serious face, engaged to Fillmore Nicholas in AS22; plays the maid in *The Primrose Way*.

Mabel **Winchester**, Bill Brewster's fiancée in 20PW/IA21, an English chorus girl who dyes her hair red; later engaged to Reggie Van Tuyl.

Dermot **Windleband**, self-described Napoleon of Finance, buys

Squibs from Roland Bleke in MM14.

Lal **Windleband**, former secretary to Dermot, now his wife in MM14.

Billy **Windsor**, 25, sub-editor of *Cosy Moments*, becomes acting editor in PJ15; a tall, wiry, loose-jointed young man with unkempt hair and the general demeanor of a caged eagle. Born on his father William's ranch in Wyoming.

Kirk **Winfield**, 26, a large and muscular would-be painter with a small private income in WH14. Amiable and rather weak, marries Ruth Bannister. Father of William, the White Hope.

William Bannister **Winfield**, the White Hope, young son of Kirk Winfield and Ruth Bannister Winfield, title character of WH14.

Rev. Hubert **Wingham**, 3rd son of the Earl of Sturridge, Old Heppenstall's new curate at Twing, edges out Bingo Little for the hand of Mary Burgess in 22MT/IJ23.

Sir Mortimer **Wingham**, host of Cyril Mulliner and Lady Wingham Bassett in 32SS. Heavy and country-squire-ish, master of Barkley Towers.

Dame Daphne Littlewood **Winkworth**, relict of a rather celebrated historian, the late P.B. Winkworth. A tall, dark, handsome lightheavyweight with a formidable personality, mother of Gertrude and Huxley, sister of Charlotte, Emmeline, Harriet and Myrtle Deverill. Aunt of Esmond Haddock, whose country house (Deverill Hall) she and her sisters infest in MS49, and Claude Duff. Headmistress of a fashionable girls' school near Eastbourne (from which she is retired in MS49 only) and godmother of Madeline Bassett. Wants to marry Lord Emsworth in BG65 and is foiled thanks to the efforts of Galahad. Fires Jeff Bennison from his job teaching drawing at her school in SB77.

Gertrude **Winkworth**, slim, blonde, fragile daughter of Dame Daphne in MS49, engaged to Catsmeat Pirbright.

Huxley **Winkworth**, only son of Dame Daphne in BG65, a small, wizened, supercilious boy with a penetrating eye.

Claude **Winnington-Bates**, slim, repellent son of Kay Derrick's erstwhile employer in SS25; went to Wrykyn with Sam Shotter and J. Willoughby Braddock. Tries to force his attentions on Kay Derrick.

Harold "Ginger" **Winship**, friend of Bertie's and his neighbor at Magdalen, former heavyweight boxer for Oxford and Drone until forced to resign by fiancée Florence Craye. Well worth looking at, muscular and well knit, a Parliamentary candidate at Steeple Bumpleigh in MO71. Marries Magnolia Glendennon.

Roland **Winter**, nephew of Mervyn Spink in SF48, a tall thin actor with a slight squint, funny-shaped mouth, and red hair.

Lord **Wisbeach** wants to marry Ann Chester in PJ17; impersonated in the Pett mansion by Gentleman Jack.

Cosmo **Wisdom**, son of the late Algernon Wisdom and Phoebe Bastable Wisdom, resident at #11 Budge Street, Chelsea. Frequently between jobs, agrees to accept authorship of his uncle Beefy Bastable's scandalous *Cocktail Time* for £200 plus royalties in CT58.

Hannah **Wisdom**, former nurse and old retainer of Berry Conway in BM31; plump and comfortable, takes a ghoulish relish in disasters at Valley Fields. Becomes engaged to police sergeant Finbow.

Phoebe **Wisdom** is Beefy Bastable's bullied sister in CT58; resembles a white rabbit. Relict of the late Algernon Wisdom and mother of Cosmo. Owns a cocker spaniel named Benjy. Courted by Albert Peasemarch.

Vera **Witherby**, niece of Ponsford Botts, is courted by Horace Bewstridge in 48EX.

Mrs. **Withers** is cook at Windles in TM22.

Chief Inspector **Witherspoon** of Scotland Yard, a Jeeves alias in SU63.

Claude **Witherspoon** proposes unsuccessfully to Gertrude Butterwick in PG72.

Katherine Travers **Witherspoon**, younger sister of T.P. Travers, wife of Sir Reginald in 30TC.

Sir Reginald **Witherspoon**, Bart., of Bleaching Court, Upper Bleaching, Hants, spouse of Tom Travers' younger sister Katherine Travers in 30TC.

Earl of **Wivelscombe**: see Ferdinand James Delamere.

Apollo **Wix**, a regular cricket player for Somerset, is brought

Aunt Agatha Wooster

in by Rev. Dacre to play for Marvis Bay in 05LB. A little shrimp of a man, with a face like a music-hall comedian.

Wildcat **Wix** ko'ed Mugsy Steptoe when he was a boxer prior to the action of QS40.

Dudley "Biffy" **Wix-Biffen**, an old Malburian and a Drone formerly engaged to Clarissa Boote, marries Catherine Jipson in 58UK.

Wolff-Lehmann, author of a treatise on the diet of pigs in SS61, deceased in PB69.

Freddie **Woosley**, club golfer in 19WW.

Agatha **Wooster** (sister of Dahlia, George Wooster [Lord Yaxley], and Bertie's late father), human snapping turtle who has savaged Bertie incessantly from childhood up, living at Woollam Chersey, Herts, and married to Spenser Gregson in 15EY (where her family name is Mannering-Phipps) and stories of the twenties (in 25WO and 11HF she is called Mrs. Spenser); by CW38 he is "the late" Spenser Gregson. Her son Thomas Gregson, a pestilential schoolboy, is under Bingo Little's tutelage in 26JI. Marries Lord Worplesdon about eighteen months before JM46; lives with him in Steeple Bumpleigh, Essex in JM46, MS49, and thereafter. Kills rats with her teeth, devours her young, eats broken bottles, and turns into a werewolf at the time of the full moon. Tall and thin, about 5' 9" topped off with a beaky nose, an eagle eye, and a lot of grey hair, looks rather like a vulture in the Gobi desert. Cold and haughty, though presumably she unbends a bit when conducting human sacrifices at the time of the full moon, as she is widely rumored to do. Doesn't like Jeeves.

Algernon **Wooster**, the first Wooster in PGW, is cousin to Lord Emsworth's nephew Percy, Lord Stockheath and a guest at Blandings Castle in SN15.

Bertram Wilberforce **Wooster,** resident at 3A Berkeley Mansions, London W.1, narrator of 10 novels and 34 stories: 16AC, 16JU, 16AS, 16JT, 17JH, 18JC, 21JS, 22AA, 22SO, 22SR, 22CB, 22SH, 22PT, 22MT, 22EC, 22BL, 22BC, IJ23, 24RA, 25CR, 25WO, 26FF, 26IC, 26JI, 27JY, 29JS, 29JD, 29SA, 29JL, 30JK, 30JO, 30IS, 30TC, RH34, TY34, RH34, CW38, JM46, MS49, JF54, 59JM, HR60, SU63, 65JG, MO71,

AA74. A graduate of Rev. Aubrey Upjohn's private school at Malvern House, Bramley-on-Sea, Eton, and Oxford, where he was in Magdalen and won his Rackets Blue in partnership with Beefy Anstruther during his last year. A Drone, his proper attire and escape from personal difficulties are attended to by his man Jeeves. His appearance is rarely hinted; in 22CB/IJ23 a Hyde Park agitator (Bingo Little in disguise) describes him as "the tall thin one with the face like a motor-mascot." Boko Fittleworth describes him as tall and slim in JM46. Normally clean-shaven, he has grown a moustache in 17JH, and another of the David Niven type in JF54, each time provoking a rift with Jeeves. His most public discomfiture was being fined £5 by magistrate Watkyn Basset for pinching a policeman's helmet on Boat Race Night. His proudest achievements include winning a prize at his first school for the best collection of wild flowers made during the summer holidays, winning a Scripture Knowledge contest at Malvern House, and writing an article for *Milady's Boudoir* entitled "What the Well-Dressed Man Is Wearing" for the "Husbands and Brothers" page (this happens in 25CR—"I don't wonder now that all these author blokes have bald heads and faces like birds who have suffered") for which his Aunt Dahlia paid him a packet of cigarettes. He also mentions having won a Choir Boys Bicycle Handicap in his younger days at a clergyman uncle's place in Kent. His middle name, as we learn in MO71, is derived from the horse who won the Grand National immediately prior to his baptism, earning Wooster Sr. a packet (presumably of something more valuable than cigarettes). His ranking aunts are Dahlia and Agatha (his late father's sisters, who regard him with a mixture of affection and contempt), but among his many kin are George Wooster (Lord Yaxley, brother of Dahlia and Agatha), an Uncle Willoughby (16JT), an eccentric Uncle Henry who kept eleven pet rabbits in his bedroom and wound up his career in some sort of a home (22SR/IJ23—mentioned in TY34 as three years dead), an Aunt Emily (mother of Claude & Eustace in 22EC/IJ23), an Uncle Clive in Worcestershire (22EC/IJ23), an Uncle James

Bertie Wooster and Jeeves

(24RA), an Uncle Percy (25WO, 26FF), and an Uncle Thomas (29JL). A sister, Mrs. Scholfield, is mentioned in 22BC. The Code of the Woosters includes the commandment "never let a pal down" and numerous other prohibitions. Aims always to be the preux chevalier, which requires that he never demur when a girl in a passing fit of despair declares that she will marry him, e.g. Florence Craye in JF54, Madeline Bassett and Florence Craye (again) in MO71, Vanessa Cook in AA74. Normally regarded with contempt by women ("Show me a woman, and I will show you someone who is going to ignore my observations"), but often seized by vain impulses to propose marriage ("It would be pretty difficult for me to go anywhere in England where there wasn't somebody who has turned me down at some time or another.") Plays the banjolele (for which Jeeves briefly leaves his service) in TY34, where Jeeves describes him to Pauline Stoker as "mentally somewhat negligible," Pauline as "one of Nature's bachelors." Aunt Agatha, his severest critic, describes him as "barely sentient" (26IC). His prototypes include Reggie Pepper and Bertie Mannering-Phipps.

Claude and Eustace **Wooster**, Bertie's twin cousins in 22SH and 22EC (IJ23), staying at Lord Wickhammersley's Twing Hall in 22SH reading for some exam with the vicar, Old Heppenstall. At school with Bertie in his last summer term, expelled from Oxford for pouring soda-water on the Senior Tutor. They infest Bertie's flat and plague the life of show-girl Marion Wardour in 22EC until tricked by Jeeves into boarding a ship for South Africa. Aunt Agatha believes they inherited the eccentricity of Bertie's late uncle Henry.

Dahlia **Wooster** (Bertie's good but amoral aunt), of Brinkley Court, Brinkley-cum-Snodsfield-in-the-Marsh, publisher for four years of an unprofitable weekly paper for the halfwitted woman called *Milady's Boudoir*, to which Bertie once contributed an article on What the Well-Dressed Man Is Wearing (in JF54 the magazine is sold to a mug up Liverpool way named L.G. Trotter), wife of Thomas P. Travers *en secondes noces* in 25CR, 27JS, RH34, CW38, JF54, 59JM, HR60, SU63, MO71, AA74. Married Tom Travers the year

Bluebottle won the Cambridgeshire; mother of Angela Travers in 27JS, 30TC, RH34, MO71. Short and solid, like a scrum half in Rugby, jovial and bonhomous, her lightest whisper is like someone calling the cattle home across the sands of Dee. Her vocal power and energetic style recall the days when she hunted foxes with the Quorn, and occasionally the Pytchley. Controls Bertie with the power of her chef Anatole's cuisine. Her son Bonzo is a pest in 29JL, where she wagers the services of Anatole that Agatha's son Thos will lose a good-behavior contest. Sister of Agatha, George Wooster (Lord Yaxley), and Bertie's father.

Poor Emily **Wooster**, Bertie's third aunt, mother of Claude & Eustace in 22EC/IJ23, and of Harold, who celebrates his sixth birthday in 24RA.

Eustace **Wooster**, Bertie's cousin, twin brother of Claude (q.v.).

George **Wooster**, Lord Yaxley, Bertie's bulging Uncle George, brother of Agatha, Dahlia, and Bertie's father—presumably his elder brother; robbed of an expensive cigarette case by Claude Wooster in 22EC/IJ23. Prominent London clubman, member of the Buffers, lives in rooms on Jermyn St. Discovered that alcohol was a food well in advance of modern medical thought; goes to Harrogate (30JO) or Carlsbad whenever his liver gives him the elbow. Favorite topic of conversation is the lining of his stomach. Reunited with his plebeian flame Maudie (Mrs. Wilberforce) in 30IS.

Sir Oscar **Wopple** of Ditchingham, a financier, shoots himself on the Friday before the action of RJ53.

Jimmy, Lord **Worfield**, was at school and Oxford with Tom Garth. Founder and co-proprietor of a short-lived New York scandal sheet called *Candor* in 06BJ, engaged to Julie Weyder.

Worple, a member of the Junior Ganymede, L.G. Trotter's valet in JF54.

Alexander **Worple**, Bruce Corcoran's rich uncle in the jute business, 51 years old in 16AC, provides Corky with a small quarterly allowance. An amateur ornithologist, marries Muriel Singer.

Bernard **Worple**, neo-vorticist sculptor friend of Lancelot

Mulliner in 32SW.

Rupert **Worple**, old friend of Bradbury Fisher and fellow-graduate of Sing-Sing (#8,097,565), just back from a graduate program there in 26KI.

Agatha **Worplesdon**: see Agatha Wooster.

Percival or Percy Craye[1], Lord **Worplesdon**, father of Lady Florence Craye, Percy Craye[2], and Edwin. In 12DO, already some years a widower, he lives in self-imposed exile, having fled his family to live on the Continent. A rather large man with elephantiasis of the temper, he came down to breakfast one morning, lifted the first cover he saw, said "Eggs! Eggs! Eggs! Damn all eggs!" in an overwrought sort of voice, and instantly legged it for France. Marries Dorothea Darrell in 12DO. A former employer of Jeeves. When Bertie was fifteen Lord W. found him smoking one of his special cigars in the stable yard and chased him a mile across difficult country with a riding crop. Was at Oxford with Bertie's Uncle Willoughby, thrown out of a music hall with him in 1887. Second husband of Agatha Wooster in JM46, MS49, and JF54; master of Bumpleigh Hall, Steeple Bumpleigh, Hampshire. A shipping magnate, owner of the Pink Funnel Line.

Orlando **Wotherspoon**, perpetual Vice-President of Our Dumb Chums League in 32OH; eyes of the piercing type one associates with owls, sergeant-majors, and Scotland Yard inspectors.

Lord **Wotwotleigh**, fortune-hunting English lord in a musical comedy alluded to by J. Washburn Stoker and others in TY34 with reference to Chuffy Chuffnell's courtship of Pauline Stoker.

Wren, a little beast from Kay's at Eckleton in HK05. Red hair.

Wrench, butler in UM16 imported from England by Algie Wetherby, formerly employed by the well-known political hostess the Dowager Duchess of Waveney.

Matthew **Wrenn**, editor of *Pyke's Home Companion* and uncle of Kay Derrick in SS25. Lives with Kay in San Rafael, Burberry Road, Valley Fields. A tall, elderly gentleman with grey hair, a scholarly stoop, and a mild and dreamy aspect.

Lady **Wroxham** is the mother of Lord Mountry and Augustus Beckford in LN13.

James **Wyatt**, step-son of Mr. Wain at Wrykyn, resident of Wain's in MK09; short, thick-set, likes to break out at night and pot at cats with an air-pistol; sent to work at the Jackson-MacPherson sheep farm in Argentina.

Pomona **Wycherly**, reporter for the Los Angeles *Chronicle* in LG36. Cf. Alma Whitaker of the Los Angeles *Times*, who reported PGW's observation that he had done nothing to earn his fees in Hollywood. Letter to Townend, 5/19/31 and Jasen, *Portrait* p. 127.

Algy **Wymondham-Wymondham**, Drone in 28RW, friend of Archibald Mulliner.

Col. Aubrey **Wyvern**, father of Jill and Chief Constable of the county of Southmoltonshire in RJ53. Short and stout, master of Wyvern Hall, a sixteen-year-old butler named Bulstrode, and a fifteen-year-old cook named Evangeline Trelawny.

Jill **Wyvern**, daughter of Col. Aubrey Wyvern in RJ53. The local veterinarian in Southmoltonshire, small, young, alert, slightly freckled, engaged to W.E.O. Belfry, ninth Earl of Towcester.

Col. Meredith **Wyvern**, father of Patricia in MN28, retired military officer. Has been quarreling with neighbor Lester Carmody of Rudge Hall and forbids his daughter's association with its manager John Carroll.

Patricia **Wyvern**, daughter of Col. Meredith Wyvern in MN28, in love with childhood companion John Carroll. A slim, slight girl with a tip-tilted nose.

Y

Lord **Yaxley**: see George Wooster.

Clarence **Yeardsley**, son of Matthew Yeardsley, married to Elizabeth Schoolbred in 13DC. A little, thin, nervous-looking painter of about 35, with hair getting grey at the temples and straggly on top. Pince-nez, drooping moustache.

Elizabeth Schoolbred **Yeardsley**: see Elizabeth Schoolbred.

Matthew **Yeardsley**, Clarence's father, amateur artist and painter of the unbearable Yeardsley Venus in 13DC.

Yorke[1], master of the Upper Fifth at St Austin's, is expected to set the Euripides exam in 02BL.

Yorke[2], a celebrated slow bowler in 03HP.

Jane **Yorke**, short, square, and solid friend of Aggie Donaldson Threepwood, whose marriage to Freddie she tries to sour in 26LE.

Leila **Yorke**, the novelist, on Claines Hall, Loose Chippings, Sussex. Author of *For True Love Only*, *Heather o' the Hills* (her first novel), *Sweet Jennie Dean* and other treacle. A large hearty woman in the early forties, built on the lines of Catherine of Russia, with bright, blue, piercing eyes and the voice of a drill sergeant. Born Elizabeth Binns. Once married to Joe Bishop, in love with former fiancé Lord Blicester in IB61.

Charlie **Yost**, Chicago gunman in England, former associate of Horace Appleby in DB68.

Yvonne, daughter of Earl Dorm of the Hills, a plain damsel in distress aided by Sir Agravaine in 12SA.

Z

Isadore **Zinzinheimer** of the Bigger, Better, & Brighter Motion Picture Co. of Hollywood, California makes an offer in 27CD.

Ben **Zizzbaum**, head of Zizzbaum-Celluloid, a motion picture corporation, in 33RM.

I.J. **Zizzbaum**, Beverly Hills dentist who attends to Reggie Havershot's wisdom tooth in LG36.

KEY TO TITLE ABBREVIATIONS

Story codes have the year of publication first (e.g. 01PP).
Novel codes have the year of publication last (e.g. PH02).

1901
01PP   The Prize Poem
01WP   When Papa Swore in Hindustani (How Papa
        Swore...)
01AF   L'Affaire Uncle John
01SD   The Strange Disappearance of Mr. Buxton-
        Smythe
01AU   Author!

1902
PH02   THE POTHUNTERS
02TT   The Tabby Terror
02BD   The Babe and the Dragon
02BL   Bradshaw's Little Story
02OT   The Odd Trick
02HP   How Paine Bucked Up
02WM   Welch's Mile Record

1903
PU03   A PREFECT'S UNCLE
03HS   Harrison's Slight Error
03HP   How Pillingshot Scored
03MC   The Manoeuvres of Charteris (Out of Bounds!)
03SA   A Shocking Affair
03IK   The Idle King
03CP   Cupid and the Paint-Brush

1904
GB04   THE GOLD BAT
WT04   WILLIAM TELL TOLD AGAIN
04AD   An Afternoon Dip (Jackson's Dip)
04BB   Blenkinsop's Benefit

KEY TO TITLE ABBREVIATIONS

04HT	Homeopathic Treatment
04JE	Jackson's Extra
04RS	The Reformation of Study Sixteen

1905

HK05	THE HEAD OF KAY'S
05RR	Ruthless Reginald (Tales of Wrykyn No. 1)
05PP	The Politeness of Princes (Tales of Wrykyn No.2)
05SC	Shields' and the Cricket Cup (Tales of Wrykyn No. 3)
05AB	An Affair of Boats (Tales of Wrykyn No. 4)
05BI	Between the Innings
05LP	The Last Place (Tales of Wrykyn No. 5)
05IA	An International Affair (Tales of Wrykyn No. 6)
05WP	The Wire-Pullers
05LB	The Lost Bowlers
05CL	A Corner in Lines
05AH	The Autograph Hunters
05TD	Tom, Dick, and Harry
05DE	The Deserter
05BL	Kid Brady—Light-Weight
05BB	How Kid Brady Broke Training

1906

LC06	LOVE AMONG THE CHICKENS (Revised in 1920)
06PI	Petticoat Influence
06TP	The Pro
06FM	The Fifteenth Man
06BW	How Kid Brady Won the Championship
06BA	How Kid Brady Assisted a Damsel in Distress
06BJ	How Kid Brady Joined the Press
06BF	How Kid Brady Fought for his Eyes
06AB	A Benefit Match
06DS	A Division of Spoil

1907

WF07	THE WHITE FEATHER

228

KEY TO TITLE ABBREVIATIONS

NG07	NOT GEORGE WASHINGTON (with H. Westbrook)
07BT	How Kid Brady Took a Sea Voyage
07PC	Personally Conducted

1908

LS08	THE LUCK STONE (with W. Townend)
08GU	The Guardian
08LG	Ladies and Gentlemen v. Players

1909

SW09	THE SWOOP!
MK09	MIKE
09OS	Out of School
09AC	Against the Clock
09RR	Reginald's Record Knock

1910

IJ10	THE INTRUSION OF JIMMY (A Gentleman of Leisure)
PC10	PSMITH IN THE CITY (The New Fold)
10GA	The Good Angel (Matrimonial Sweepstakes)
10MU	The Man Upstairs
10AB	Archibald's Benefit
10RH	Rough-Hew Them How We Will
10DW	Deep Waters
10MM	The Man, the Maid, and the Miasma
10BA	By Advise of Counsel
10PP	The Pitcher and the Plutocrat
10WD	When Doctors Disagree
10MI	Misunderstood
10PD	Pillingshot, Detective
10LM	Love Me, Love My Dog (The Watch Dog/A Dog-Eared Romance)
10SW	Stone and the Weed

1911

11AS	Ahead of Schedule

KEY TO TITLE ABBREVIATIONS

11AT	Absent Treatment
11PP	Pillingshot's Paper
11TD	Three from Dunsterville
11EA	Educating Aubrey
11HF	Helping Freddie
11PO	Pots o' Money
11IA	In Alcala
11BS	The Best Sauce

1912

PA12	THE PRINCE AND BETTY (New York: Watt, 2/14/12)
PB12	THE PRINCE AND BETTY (London: Mills & Boon, 5/1/12)[1]
12MC	The Man Who Disliked Cats
12SA	Sir Agravaine (Roderick the Runt)
12RE	Ruth in Exile
12TM	The Tuppenny Millionaire
12RR	Rallying Round Old George (Brother Alfred)
12GK	The Goal-Keeper and the Plutocrat
12DO	Disentangling Old Percy (Disentangling Old Duggie)

1913

LN13	THE LITTLE NUGGET
13ST	Something To Worry About
13EC	The Eighteen-Carat Kid
13DC	Doing Clarence A Bit of Good
13JW	A Job of Work
13KI	Keeping It from Harold
13ML	Mike's Little Brother

1914

MM14	A MAN OF MEANS

---

[1] "Aside from the romance in the Mervian plot, this is a completely different story." —David A. Jasen, *A Bibliography and Reader's Guide to the First Editions of P.G. Wodehouse.* Archon Books (1970), p. 41.

KEY TO TITLE ABBREVIATIONS

WH14	THE WHITE HOPE (Their Mutual Child/The Coming of Bill)
14OT	One Touch of Nature (Brother Fans)
14ST	A Sea of Troubles
14DE	Death at the Excelsior (The Education of Detective Oakes/The Harmonica Mystery)
14CI	Creatures of Impulse

1915

SN15	SOMETHING NEW (Something Fresh)
PJ15	PSMITH, JOURNALIST
15AA	Aubrey's Arrested Individuality
15CA	Concealed Art
15PW	A Prisoner of War
15SP	The Secret Pleasures of Reginald
15DP	The Disappearance of Podmarsh
15MI	The Military Invasion of America
15RU	The Romance of an Ugly Policeman
15BB	Bill the Bloodhound
15CH	Crowned Heads
15MM	The Making of Mac's (The Romance of Mac's)
15BL	Black For Luck (A Black for Cat Luck)
15WH	Wilton's Vacation (Wilton's Holiday)
15AG	At Geisenheimer's (The Love-r-ly Silver Cup)
15EY	Extricating Young Gussie
15TM	The Mixer: He Meets a Shy Gentleman (A Very Shy Gentleman)
15MS	The Mixer: He Moves in Society (Breaking into Society)
15TC	The Test Case

1916

UM16	UNEASY MONEY
16AC	Artistic Career of Corky (Leave It to Jeeves)
16TL	The Man with Two Left Feet
16AS	The Aunt and the Sluggard
16JT	Jeeves Takes Charge
16JU	Jeeves and the Unbidden Guest

KEY TO TITLE ABBREVIATIONS

1917
PJ17   PICCADILLY JIM
17JH   Jeeves and the Hard Boiled Egg

1918
18JC   Jeeves and the Chump Cyril

1919
DD19   A DAMSEL IN DISTRESS
19WW   A Woman is Only a Woman
19OG   Ordeal By Golf (A Kink in His Character)
19SF   The Spring Frock (The Spring Suit)

1920
LW20   THE LITTLE WARRIOR (Jill the Reckless)
20MH   The Man Who Married a Hotel
20AS   Archie and the Sausage Chappie
20DO   Dear Old Squiffy
20MT   A Mixed Threesome
20DF   Doing Father a Bit of Good
20PW   Paving the Way for Mabel
20WM   Washy Makes His Presence Felt
20RH   A Room at the Hermitage
20FA   First Aid for Looney Biddle
20RS   The Rough Stuff
20MK   Mother's Knee
20GF   The Golden Flaw
20SH   Sundered Hearts

1921
IA21   INDISCRETIONS OF ARCHIE (see also collections)
21SE   Strange Experience of an Artist's Model
21WV   The Wigmore Venus
21CG   The Coming of Gowf
21SG   The Salvation of George Mackintosh
21LH   The Long Hole

KEY TO TITLE ABBREVIATIONS

21UC	The (Unexpected) Clicking of Cuthbert (Cuthbert Unexpectedly Clicks)
21HA	The Heel of Achilles
21JS	Jeeves in the Springtime

1922

TM22	THREE MEN AND A MAID (The Girl on the Boat)
AS22	THE ADVENTURES OF SALLY (Mostly Sally)
22SO	Scoring Off Jeeves (Bertie Gets Even)
22SR	Sir Roderick Comes To Lunch (Jeeves and the Blighter)
22AA	Aunt Agatha Takes the Count (Aunt Agatha Makes a Bloomer)
22CB	Comrade Bingo
22SH	The Great Sermon Handicap
22PT	The Purity of the Turf
22BC	Bertie Changes His Mind (Bertie Gets His Chance)
22MT	The Metropolitan Touch
22BL	Bingo and the Little Woman
22EC	The Exit of Claude and Eustace (The Delayed Exit of Claude and Eustace)
22MP	The Magic Plus Fours (Plus Fours)

1923

IJ23	THE INIMITABLE JEEVES (Jeeves) see also Collections
LP23	LEAVE IT TO PSMITH
23AR	The Awakening of Rollo Podmarsh
23UD	Ukridge's Dog College
23UA	Ukridge's Accident Syndicate (Ukridge, Teddy Weeks & the Tomato)
23DB	The Debut of Battling Billson
23FA	First Aid for Dora
23CF	Chester Forgets Himself
23RB	The Return of Battling Billson
23HG	The Heart of a Goof

KEY TO TITLE ABBREVIATIONS

23US	Ukridge Sees Her Through
23NW	No Wedding Bells for Him
23LA	The Long Arm of Looney Coote
23EB	The Exit of Battling Billson

1924

BC24	BILL THE CONQUEROR
24UR	Ukridge Rounds a Nasty Corner
24RF	Rodney Fails to Qualify
24RA	The Rummy Affair of Old Biffy
24JG	Jane Gets off the Fairway
24CP	The Custody of the Pumpkin
24SS	Something Squishy

1925

SS25	SAM THE SUDDEN (Sam in the Suburbs)
25HC	Honeysuckle Cottage
25CR	Clustering Round Young Bingo
25AG	The Awful Gladness of the Mater
25WO	Without the Option
25PR	The Purification of Rodney Spelvin
25HS	High Stakes
25BD	Buttercup Day
25BL	A Bit of Luck for Mabel

1926

26PT	Mr. Potter Takes a Rest Cure (The Rest Cure)
26KI	Keeping in with Vosper
26IC	The Inferiority Complex of Old Sippy
26LB	The Level Business Head
26LE	Lord Emsworth Acts for the Best
26TA	The Truth About George
26SL	A Slice of Life
26MB	Mulliner's Buck-U-Uppo
26JI	Jeeves and the Impending Doom
26FF	Fixing It for Freddie

KEY TO TITLE ABBREVIATIONS

1927

SB27	THE SMALL BACHELOR
27RB	The Romance of a Bulb-Squeezer
27SW	The Story of William (It Was Only a Fire)
27TP	Those in Peril at the Tee
27CD	Came the Dawn
27PH	Pig-Hoo-o-o-o-ey!
27BM	The Bishop's Move
27PD	Portrait of a Disciplinarian
27JY	Jeeves and the Yule-Tide Spirit

1928

MN28	MONEY FOR NOTHING
28UO	Ukridge and the Old Stepper
28PA	The Passing of Ambrose
28RW	The Reverent Wooing of Archibald
28CG	Company for Gertrude
28EG	Lord Emsworth and the Girl Friend
28OO	The Ordeal of Osbert Mulliner

1929

FP29	FISH PREFERRED (Summer Lightning)
29UB	Unpleasantness at Bludleigh Court
29GU	The Man Who Gave Up Smoking
29SC	The Story of Cedric
29BG	Back to the Garage (Franklin's Favorite Daughter)
29PW	Prospects for Wambledon
29JS	Jeeves and the Song of Songs
29JD	Jeeves and the Dog McIntosh
29JL	Jeeves and the Love That Purifies
29SA	Jeeves and the Spot of Art

1930

30BS	Best Seller (Parted Ways)
30JK	Jeeves and the Kid Clementina
30JO	Jeeves and the Old School Chum
30IS	Indian Summer of an Uncle

235

30TC	Tuppy Changes His Mind (The Ordeal of Young Tuppy)
30GN	Gala Night

1931

BM31	BIG MONEY
IW31	IF I WERE YOU
31UH	Ukridge and the Home from Home
31GG	Go-Getter (Sales Resistance)
31KQ	The Knightly Quest of Mervyn (Quest)
31MG	The Medicine Girl (DS32 Doctor Sally)
31FA	Fate
31SW	The Smile That Wins (Adrian Mulliner, Detective/Mr. Mulliner, Private Detective)
31VP	The Voice from the Past (The Missing Mystery)

1932

DS32	DOCTOR SALLY (31MG The Medicine Girl)
HW32	HOT WATER
32SS	Strychnine in the Soup
32SW	The Story of Webster (The Bishop's Cat)
32CC	Cats Will Be Cats (The Bishop's Folly)
32OH	Open House
32MB	Monkey Business (A Cagey Gorilla)

1933

HW33	HEAVY WEATHER
33NO	The Nodder (Love Birds)
33JO	The Juice of an Orange (Love on a Diet)
33RM	The Rise of Minna Nordstrom
33CA	The Castaways
33AH	The Amazing Hat Mystery
33LS	The Luck of the Stiffhams

1934

TY34	THANK YOU, JEEVES
RH34	RIGHT HO, JEEVES (Brinkley Manor)
34NO	Noblesse Oblige

KEY TO TITLE ABBREVIATIONS

34GB	Good-Bye to All Cats
34FW	The Fiery Wooing of Mordred

1935

LB35	THE LUCK OF THE BODKINS
35CM	The Code of the Mulliners
35TD	Trouble Down at Tudsleigh
35CB	The Come-Back of Battling Billson
35UF	Uncle Fred Flits By
35FL	Farewell to Legs
35AM	Archibald and the Masses
35TF	Tried in the Furnace

1936

LG36	LAUGHING GAS
36LL	The Letter of the Law
36AG	There's Always Golf! (Not Out of Distance)
36BT	Buried Treasure (Hidden Treasure)
36CW	The Crime Wave at Blandings
36MT	The Masked Troubadour (Reggie and the Greasy Bird)

1937

SM37	SUMMER MOONSHINE
37AW	All's Well with Bingo
37RD	Romance at Droitgate Spa
37BP	Bingo and the Peke Crisis
37AG	Anselm Gets His Chance

1938

CW38	THE CODE OF THE WOOSTERS

1939

UF39	UNCLE FRED IN THE SPRINGTIME
39ER	The Editor Regrets
39SB	Sonny Boy
39BI	Bramley Is So Bracing

KEY TO TITLE ABBREVIATIONS

1940
QS40   QUICK SERVICE
40SM   Scratch Man (Tee for Two)
40WS   The Word in Season (Bingo Little's Wild Night Out)
40DI   Dudley Is Back to Normal

1941-42
MB42   MONEY IN THE BANK

1943-46
JM46   JOY IN THE MORNING

1947
FM47   FULL MOON
47SS   Success Story (Ukie Invests in Human Nature)
47RA   The Right Approach

1948
SF48   SPRING FEVER
UD48   UNCLE DYNAMITE
48TH   Tangled Hearts (I'll Give You Some Advice)
48EX   Excelsior (The Hazards of Horace Bewstridge)
48FO   Freddie, Oofy, and the Beef Trust

1949
MS49   THE MATING SEASON
49RR   Rodney Has a Relapse

1950
50BS   Birth of a Salesman
50FC   Feet of Clay (A Slightly Broken Romance)
50SP   The Shadow Passes
50MM   Mr. McGee's Big Day

1951
OR51   THE OLD RELIABLE (Phipps to the Rescue)
51UF   Up from the Depths

KEY TO TITLE ABBREVIATIONS

51HT   How's That, Umpire?

1952
BW52   BARMY IN WONDERLAND (Angel Cake)
PW52   PIGS HAVE WINGS
52BB   Big Business

1953
RJ53   RING FOR JEEVES (The Return of Jeeves)

1954
JF54   JEEVES AND THE FEUDAL SPIRIT (Bertie
        Wooster Sees It Through)
54OB   The Ordeal of Bingo Little
54LA   Leave It to Algy (Hats Off to Algernon)

1955
55TC   A Tithe for Charity

1956
FL56   FRENCH LEAVE
56JB   Joy Bells for Walter (Keep Your Temper, Wal-
        ter)

1957
SF57   SOMETHING FISHY (The Butler Did It)
57WT   Ways to Get a Gal (cf. 11AS Ahead of Schedule)

1958
CT58   COCKTAIL TIME
58FL   The Fat of the Land
58UK   Unpleasantness at Kozy Kot

1959
59DN   From a Detective's Notebook (Adrian Mulliner's
        Greatest Triumph)
59JM   Jeeves Makes an Omelet (Jeeves and the Stolen
        Venus)

KEY TO TITLE ABBREVIATIONS

1960

HR60   HOW RIGHT YOU ARE, JEEVES (Jeeves in the Offing)

1961

IB61   ICE IN THE BEDROOM
SS61   SERVICE WITH A SMILE

1962-63

SU63   STIFF UPPER LIP, JEEVES

1964

BM64   BIFFEN'S MILLIONS (Frozen Assets)

1965

BG65   THE BRINKMANSHIP OF GALAHAD THREEPWOOD (Galahad at Blandings)
65BB   Bingo Bans the Bomb
65SS   Stylish Stouts
65ST   Sleepy Time (The Battle of Squashy Hollow)
65JG   Jeeves and the Greasy Bird

1966

66SW   Sticky Wicket at Blandings (First Aid for Freddie)
66LF   Life with Freddie

1967

PP67   THE PURLOINED PAPERWEIGHT (Company for Henry)
67GA   George and Alfred
67US   Ukridge Starts a Bank Account
67GC   A Good Cigar Is a Smoke

1968

DB68   DO BUTLERS BURGLE BANKS?

1969

PB69   A PELICAN AT BLANDINGS (No Nudes Is

Good Nudes)

1970
GB70   THE GIRL IN BLUE
70AC   Another Christmas Carol

1971
MO71   MUCH OBLIGED, JEEVES (Jeeves and the Tie
        That Binds)

1972
PG72   PEARLS, GIRLS, AND MONTY BODKIN (The
        Plot That Thickened)

1973
BA73   BACHELORS ANONYMOUS

1974
AA74   AUNTS AREN'T GENTLEMEN (The Cat
        Nappers)

1977
SB77   SUNSET AT BLANDINGS

ALPHABETICAL LIST OF TITLES

Besides the titles that Wodehouse himself gave his stories, novels, and collections, many have been made up by later editors and publishers. The following is an attempt to account for all titles appended to Wodehouse fiction.

Novels (in caps) and stories are listed below alphabetically, with alternate titles in parentheses. As before, story codes have the year of publication first (e.g. 11AT); novel codes have the year of publication last (e.g. AS22).

Absent Treatment 11AT
Adrian Mulliner, Detective 31SW (The Smile That Wins/Mr. Mulliner, Private Detective)
Adrian Mulliner's Greatest Triumph 59DN (From a Detective's Notebook)
THE ADVENTURES OF SALLY AS22 (Mostly Sally)
An Affair of Boats 05AB
An Afternoon Dip 04AD (Jackson's Dip)
Against the Clock 09AC
Ahead of Schedule 11AS
All's Well Ch. XVIII of IJ23, second part of 22BL
All's Well with Bingo 37AW
The Amazing Hat Mystery 33AH
ANGEL CAKE BW52 (Barmy in Wonderland)
Another Christmas Carol 70AC
Anselm Gets His Chance 37AG
Archibald and the Masses 35AM
Archibald's Benefit 10AB
Archie and the Sausage Chappie 20AS (The Sausage Chappie)
Artistic Career of Corky 16AC (Leave It to Jeeves)
At Geisenheimer's 15AG (The Love-r-ly Silver Cup)
Aubrey's Arrested Individuality 15AA
Aunt Agatha Makes a Bloomer 22AA (Aunt Agatha Takes the Count)

ALPHABETICAL LIST OF TITLES

Aunt Agatha Speaks Her Mind Ch. III of IJ23, first part of 22AA

Aunt Agatha Takes the Count 22AA (Aunt Agatha Makes a Bloomer)

The Aunt and the Sluggard 16AS

AUNTS AREN'T GENTLEMEN AA74 (The Cat Nappers)

Author! 01AU

The Autograph Hunters 05AH

The Awakening of Rollo Podmarsh 23AR

The Awful Gladness of the Mater 25AG

The Babe and the Dragon 02BD

BACHELORS ANONYMOUS BA73

Back to the Garage 29BG (Franklin's Favorite Daughter)

BARMY IN WONDERLAND BW52 (Angel Cake)

The Battle of Squashy Hollow 65ST (Sleepy Time)

A Benefit Match 06AB

Bertie Changes His Mind 22BC (Bertie Gets His Chance)

Bertie Gets Even 22SO (Scoring off Jeeves)

Bertie Gets His Chance 22BC (Bertie Changes His Mind)

BERTIE WOOSTER SEES IT THROUGH JF54 (Jeeves and the Feudal Spirit)

The Best of Wodehouse (1949) See Collections

The Best Sauce 11BS (A Dinner of Herbs)

Best Seller 30BS (Parted Ways)

Between the Innings 05BI

BIFFEN'S MILLIONS BM64 (Frozen Assets)

Big Business 52BB

BIG MONEY BM31

Bill the Bloodhound 15BB

BILL THE CONQUEROR BC24

Bingo and the Little Woman 22BL

Bingo and the Peke Crisis 37BP

Bingo Bans the Bomb 65BB

Bingo Has a Bad Goodwood Ch. XII of IJ23, second part of 22CB

Bingo Little's Wild Night Out 40WS (The Word in Season)

Birth of a Salesman   50BS
The Bishop's Cat   32SW (The Story of Webster)
The Bishop's Folly   32CC (Cats Will Be Cats)
The Bishop's Move   27BM
A Bit of All Right 20RH (A Room at the Hermitage)
A Bit of Luck for Mabel   25BL
Black for Luck   15BL (A Black for Cat Luck)
Blandings Castle and Elsewhere (1935) See Collections
Blenkinsop's Benefit   04BB
The Borrowed Dog   29JD (Jeeves and the Dog McIntosh)
Bradshaw's Little Story   02BL
Bramley Is So Bracing   39BI
Breaking into Society   15MS (The Mixer: He Moves in
    Society)
BRINKLEY MANOR   RH34   (Right Ho, Jeeves)
THE BRINKMANSHIP OF GALAHAD THREEPWOOD
    BG65   (Galahad at Blandings)
Brother Alfred   12RR (Rallying Round Old George)
Brother Fans   14OT (One Touch of Nature)
Buried Treasure   36BT (Hidden Treasure)
THE BUTLER DID IT   SF57   (Something Fishy)
Buttercup Day   25BD
By Advise of Counsel   10BA

A Cagey Gorilla   32MB (Monkey Business)
Came the Dawn   27CD
Carry On, Jeeves (1925, 1927) See Collections
The Castaways   33CA
THE CAT NAPPERS   AA74   (Aunts Aren't Gentlemen)
Cats Will Be Cats   32CC (The Bishop's Folly)
Chester Forgets Himself · 23CF
The Clicking of Cuthbert   21UC (The Unexpected Clicking
    of Cuthbert, Cuthbert Unexpectedly Clicks))
The Clicking of Cuthbert (1922) See Collections
Clustering Round Young Bingo   25CR
COCKTAIL TIME   CT58
The Code of the Mulliners   35CM
THE CODE OF THE WOOSTERS   CW38

The Come-Back of Battling Billson 35CB
THE COMING OF BILL WH14 (The White Hope/Their
   Mutual Child)
The Coming of Gowf 21CG
Company For Gertrude 28CG
COMPANY FOR HENRY PP67 (The Purloined Paper-
   weight)
Compromised 31FA (Fate)
Comrade Bingo 22CB
Concealed Art 15CA
A Corner in Lines 05CL
Creatures of Impulse 14CI
Crime Wave at Blandings 36CW
Crime Wave at Blandings (1937) See Collections
Crowned Heads 15CH
Cupid and the Paint-Brush 03CP
The Custody of the Pumpkin 24CP
Cuthbert Unexpectedly Clicks 21UC (The Unexpected
   Clicking of Cuthbert)

A DAMSEL IN DISTRESS DD19
Dear Old Squiffy 20DO
Death at the Excelsior 14DE (The Education of Detective
   Oakes/The Harmonica Mystery)
The Debut of Battling Billson 23DB
Deep Waters 10DW
The Delayed Exit of Claude and Eustace 22EC (The Exit of
   Claude and Eustace)
The Deserter 05DE
A Dinner of Herbs 11BS (The Best Sauce)
The Disappearance of Podmarsh 15DP
Disentangling Old Duggie 12DO (Disentangling Old Percy)
Disentangling Old Percy 12DO (Disentangling Old Duggie)
A Division of Spoil 06DS
Divots (1927) See Collections
DO BUTLERS BURGLE BANKS? DB68
DOCTOR SALLY DS32 (The Medicine Girl 31MG)
A Dog-Eared Romance 10LM (Love Me, Love My Dog/The

Watch Dog)
Doing Clarence a Bit of Good   13DC
Doing Father a Bit of Good   20DF
Dudley Is Back to Normal   40DI

The Editor Regrets   39ER
Educating Aubrey   11EA
The Education of Detective Oakes   14DE (Death at the
  Excelsior/The Harmonica Mystery)
Eggs, Beans, and Crumpets (1940) See Collections
The Eighteen-Carat Kid   13EC
The 18-Carat Kid and Other Stories (1980) See Collections
ENTER PSMITH (the second half of MK09 as reissued in
  1935 by A&C Black. Cf. MIKE AND PSMITH)
Episode of the Dog McIntosh   29JD (Jeeves and the Dog
  McIntosh) (The Borrowed Dog)
Excelsior   48EX (The Hazards of Horace Bewstridge)
The Exit of Battling Billson   23EB
The (Delayed) Exit of Claude and Eustace   22EC
Extricating Young Gussie   15EY

Farewell to Legs   35FL
The Fat of the Land   58FL
Fatal Kink in Algernon   12MC (The Man Who Disliked
  Cats)
Fate   31FA (Compromised)
Feet of Clay   50FC (A Slightly Broken Romance)
A Few Quick Ones (1959) See Collections
The Fiery Wooing of Mordred   34FW
The Fifteenth Man   06FM
First Aid for Dora   23FA
First Aid for Freddie   66SW (Sticky Wicket At Blandings)
First Aid for Looney Biddle   20FA
FISH PREFERRED   FP29   (Summer Lightning)
Fixing It for Freddie   26FF
Fore! The Best of Wodehouse on Golf (1983) See Collec-
  tions
Franklin's Favorite Daughter   29BG (Back to the Garage)

ALPHABETICAL LIST OF TITLES

Freddy, Oofy, and the Beef Trust 48FO (Oofy, Freddy and the Beef Trust)

FRENCH LEAVE FL56

From a Detective's Notebook 59DN (Adrian Mulliner's Greatest Triumph)

FROZEN ASSETS BM64 (Biffen's Millions)

FULL MOON FM47

Gala Night 30GN

GALAHAD AT BLANDINGS BG65 (The Brinkmanship of Galahad Threepwood)

A GENTLEMAN OF LEISURE IJ10 (The Intrusion of Jimmy)

George and Alfred 67GA

THE GIRL IN BLUE GB70

THE GIRL ON THE BOAT TM22 (Three Men and a Maid)

The Goal-Keeper and the Plutocrat 12GK

Go-Getter 31GG (Sales Resistance)

The Good Angel 10GA (Matrimonial Sweepstakes)

Good-Bye to All Cats 34GB

A Good Cigar Is a Smoke 67GC

THE GOLD BAT GB04

The Golden Flaw 20GF

The Golf Omnibus (1973) See Collections

Golf Without Tears (1924) See Collections

The Great Sermon Handicap 22SH

The Guardian 08GU

The Harmonica Mystery 14DE (Death at the Excelsior/The Education of Detective Oakes

Harrison's Slight Error 03HS

Hats Off to Algernon 54LA (Leave It to Algy)

The Hazards of Horace Bewstridge 48EX (Excelsior)

He Rather Enjoyed It (1926) See Collections

THE HEAD OF KAY'S HK05

The Heart of a Goof 23HG

The Heart of a Goof (1926) See Collections

HEAVY WEATHER HW33

247

ALPHABETICAL LIST OF TITLES

The Heel of Achilles 21HA
Helping Freddie 11HF (Lines and Business)
The Hero's Reward Ch. VI of IJ23, second part of 22SO
Hidden Treasure 36BT (Buried Treasure)
High Stakes 25HS
The Hollywood Omnibus (1985) See Collections
Homeopathic Treatment 04HT
Honeysuckle Cottage 25HC
HOT WATER HW32
How Kid Brady Assisted a Damsel in Distress 06BA
How Kid Brady Broke Training 05BB
How Kid Brady Fought for his Eyes 06BF
How Kid Brady Joined the Press 06BJ
How Kid Brady Took a Sea Voyage 07BT
How Kid Brady Won the Championship 06BW
How Paine Bucked Up 02HP
How Papa Swore in Hindustani 01WP (When Papa Swore...)
How Pillingshot Scored 03HP
HOW RIGHT YOU ARE, JEEVES HR60 (Jeeves in the
    Offing)
How's That, Umpire? 51HT

THE ICE IN THE BEDROOM IB61
The Idle King 03IK
IF I WERE YOU IW31
I'll Give You Some Advice 48TH (Tangled Hearts)
In Alcala 11IA
Indian Summer of an Uncle 30IS
INDISCRETIONS OF ARCHIE IA21 (An episodic novel,
    first published as stories—see Collections)
The Inferiority Complex of Old Sippy 26IC
THE INIMITABLE JEEVES IJ23 (An episodic novel, first
    published as stories—see Collections)
An International Affair 05IA
Introducing Claude and Eustace Ch. VII of IJ23, first part
    of 22SR
THE INTRUSION OF JIMMY IJ10 (A Gentleman of
    Leisure)

It Was Only a Fire 27SW (The Story of William)

Jackson's Dip 04AD (An Afternoon Dip)
Jackson's Extra 04JE
JACKSON JUNIOR (part 1 of MK09 as serialized in *The Captain*)
Jane Gets Off the Fairway 24JG
Jeeves (1923) See Collections
Jeeves and the Blighter 22SR (Sir Roderick Comes to Lunch)
Jeeves and the Chump Cyril 18JC
Jeeves and the Dog McIntosh 29JD (The Borrowed Dog) (Episode of the Dog McIntosh)
JEEVES AND THE FEUDAL SPIRIT JF54 (Bertie Wooster Sees It Through)
Jeeves and the Greasy Bird 65JG
Jeeves and the Hard-Boiled Egg 17JH
Jeeves and the Impending Doom 26JI
Jeeves and the Kid Clementina 30JK
Jeeves and the Love That Purifies 29JL (The Love That Purifies)
Jeeves and the Old School Chum 30JO
Jeeves and the Song of Songs 29JS
Jeeves and the Spot of Art 29SA (The Spot of Art)
Jeeves and the Stolen Venus 59JM (Jeeves Makes an Omelet)
JEEVES AND THE TIE THAT BINDS MO71 (Much Obliged, Jeeves)
Jeeves and the Unbidden Guest 16JU
Jeeves and the Yule-Tide Spirit 27JY
Jeeves Exerts the Old Cerebellum Ch. I of IJ23, first part of 21JS
JEEVES IN THE MORNING JM46 (Joy in the Morning)
JEEVES IN THE OFFING HR60 (How Right You Are, Jeeves)
Jeeves in the Springtime 21JS
Jeeves, Jeeves, Jeeves (1976) See Collections
Jeeves Makes an Omelet 59JM (Jeeves and the Stolen

Venus)
Jeeves Omnibus (1931) See Collections
Jeeves Takes Charge 16JT
JILL THE RECKLESS LW20 (The Little Warrior)
A Job of Work 13JW
Joy Bells for Barmy 47RA (The Right Approach)
Joy Bells for Walter 56JB (Keep Your Temper, Walter)
JOY IN THE MORNING JM46
The Juice of an Orange 33JO (Love on a Diet)

Keep Your Temper, Walter 56JB (Joy Bells for Walter)
Keeping in with Vosper 26KI
Keeping It from Harold 13KI
Kid Brady—Light-Weight 05BL
A Kink in His Character 19OG (Ordeal By Golf)
The Knightly Quest of Mervyn 31KQ (Quest)

Ladies and Gentlemen v. Players 08LG
L'Affaire Uncle John 01AF
The Last Place 05LP
LAUGHING GAS LG36
Leave It to Algy 54LA (Hats Off to Algernon)
Leave It to Jeeves 16AC (Artistic Career of Corky)
LEAVE IT TO PSMITH LP23
A Letter of Introduction Ch. 9 of IJ23, first part of 18JC
The Letter of the Law 36LL (A Triple Threat Man)
The Level Business Head 26LB
Life with Freddie 66LF
Life with Jeeves (1981) See Collections
Lines and Business 11HF (Helping Freddie)
THE LITTLE NUGGET LN13
THE LITTLE WARRIOR LW20 (Jill the Reckless)
The Long Arm of Looney Coote 23LA
The Long Hole 21LH
Lord Emsworth Acts for the Best 26LE
Lord Emsworth and the Girl Friend 28EG
Lord Emsworth and Others (1937) See Collections
The Lost Bowlers 05LB

ALPHABETICAL LIST OF TITLES

THE LOST LAMBS (pt. 2 of MK09 as serialized in *The Captain*)

LOVE AMONG THE CHICKENS LC06

Love Birds 33NO (The Nodder)

Love Me, Love My Dog 10LM (The Watch Dog/A Dog-Eared Romance)

Love on a Diet 33JO (The Juice of an Orange)

The Love That Purifies 29JL (Jeeves and the Love That Purifies)

The Love-r-ly Silver Cup 15AG (At Geisenheimer's)

THE LUCK OF THE BODKINS LB35

The Luck of the Stiffhams 33LS

THE LUCK STONE LS08

The Magic Plus Fours 22MP (Plus Fours)

The Making of Mac's 15MM (The Romance of Mac's)

A MAN OF MEANS MM14

The Man, the Maid, and the Miasma 10MM

The Man Upstairs 10MU

The Man Upstairs (1914) See Collections

The Man Who Disliked Cats 12MC (Fatal Kink in Algernon)

The Man Who Gave Up Smoking 29GU

The Man Who Married a Hotel 20MH

The Man With Two Left Feet 16TL

The Man With Two Left Feet (1917) See Collections

The Manoeuvres of Charteris 03MC (Out of Bounds!)

The Masked Troubadour 36MT (Reggie and the Greasy Bird)

THE MATING SEASON MS49

Matrimonial Sweepstakes 10GA (The Good Angel)

The Medicine Girl 31MG (DOCTOR SALLY DS32)

Meet Mr. Mulliner (1927, 1928) See Collections

Methuen's Library of Humour. P.G. Wodehouse (1934) See Collections

The Metropolitan Touch 22MT

MIKE MK09 (Jackson Junior + The Lost Lambs/Mike at Wrykyn + Mike and Psmith)

MIKE AND PSMITH (Part II of MK09 as reissued in 1953 by Herbert Jenkins)

MIKE AT WRYKYN (Part I of MK09 as reissued in 1953 by Herbert Jenkins)

Mike's Little Brother 13ML

The Military Invasion of America 15MI

The Missing Mystery 32SS (Strychnine in the Soup)

Mr. McGee's Big Day 50MM

Mr. Mulliner, Private Detective 31SW (The Smile That Wins /Adrian Mulliner, Detective

Mr. Mulliner Speaking (1929, 1930) See Collections

Mr. Potter Takes a Rest Cure 26PT (The Rest Cure)

Misunderstood 10MI

A Mixed Threesome 20MT

The Mixer: He Meets a Shy Gentleman 15TM (A Very Shy Gentleman)

The Mixer: He Moves in Society 15MS (Breaking into Society)

MONEY FOR NOTHING MN28

MONEY IN THE BANK MB42

Monkey Business 32MB (A Cagey Gorilla)

The Most of P.G. Wodehouse (1960) See Collections

MOSTLY SALLY AS22 (The Adventures of Sally)

Mother's Knee 20MK

MUCH OBLIGED, JEEVES MO71 (Jeeves and the Tie That Binds)

Mulliner Nights (1933) See Collections

Mulliner Omnibus (1935) See Collections

Mulliner's Buck-U-Uppo 26MB

My Man Jeeves (1919) See Collections

THE NEW FOLD PC10 (Psmith in the City)

NO NUDES IS GOOD NUDES PB69 (A Pelican at Blandings)

No Wedding Bells for Bingo Ch. II of IJ23, second part of 21JS

No Wedding Bells for Him 23NW

Noblesse Oblige 34NO

The Nodder 33NO
NOT GEORGE WASHINGTON NG07 [With Herbert
  Westbrook]
Not out of Distance 36AG (There's Always Golf)
Nothing But Wodehouse (1932) See Collections
Nothing Serious (1950, 1951) See Collections

The Odd Trick 02OT
THE OLD RELIABLE OR51 (Phipps to the Rescue)
One Touch of Nature 14OT (Brother Fans)
Oofy, Freddy and the Beef Trust 48FO (Freddy, Oofy and
  the Beef Trust)
Open House 32OH
Ordeal By Golf 19OG (A Kink in His Character)
The Ordeal of Bingo Little 54OB
The Ordeal of Osbert Mulliner 28OO
The Ordeal of Young Tuppy 30TC (Tuppy Changes His
  Mind)
Out of Bounds! 27OB (The Manoeuvres of Charteris)
Out of School 09OS

P.G. Wodehouse Short Stories (1983) See Collections
Parted Ways 30BS (Best Seller)
The Passing of Ambrose 28PA
Paving the Way for Mabel 20PW
PEARLS, GIRLS, & MONTY BODKIN PG72 (The Plot
  That Thickened)
Pearls Mean Tears Ch. IV of IJ23, second part of 22AA
A PELICAN AT BLANDINGS PB69 (No Nudes Is Good
  Nudes)
Personally Conducted 07PC
Petticoat Influence 06PI
PHIPPS TO THE RESCUE OR51 (The Old Reliable)
PICCADILLY JIM PJ17
PIGS HAVE WINGS PW52
Pig-Hoo-o-o-o-ey! 27PH
Pillingshot, Detective 10PD
Pillingshot's Paper 11PP

ALPHABETICAL LIST OF TITLES

The Pitcher and the Plutocrat 10PP (Cf. 12GK, The Goal-
Keeper and the Plutocrat)
THE PLOT THAT THICKENED PG72 (Pearls, Girls, &
Monty Bodkin)
Plum Pie (1966, 1967) See Collections
Plus Fours 22MP (The Magic Plus Fours)
The Politeness of Princes 05PP
Portrait of a Disciplinarian 27PD
THE POTHUNTERS PH02
The Pothunters and Other School Stories (1985) See Collec-
tions
Pots o' Money 11PO
A PREFECT'S UNCLE PU03
The Pride of the Woosters Is Wounded Ch. V of IJ23, first
part of 22SO
THE PRINCE AND BETTY [New York: Watt, 2/14/12]
PA12
THE PRINCE AND BETTY [London: Mills & Boon,
5/1/12] PB12
A Prisoner of War 15PW
The Prize Poem 01PP
The Pro 06TP
Prospects for Wambledon 29PW
PSMITH IN THE CITY PC10 (serialized in *The Captain* as
The New Fold)
PSMITH, JOURNALIST PJ15
The Purification of Rodney Spelvin 25PR
The Purity of the Turf 22PT
THE PURLOINED PAPERWEIGHT PP67 (Company for
Henry)

Quest 31KQ (The Knightly Quest of Mervyn)
QUICK SERVICE QS40

Rallying Round Old George 12RR (Brother Alfred)
The Reformation of Study Sixteen 04RS
Reggie and the Greasy Bird 36MT (The Masked Trouba-
dour)

Reginald's Record Knock 09RR
The Rest Cure 26PT (Mr. Potter Takes a Rest Cure)
The Return of Battling Billson 23RB
THE RETURN OF JEEVES RJ53 (Ring for Jeeves)
The Reverent Wooing of Archibald 28RW
The Right Approach 47RA (Joy Bells For Barmy)
RIGHT HO, JEEVES RH34 (Brinkley Manor)
RING FOR JEEVES RJ53 (The Return of Jeeves)
The Rise of Minna Nordstrom 33RM (A Star Is Born)
Roderick, the Runt 12RA (Sir Agravaine)
Rodney Fails to Qualify 24RF
Rodney Has a Relapse 49RR (Rupert Has a Relapse)
Romance at Droitgate Spa 37RD
The Romance of a Bulb-Squeezer 27RB
The Romance of an Ugly Policeman 15RU
The Romance of Mac's 15MM (The Making of Mac's)
A Room at the Hermitage 20RH (A Bit of All Right)
Rough-Hew Them How We Will 10RH
The Rough Stuff 20RS
The Rummy Affair of Old Biffy 24RA
Rupert Has a Relapse 49RR (Rodney Has a Relapse)
Ruth in Exile 12RE
Ruthless Reginald 05RR

Sales Resistance 31GG (Go-Getter)
The Salvation of George Mackintosh 21SG
SAM IN THE SUBURBS SS25 (Sam the Sudden)
SAM THE SUDDEN SS25 (Sam in the Suburbs)
The Sausage Chappie 20AS (Archie and the Sausage Chappie)
Scoring Off Jeeves 22SO (Bertie Gets Even)
Scratch Man 40SM (Tee For Two)
A Sea of Troubles 14ST
The Secret Pleasures of Reginald 15SP
Selected Stories By P.G. Wodehouse (1958) See Collections
SERVICE WITH A SMILE SS61
The Shadow Passes 50SP
Shields' and the Cricket Club 05SC

ALPHABETICAL LIST OF TITLES

A Shocking Affair 03SA
Sir Agravaine 12SA (Roderick, the Runt)
Sir Roderick Comes To Lunch 22SR (Jeeves and the Blighter)
Sleepy Time 65ST (The Battle of Squashy Hollow)
A Slice of Life 26SL
A Slightly Broken Romance 50FC (Feet of Clay)
THE SMALL BACHELOR SB27
The Smile That Wins 31SW (Adrian Mulliner, Detective/Mr. Mulliner, Private Detective)
SOMETHING FISHY SF57 (The Butler Did It)
SOMETHING FRESH SN15 (Something New)
SOMETHING NEW SN15 (Something Fresh)
Something Squishy 24SS
Something to Worry About 13ST
The Song of Songs 29JS (Jeeves and the Song of Songs)
Sonny Boy 39SB
The Spot of Art 29SA (Jeeves and the Spot of Art)
SPRING FEVER SF48
The Spring Frock 19SF (The Spring Suit)
The Spring Suit 19SF (The Spring Frock)
A Star Is Born 33RM (The Rise of Minna Nordstrom)
Startling Dressiness of a Lift Attendant Ch. X of IJ23, second part of 18JC
Sticky Wicket at Blandings 66SW (First Aid for Freddy)
STIFF UPPER LIP, JEEVES SU63
Stone and the Weed 10SW
The Story of Cedric 29SC
The Story of Webster 32SW (The Bishop's Cat)
The Story of William 27SW (It Was Only a Fire)
Strange Experiences of an Artist's Model 21SE
Strychnine in the Soup 32SS (The Missing Mystery)
Stylish Stouts 65SS
Success Story 47SS (Ukie Invests in Human Nature)
SUMMER LIGHTNING FP29 (Fish Preferred)
SUMMER MOONSHINE SM37
Sundered Hearts 20SH
SUNSET AT BLANDINGS SB77

THE SWOOP! SW09
The Swoop! and Other Stories (1979) See Collections

The Tabby Terror 02TT
Tales of St Austin's (1903) See Collections
Tangled Hearts 48TH (I'll Give You Some Advice)
Tee for Two 42SM (Scratch Man)
The Test Case 15TC
THANK YOU, JEEVES TY34
THEIR MUTUAL CHILD WH14 (The White Hope/The
  Coming of Bill)
There's Always Golf! 36AG (Not Out of Distance)
Those in Peril at the Tee 27TP
Three from Dunsterville 11TD
THREE MEN AND A MAID TM22 (The Girl on the
  Boat)
A Tithe for Charity 55TC
Tom, Dick, and Harry 05TD
Tried in the Furnace 35TF
A Triple Threat Man 36LL (The Letter of the Law)
Trouble Down at Tudsleigh 35TD
The Truth About George 26TA
The Tuppenny Millionaire 12TM
Tuppy Changes His Mind 30TC (The Ordeal of Young
  Tuppy)

Ukie Invests in Human Nature 47SS (Success Story)
Ukridge (1924) See Collections
Ukridge and the Home from Home 31UH
Ukridge and the Old Stepper 28UO
Ukridge Rounds a Nasty Corner 24UR
Ukridge Sees Her Through 23US
Ukridge Starts a Bank Account 67US
Ukridge's Accident Syndicate 23UA (Ukridge, Teddy Weeks
  and the Tomato)
Ukridge's Dog College 23UD
Ukridge, Teddy Weeks and the Tomato 23UA (Ukridge's
  Accident Syndicate)

UNCLE DYNAMITE UD48
Uncle Fred Flits By 35UF
UNCLE FRED IN THE SPRINGTIME UF39
The Uncollected Wodehouse (1976) See Collections
UNEASY MONEY UM16
The Unexpected Clicking of Cuthbert 21UC (Cuthbert
 Unexpectedly Clicks)
Unpleasantness at Bludleigh Court 29UB
Unpleasantness at Kozy Kot 58UK
Up from the Depths 51UF

Very Good, Jeeves (1930) See Collections
A Very Shy Gentleman 15TM (The Mixer: He Meets a Shy
 Gentleman)
Vintage Wodehouse (1977) See Collections
The Voice From the Past 31VP

Washy Makes His Presence Felt 20WM
The Watch Dog 10LM (Love Me, Love My Dog/A Dog-
 Eared Romance)
Ways to Get a Gal 57WT (cf. 11AS Ahead of Schedule)
Week-End Wodehouse (1939) See Collections
Welch's Mile Record 02WM
When Doctors Disagree 10WD
When Papa Swore in Hindustani 01WP (How Papa Swore
 ...)
THE WHITE FEATHER WF07
THE WHITE HOPE WH14 (Their Mutual Child/The Com-
 ing of Bill)
The Wigmore Venus 21WV
WILLIAM TELL TOLD AGAIN WT04
Wilton's Holiday 15WH (Wilton's Vacation)
The Wire-Pullers 05WP
Without the Option 25WO
A Wodehouse Bestiary (1985) See Collections
Wodehouse on Crime (1981) See Collections
Wodehouse on Golf (1940) See Collections
A Woman Is Only a Woman 19WW

The Word In Season 40WS (Bingo Little's Wild Night Out)
The World of Blandings (1976) See Collections
The World of Jeeves (1967) See Collections
The World of Psmith (1974) See Collections
The World of Mr. Mulliner (1972, 1974) See Collections
The World of Ukridge (1975) See Collections
The World of Wodehouse Clergy (1984) See Collections

Young Men In Spats (1936) See Collections

WODEHOUSE COLLECTIONS

Listed Chronologically

Tales of St Austin's [London: A&C Black, 1903]: includes
01PP, 01AF, 01AU, 02TT, 02OT, 02BL, 02BD, 02HP, 03HS,
03HP, 03MC, 03SA, and five essays.

The Man Upstairs [London: Methuen, 1914]: includes 09OS,
10GA, 10MU, 10AB, 10RH, 10DW, 10MM, 10BA, 12GK,
10WD, 11AS, 11TD, 11PO, 11IA, 12MC, 12SA, 12RE, 12TM,
13ST.

The Man with Two Left Feet [London: Methuen, 1917]:
includes 14OT, 14ST, 15RU, 15BB, 15CH, 15MM, 15BL,
15WH, 15AG, 15EY, 15TM, 15MS, 16TL.
The Man with Two Left Feet [New York: A.L. Burt, 1933]:
includes 11AT, 12RR, 13DC, 14OT, 14ST, 15RU, 15BB,
15MM, 15BL, 15AG, 15EY, 16TL.

My Man Jeeves [London: George Newnes, 1919]: includes
11AT, 11HF, 12RR, 13DC, 16AC, 16AS, 16JU, 17JH.

Indiscretions of Archie [London: Herbert Jenkins, 1921]: an
episodic novel first published as stories; includes 20MH,
20AS, 20DO, 20DF, 20PW, 20WM, 20RH, 20FA, 20MK,
21SE, 21WV.
Indiscretions of Archie [New York: George H. Doran, 1921]:
same contents as foreg.

The Clicking of Cuthbert [London: Herbert Jenkins, 1922]:
includes 19WW, 19OG, 20MT, 20RS, 20SH, 21CG, 21SG,
21LH, 21UC, 21HA.
Golf Without Tears (=foreg.) [New York: George H. Doran,
1924]: same contents as foreg.

The Inimitable Jeeves [London: Herbert Jenkins, 1923]: an episodic novel first published as stories; includes 18JC, 21JS, 22SO, 22SR, 22AA, 22CB, 22SH, 22PT, 22MT, 22BL, 22EC.
Jeeves (=foreg.) [New York: George H. Doran, 1923]: same contents as foreg.

Ukridge [London: Herbert Jenkins, 1924]: includes 23UD, 23UA, 23DB, 23FA, 23RB, 23US, 23NW, 23LA, 23EB, 24UR.
He Rather Enjoyed It (=foreg.) [New York: George H. Doran, 1926]: same contents as foreg.

Carry On, Jeeves [London: Herbert Jenkins, 1925]: includes 16JT, 16AC, 16JU, 17JH, 16AS, 22RA, 25WO, 26FF, 25CR, 22BC.
Carry On, Jeeves [New York: George H. Doran, 1927]: omits 16AC and 16AS

The Heart of a Goof [London: Herbert Jenkins, 1926]: includes 22MP, 23AR, 23CF, 23HG, 24RF, 24JG, 25PR, 25HS, 26KI.
Divots (=foreg.) [New York: George H. Doran, 1927]: same contents as foreg.

Meet Mr. Mulliner [London: Herbert Jenkins, 1927]: includes 26TA, 26SL, 26MB, 27BM, 27CD, 27SW, 27PD, 27RB, 25HC.
Meet Mr. Mulliner [Garden City, NY: Doubleday, Doran, 1928]: same contents as foreg.

Mr. Mulliner Speaking [London: Herbert Jenkins, 1929]: includes 24SS, 25AG, 27TP, 28PA, 28RW, 28OO, 29UB, 29GU, 29SC.
Mr. Mulliner Speaking [Garden City, NY: Doubleday, Doran, 1930]: same contents as foreg.

Very Good, Jeeves [Garden City, NY: Doubleday, Doran, 1930]: includes 26JI, 26IC, 27JY, 29JS, 29JD, 29SA, 30JK, 30JO, 29JL, 30IS, 30TC.

Very Good, Jeeves [London: Herbert Jenkins, 1930]: omits 30TC.

Jeeves Omnibus [London: Herbert Jenkins, 1931]: includes 16JT, 21JS, 22SO, 22SR, 22AA, 16AC, 18JC, 16JU, 17JH, 16AS, 22CB, 22SH, 22PT, 22MT, 22EC, 22BL, 24RA, 25WO, 26FF, 25CR, 26JI, 26IC, 27JY, 29JS, 29JD, 29SA, 30JK, 29JL, 30JO, 30IS, 30TC.

Nothing but Wodehouse [Garden City, NY: Doubleday, Doran, 1932]: includes six chapters of IJ23: 1, 2, 7, 8, 22SH, and 22PT; also 27JY, 29JS, 29JL, 30JO, 30IS, 23UD, 23UA, 23FA, 23US, 23NW, 24UR, 26TA, 28OO, 29UB, 24SS, LP23.

Mulliner Nights [London: Herbert Jenkins, 1933]: includes 30BS, 30GN, 31KQ, 31SW, 31VP, 32SW, 32SS, 32OH, 32CC.
Mulliner Nights [Garden City, NY: Doubleday, Doran, 1933]: same contents as foreg.

Mulliner Omnibus [London: Herbert Jenkins, 1935]: includes 26TA, 26SL, 26MB, 27BM, 27CD, 27SW, 27PD, 27RB, 25HC, 28RW, 29GU, 29SC, 28OO, 29UB, 27TP, 24SS, 25AG, 28PA, 31SW, 32SW, 32CC, 31KQ, 31VP, 32OH, 30BS, 32SS, 30GN, 32MB, 33NO, 33JO, 33RM, 33CA.

Blandings Castle and Elsewhere [London: Herbert Jenkins, 1935]: includes 24CP, 26LE, 27PH, 28CG, 31GG, 28EG, 26PT, 32MB, 33NO, 33JO, 33RM, 33CA.
Blandings Castle and Elsewhere [Garden City, NY: Doubleday, Doran, 1935]: same contents as foreg.

Young Men in Spats [London: Herbert Jenkins, 1936]: includes 31FA, 35TF, 35TD, 33AH, 34GB, 33LS, 34NO, 35UF, 35AM, 35CM, 34FW.
Young Men in Spats [Garden City, NY: Doubleday, Doran, 1936]: includes 31FA, 33AH, 33LS, 34NO, 34GB, 34FW, 35AM, 35CM, 35UF, 35FL, 36LL, 36AG.

Lord Emsworth and Others [London: Herbert Jenkins, 1937]: includes 26LB, 31UH, 35CB, 35FL, 36LL, 36AG, 36BT, 36CW, 36MT.

Crime Wave at Blandings (cf. foreg.) [Garden City, NY: Doubleday, Doran, 1937]: includes 31MG, 35TF, 36BT, 36CW, 36MT, 37AW, 37RD.

The Week-End Wodehouse [New York: Doubleday, Doran, 1939]: includes 35AM, 32MB, 33RM, 31VP, 31SW, 32CC, 30BS, 32SS, 22MT, 16JT, 17JH, 25CR, 22BC, 26JI, 29SA, 37AW, 36MT, 35TF, 27PH, 31GG, FP29.

Week-End Wodehouse [London: Herbert Jenkins, 1939]: includes stories and fragments as follows: 35UF, "Galahad on Tea," "My Gentle Readers," 21SG, "The Artistry of Archibald," "Old Bill Townend," "Gussie Presents the Prizes," "Good News from Denmark," "Inside Information," "The Feudal Spirit," "Golfing Tigers and Literary Lions," "The Soupiness of Madeline," 28EG, "One Moment!," "The First Time I Went to New York," 34FW, "Le Vodehouse," "Mr. Bennett and the Bulldog, Smith," 34GB, "The Penurious Aristocracy," "I Explode the Haggis," "Diet and the Omnibus," 23UA, 25HS, "Archibald Goes Slumming," "Two Ways of...," "...Saying the Same Thing," "Conversation Piece," 27PH, "Americans 'A' and 'B'," "To W. Townend," "Back to Whiskers," 36BT, "The Defeat of a Critic," 21UC, "The Saga Habit," "Gallant Rescue By Well-Dressed Young Man," 23NW, "Good Gnus," "The Pinheadedness of Archibald," "The Sinister Cudster," "In Which a Mother Pleads for Her Son," 23CF, "A Damsel in Distress," "Fore!", "Hollywood Interlude," "Sinister Behaviour of a Yacht-Owner."

Wodehouse on Golf [New York: Doubleday, Doran, 1940]: includes Divots (1927—see Collections), Golf Without Tears (1924—see Collections), DS32, 36AG, 36LL, 10AB.

Eggs, Beans, and Crumpets [London: Herbert Jenkins, 1940]: includes 25BD, 25BL, 28OO, 37AW, 37RD, 37BP, 37AG,

39ER, 39SB.

Eggs, Beans, and Crumpets [Garden City, NY: Doubleday, Doran, 1940]: includes 25BD, 25BL, 26LB, 28OO, 31UH, 35TD, 35CB, 37BP, 37AG, 39ER, 39SB, 39BI, 40SM.

The Best of Wodehouse [New York: Pocket Books, 1949]: includes 27JY, 35TD, Good-Bye to Butlers, 32SS, 26LB, 36CW, 39SB, 36LL, 35TF, 48FO.

Nothing Serious [London: Herbert Jenkins, 1950]: includes 39BI, 47SS, 48IG, 48EX, 50BS, 50SB, 50SP, 51UF, 51HT.
Nothing Serious [Garden City, NY: Doubleday, Doran, 1951]: same contents as foreg.

Selected Stories by P.G. Wodehouse [Random House: Modern Library, 1958]: includes 16JT, 16AC, 16JU, 16AS, 24RA, 25CR, 22BC, 26JI, 27JY, 29JS, 29JD, 30JK, 29JL, 30JO, 30TC.

A Few Quick Ones [New York: Simon & Schuster, 1959]: includes 40SM, 40WS, 47RA, 48FO, 52BB, 54LA, 56JB, 58FL, 58UK, 59JM.
A Few Quick Ones [London: Herbert Jenkins, 1959]: includes 40SM, 40WS, 47RA, 48FO, 52BB, 54LA, 55TC, 56JB, 58FL, 59JM.
A Few Quick Ones [Coronet Edition. London: Hodder & Stoughton, 1978]: like Jenkins edn. but omits 52BB, 56JB and adds 50BS.

The Most of P.G. Wodehouse [New York: Simon & Schuster, 1960]: includes 31FA, 35TF, 33AH, 34NO, 34GB, 37AW, 35UF, 26TA, 26SL, 26MB, 28RW, 28OO, 32MB, 31SW, 32SS, 23UD, 23UA, 25BL, 25BD, 28UO, 27PH, 21CG, 23AR, 21UC, 25HS, 21HA, 22PT, 22SH, 22MT, 29JS, 26JI, QS40.

Plum Pie [London: Herbert Jenkins, 1966]: includes 65BB, 65SS, 65ST, 65JG, 66SW, 66LF, 67GA, 67US, 67GC.

Plum Pie [New York: Simon & Schuster, 1967]: same contents as foreg.

Plum Pie [Coronet Edition. London: Hodder & Stoughton, 1978]: substitutes 47SS for 65JG.

The World of Jeeves [London: Herbert Jenkins, 1967, rp. Harper & Row 1988]: includes 16JT, 21JS, 22SO, 22SR, 22AA, 16AC, 18JC, 16JU, 17JH, 16AS, 22CB, 22SH, 22PT, 22MT, 22EC, 22BL, 24RA, 25WO, 26FF, 25CR, 26JI, 26IC, 27JY, 29JS, 29JD, 29SA, 30JK, 29JL, 30JO, 30IS, 30TC, 22BC, 59JM, 65JG.

The World of Mr. Mulliner [London: Barrie & Jenkins, 1972]: includes 26TA, 26SL, 26MB, 27BM, 27CD, 27SW, 27PD, 27RB, 25HC, 28RW, 29GU, 29SC, 28OO, 29UB, 27TP, 24SS, 25AG, 28PA, 31SW, 32SW, 32CC, 31KQ, 31VP, 32OH, 30BS, 32SS, 30GN, 32MB, 33NO, 33JO, 33RM, 33CA, 35AM, 35CM, 34FW, 36BT, 37AG, 47RA, 52BB, 67GA, 70AC, 59DN.

The World of Mr. Mulliner [New York: Taplinger, 1974]: same contents as foreg.

The Golf Omnibus [London: Barrie & Jenkins, 1973]: includes 10AB, 21UC, 19WW, 20MT, 20SH, 21SG, 19OG, 21LH, 21HA, 20RS, 21CG, 23HG, 25HS, 26KI, 23CF, 22MP, 23AR, 24RF, 24JG, 25PR, 27TP, 36LL, 35FL, 36AG, 51UF, 50FC, 48EX, 49RR, 48TH, 40SM, 65ST.

The World of Psmith [London: Barrie & Jenkins, 1974]: includes Mike and Psmith (Pt. II of MK09), PC10, PJ15, LP23.

The World of Ukridge [London: Barrie & Jenkins, 1975]: includes 23UD, 23UA, 23DB, 23FA, 23RB, 23US, 23NW, 23LA, 23EB, 24UR, 47SS, 67US, 25BL, 25BD, 28UO, 55TC, 31UH, 35CB, 26LB.

The World of Blandings [London: Barrie & Jenkins, 1976]:

includes SF15, 24CP, 26LE, 27PH, SL29.

Jeeves, Jeeves, Jeeves [New York: Avon Books, 1976]: includes HR60, SU63, MO71.

The Uncollected Wodehouse [New York: Seabury Press, 1976]: includes sixteen articles and 01WP, 05CL, 05AH, 05TD, 10GA, 10MU, 10MI, 10PD, 10WD, 11BS, 11PO, 12RE, 14DE, 15TC, 15SP.

Vintage Wodehouse [London: Barrie & Jenkins, 1977]: includes 21UC, 27JY, 37AG, 48RR, 35UF, 28EG, 25HC, 33AH, 27PH, 35TF, 37RD, 39BI, 23UA, and excerpts from PH02, MK09, SN15, FM47, two from LB35, two from UF39, RH34, MB42, PB69, HR60, FP29, CW38, SS61, CT58, two from FP29, PB69, IB61, LN13, 65ST, Bring On the Girls, Over Seventy, and The Performing Flea.

The Swoop! and Other Stories [New York: Seabury Press, 1979]: includes SW09, 02BL, 03SA, 05PP, 05SC, 05IA, 08GU, 13ST, 12TM, 10DW, 12GK.

The Eighteen-Carat Kid and Other Stories [New York: Seabury Press, 1980]: includes 13EC, 05WP, 01PP, WT04.

Wodehouse on Crime [New Haven: Ticknor & Fields, 1981]: includes 32SS, 36CW, 67US, 22PT, 31SW, 25PR, 25WO, 27RB, 22AA, 34FW, 23UA, IA21.

Life with Jeeves [Harmondsworth: Penguin Books, 1981]: includes RH34, IJ23, Very Good, Jeeves (1930—see Collections).

Tales from the Drones Club [London: Hutchinson, 1982]: includes 31FA, 35TF, 35TD, 33AH, 34GB, 33LS, 34NO, 35UF, 36MT, 37AW, 37BP, 39ER, 39SB, 50SP, 39BI, 58FL, 40WS, 54LA, 48FO, 65BB, 65SS.

Fore! The Best of Wodehouse on Golf [New Haven: Ticknor & Fields, 1983]: includes 21CG, 21SG, 25HS, 23CF, 48TH, 23AR, 21HA, 24RF, 23HG, 20MT, 48EX, 21LH.

P.G. Wodehouse Short Stories [London: The Folio Society, 1983]: includes 22SH, 26FF, 59JM, 16AS, 26JI, 29JS, 24CP, 27PH, 31GG, 31UH, 23UA, 32SW, 35AM, 33NO, 21UC, 40SM, 21CG, 34GB, 33AH.

The World of Wodehouse Clergy [London: Hutchinson, 1984]: includes 26MB, 27BM, 32SW, 32CC, 31VP, 30GN, 37AG, 22AA, 22SH, 22PT, 22MT, 35TF, 25BD, 28CG, 39BI, extracts from MS49, UD48, CW38, SS61, SU63, and 19 nuggets from various novels and stories.

The Hollywood Omnibus [London: Hutchinson, 1985]: includes LG36, 32MB, 33NO, 33JO, 33RM, 33CA, 67GA, and one autobiographical section each from Over Seventy, Bring On the Girls, and The Performing Flea.

A Wodehouse Bestiary [New York: Ticknor & Fields, 1985]: includes 29UB, 22SR, 24SS, 27PH, 22CB, 32MB, 26JI, 32OH, 23UD, 32SW, 31GG, 30JO, 35UF, 15TM.

The Pothunters and Other School Stories [Harmondsworth: Penguin, 1985]: includes PH02, PU03, and Tales of St Austin's (see collections, 1903).

The Gold Bat and Other School Stories [Harmondsworth: Penguin, 1986]: includes GB04, WF07, HK05.

APPENDIX I: Drones

Samuel Galahad Bagshott
William Egerton Bamfylde Ossingham Belfry, 9th Earl of Towcester
Montague Bodkin
Godfrey Edward Winstanley Brent, Lord Biskerton
Tubby, Lord Bridgenorth
Freddie Bullivant
Hugh Carmody
G. D'Arcy Cheesewright
Marmaduke Chuffnell, 5th Baron Chuffnell
Nelson Cork
Algernon P. Crufts
Dudley Finch
Augustus Fink-Nottle
Ronald Overbury Fish
George Webster Fittleworth
Aubrey Fothergill
Cyril Fotheringay-Phipps
Hildebrand Glossop
Richard P. Little
Algernon Martyn
Archibald Mulliner
Freddie Oaker
Horace Pendlebury-Davenport
Barmy Phipps
Tipton Plimsoll
Claude Cattermole Potter-Pirbright
Alexander Charles Prosser
Rupert Eustace Psmith
Freddie Rooke
Oofy Simpson
Reginald Swithin, 3rd Earl of Havershot
Reggie Tennyson
Freddie Threepwood
Reginald G. Twistleton-Twistleton
Hugo Walderwick

APPENDIX I: DRONES

Capt. J.G. Walkinshaw
Frederick Fotheringay Widgeon
Ambrose Wiffin
Percy Wimbolt
Percy Wimbush
Harold Winship
Dudley Wix-Biffin
Bertram Wilberforce Wooster
Algy Wymondham-Wymondham

Staff:

Bashford[2] (Porter)
Bates (Porter)
McGarry (Bartender)
Robinson[2] (Cloakroom Waiter)

APPENDIX II: Butlers (employer in parentheses)

J.B. Attwater (ret.)
Bagshaw (R.P. Little)
Bagshot[1] (Sir Rackstraw Cammarleigh)
Barlow (Headmaster at Sedleigh)
Barter (Julia Ukridge)
Bastable (Rupert Bingley)
Baxter (Julia Ukridge)
Bayliss (Bingley Crocker)
Sebastian Beach (Lord Emsworth)
Benson (Agatha Gregson)
Bewstridge (Jeremiah Briggs)
Biggleswade (Lord Prenderby)
Binstead (Sir Gregory Parsloe)
Blizzard (Bradbury Fisher)
Bosher (Ivor Llewellyn)
Bowles (ret.)
Briggs (Richard Morrison)
Brookfield[1] (Rev. Francis Heppenstall)
Bulstrode[1] (C. Hamilton Brimble)
Bulstrode[2] (Col. Wyvern)
Butterfield (Sir Watkyn Bassett)
Chaffinch (T.P. Brinkmeyer)
Sidney Chibnall (Howard Steptoe)
Coggs (Lord Ickenham)
Eustace Coleman (Mike Bond)
Croome (unnamed narrator of 06FM)
Dobson (Roderick Glossop)
Andrew Ferris (Henry Paradene)
Rupert Antony Ferris (S. Waddington)
Fotheringay (Earl of Biddlecombe/Lady Widdrington)
Gascoigne (F.J. Delamere)
Keggs[1] (the Keiths)
Keggs[2] (John Bannister/the Winfields)
Keggs[3] (Lord Marshmoreton)
Augustus Keggs[1] (the Keiths)
Augustus Keggs[2] (ret.)
Maple (Lord Worplesdon)
Meadows (J.W. Biggs)

APPENDIX II: BUTLERS

Morris (Sir William Romney)
Mulready (Sir Reginald Witherspoon)
Murgatroyd[1] (Sir Jasper ffinch-ffarowmere)
Murgatroyd[3] (formerly T.P. Travers)
Oakshott[1] (Bertie's Uncle Willoughby)
Oakshott[2] (Julia Ukridge)
Parker[1] (headmaster at St Austin's)
Parker[3] (Mrs. Drassilis)
Parker[5] (Beatrice Bracken)
Parkinson (Dermot Windleband)
A.E. Peasemarch (ret.)
Perks (Colonel Stewart)
George Phipps (Lord Bromborough)
James Phipps (Adela Shannon Cork)
Pollen (Sir Buckstone Abbott)
Ponsonby[2] (Harold Bodkin)
Purvis (Spenser Gregson)
Riggs (Dora Garland)
Augustus Robb (Stanwood Cobbold)
Roberts[2] (Cooley Paradene)
Saunders[3] (Sir Thomas Blunt/Lord Dreever)
Seppings (T.P. Travers)
Charlie Silversmith (Esmond Haddock)
Simmons[2] (Lady Wickham)
Skidmore (Roscoe Bunyan)
Sleddon (J. Willoughby Braddock)
Ted Slingsby (Lord Droitwich)
Spenser (Agatha Gregson)
Mervyn Spink (Lord Shortlands)
Staniforth (Willoughby Gudgeon)
Horace Stout (formerly Julia Ukridge)
Sturgis (Lester Carmody)
Teal (Lord Evenwood)
Hildebrand Vosper (Bradbury Fisher)
Wace (Sinclair Hammond)
Watson[2] (headmaster at Eckleton)
Weeks (Master Peter's family)
Wilberforce[2] or Willoughby (Myrtle Beenstock)

APPENDIX II: BUTLERS

Wrench (Algie Wetherby)

also—

Cakebread, pseud. of Lord Uffenham in MB42 (Lord Uffenham)

Chippendale, a broker's man (Crispin Scrope)

The Greaser, butler-bootboy in school house, St Austin's

Jorkins, pseud. of Cyril Bunting (G.A. Pyke, Lord Tilbury)

Merridew, underbutler at Blandings in SN15.

William, known as the Moke, butler-bootboy at Merevale's, St Austin's

Skinner, pseud of Bingley Crocker in PJ17 (Peter Pett).

Swordfish, pseud. of Roderick Glossop in HR60 (T.P. Travers)

White, butler-detective at Sanstead House—see Smooth Sam Fisher

William, butler-bootboy at Leister's, Beckford

APPENDIX III: Valets (employer in parentheses)

Horace Barker (Freddie Rooke)
Richard Belsey (Stanley Briggs)
Benstead (George Stoker)
Bessemer (Ronnie Fish)
Blenkinsop[2] (Eustace Mulliner)
Brinkley or Bingley (Bertie Wooster)
Bryce (Roland Attwater)
Clarkson (J. Wendell Stickney)
Corker (Oofy Prosser)
Dixon[2] (Arthur Mifflin)
Ferris (Lord Stockheath)
Jeeves (Bertie Mannering-Phipps)
Reginald Jeeves (Bertie Wooster)
Jevons (Sir Godfrey Tanner)
Judson (Freddie Threepwood)
Meadowes[1] (Bertie Wooster)
Meadowes[2] (Archibald Mulliner)
Meadowes[3] (Gussie Fink-Nottle)
Meekyn (Aubrey Fothergill)
Frederick Mullet (George Finch)
Parker[4] (Osbert Mulliner)
Herbert Parker (Daniel Brewster)
Ridgeway (Bill West)
Smethurst (Col. Mainwaring-Smith)
Smith[5] (Peter Burns)
Spencer[2] (Looney Coote)
Stevens (Sir George Wooster)
Venner (Lord Biskerton)
Harold Voules (Reggie Pepper)
Webster[2] (Horace Pendlebury-Davenport)
Montagu Webster (J. Rufus Bennett)
Wilberforce[1] (Reggie Pepper)
Wilson[2] (Barmy Barminster)
James Wilson (Rollo Finch)
Worple (L.G. Trotter)

APPENDIX III: VALETS

also—

Ashe Marson poses as Freddie Threepwood's valet in SN15.

Wilfred Mulliner poses as a valet named Straker in 26SL.

Joss Weatherby takes charge as Howard Steptoe's valet in QS40.

Catsmeat Potter-Pirbright plays Bertie's man Meadowes in MS49.

Appendix IV

UNCOLLECTED WODEHOUSE

Against the Clock   09AC
(*Pearson's Magazine* [London] vol. 27, no. 162 (6/09), pp. 586-595)

An Affair of Boats (Tales of Wryken No. 4)   05AB
(*The Captain* vol. 13, pp. 319-324 7/05)

An Afternoon Dip   04AD (Jackson's Dip)
(*Pearson's Magazine* (London) 9/04, pp. 314-318)
(*Greyfriar's Holiday Annual*, 1925, pp. 12-17)

Aubrey's Arrested Individuality   15AA "By P. Brooke Haven"
(*Vanity Fair* vol. 4 #3 5/15, pp. 53, 92)

Back to the Garage   29BG (Franklin's Favorite Daughter)
(*The Strand*, 7/29, pp. 2-13; *Cosmopolitan* vol. 87, pp. 42-45, 217-220, July 1929)

A Benefit Match   06AB
(*Windsor Magazine* vol. 24, Jun-Nov 1906, pp. 330-336)

Between the Innings   05BI
(*Novel Magazine* vol. 1, 7/05, 438-442)

Blenkinsop's Benefit   04BB
(*The Captain* vol. 11, Aug 1904, 456-463)

Concealed Art   15CA
(*The Strand* 2/15, pp. 145-153; *Pictorial Review* 7/15)

Creatures of Impulse   14CI
(*The Strand* 10/14, *McClure's* 10/14, 48-55)

Cupid and the Paint-Brush   03CP
(*Windsor Magazine* vol. 17, pp. 687-690 April 1903)

The Deserter   05DE
(*Royal Magazine* vol. 14, 8/05, pp. 299-303)

The Disappearance of Podmarsh   15DP
(*Vanity Fair* vol. 4 #4 6/15, p. 43)

Disentangling Old Duggie   12DO
(*Colliers* 3/30/12 vol. 19, pp. 17-19, 39-40)

Disentangling Old Percy   12DO
(*The Strand* 8/12, pp. 219-229), *Newnes Summer Annual* I 11-22 (1915)

APPENDIX IV: UNCOLLECTED WODEHOUSE

A Division of Spoil 06DS
(*The Captain* vol. 15, 9/06, 502-506)
Dudley Is Back to Normal 40DI
(*The Strand* 12/39)
Educating Aubrey 11EA
(*London Magazine* vol. 26 #7, May 1911, pp. 409-418)
The Fifteenth Man 06FM
(*Windsor Magazine* vol. 25, pp. 169-176 Dec. 1906)
The Golden Flaw 20GF
(*McClure's* 3-4/20, pp. 28-29, 74-77, 80-83)
Homeopathic Treatment 04HT
(*Royal Magazine* Vol. 12, 8/04, pp. 296-300; *Boy's Life Magazine* 4/31)
How Kid Brady Assisted a Damsel in Distress 06BA
(*Pearsons* NY 3/06, pp. 313-318 [Pt. 4 of 7])
How Kid Brady Broke Training 05BB
(*Pearsons* NY 11/05, pp. 463-468 [Pt. 2 of 7])
How Kid Brady Fought for his Eyes 06BF
(*Pearsons* NY 7/06, pp. 65-70 [Pt. 6 of 7])
How Kid Brady Joined the Press 06BJ
(*Pearsons* NY 5/06, pp. 528-534 [Pt. 5 of 7])
How Kid Brady Won the Championship 06BW
(*Pearsons* NY 1/06, pp. 33-38 [Pt. 3 of 7])
How Kid Brady Took a Sea Voyage 07BT
(*Pearsons* NY 3/07, pp. 318-324 [Pt. 7 of 7])
The Idle King 03IK
(*The Sunday Magazine* XXXII 455-457 [5/03])
Jackson's Extra 04JE
(*Royal Magazine* vol. 12, 6/04, pp. 157-161)
A Job of Work 13JW
(*The Strand Magazine* 1/13, Colliers 9/6/13)
Keeping It from Cuthbert =13KI
(*Liberty* vol. 2 #43 2/27/26, 7-10)
Keeping it from Harold 13KI
(*The Strand* vol. 46 Jul-Dec 1913 pp. 656-663)
Kid Brady—Lightweight 05BL
(*Pearsons* US 9/05, pp. 235-241 [Pt. 1 of 7])
Ladies and Gentlemen v. Players 08LG

(*Windsor Magazine* vol. 28 (Aug. 1908), pp. 275-281)
The Last Place (Tales of Wrykyn No. 5) 05LP
(*The Captain* vol. 13, pp. 426-431 8/05)
The Lost Bowlers   05LB
(*The Strand Magazine* 9/05, 298-303)
Love Me, Love My Dog   10LM (Watch Dog/A Dog-Eared
Romance) (*The Strand*, vol. 40 Jul-Dec 1910 pp. 184-193)
THE LUCK STONE LS08 ("by Basil Windham")
(*Chums* vol. 17, 9/16/08 - 1/20/09
A MAN OF MEANS   MM14 (with C.H. Bovill)
The Episode of the Landlady's Daughter
The Episode of the Financial Napoleon/The Bolt from the
Blue
The Episode of the Theatrical Venture
The Episode of the Live Weekly
The Diverting Episode of the Exiled Monarch
The Episode of the Hired Past
(*The Strand* vols. 47-48: April-Sept 1914, pp. 460-467, 577-
586, 674-683, 56-65, 177-184, 260-268; *Pictorial Review*, 5/16-
10/16)
Mike's Little Brother   13ML
(*Pall Mall Magazine* vol. 52 #246, 451-456 Oct 1913)
The Military Invasion of America   15MI
(*Vanity Fair* vol. 4 #5 7/15, pp. 53-54, 82 and vol. 4 #6 8/15,
pp. 58-59)
Mr. McGee's Big Day   50MM
(*Ellery Queen's Mystery Magazine* 11/50, pp. 37-42)
The Ordeal of Bingo Little   54OB
(*Bluebook Magazine* vol. 99 #1 (5/54). pp. 6-12)
Personally Conducted   07PC
(*Cassell's Magazine* 7/07)
Petticoat Influence   06PI
(*The Strand Magazine* 2/06, 207-214)
Pillingshot's Paper   11PP
(*The Captain* 2/11)
The Pitcher and the Plutocrat   10PP
(*Collier's* 9/24/10, 17-18, 29-31)
A Prisoner of War   15PW

APPENDIX IV: UNCOLLECTED WODEHOUSE

(*The Strand* 3/15, pp. 305-314; *Illustrated Sunday Magazine* 2/13/16)

The Pro 06TP
  (*Pearson's Magazine* (London) 8/06, pp. 170-177)
Prospects for Wambledon 29PW
  (*The Strand* vol. 78 Aug 1929, pp. 123-129)
The Reformation of Study Sixteen 04RS
  (*Royal Magazine* vol. 13 Nov 1904, pp. 45-50)
Reginald's Record Knock 09RR
  (*Pearson's Magazine* [London] 7/09, pp. 60-68)
Ruthless Reginald (Tales of Wrykyn No. 1) 05RR
  (*The Captain* vol. 13, pp. 76-81 4/05)
The Spring Frock 19SF
  (*The Strand* vol. 58 Jul-Dec 1919, pp. 517-525)
Spring Suit 19SF
  (*Saturday Evening Post* vol. 192 #2 7/12/19 pp. 18-19, 50, 52)
Stone and the Weed 10SW
  (*The Captain* 5/10)
The Strange Disappearance of Mr. Buxton-Smythe 01SD
  (*Public School Magazine* vol. 8, pp. 504-506 Dec. 1901)
The Watch Dog 10LM (Love Me, Love My Dog/A Dog-Eared Romance) (*Hampton's Magazine* vol. 25 #1 July 1910, pp. 47-56)
Ways to Get a Gal 57WT
  (*Dream World* vol. I #1 24-34 Feb 1957) Based on 11AS
Welch's Mile Record 02WM
  (*The Captain* vol. 8 Nov 1902, 164-167)

A NOTE ON THE ILLUSTRATOR

We were familiar with Peter van Straaten's illustrations, not only from the cover of the first edition of this book, but from his brilliant tapestry of Wodehouse episodes commissioned by James Heineman for the Wodehouse Centenary. On enquiring with Mr. Heineman about using these for this volume, we were delighted to discover a whole trove of further illustrations, which are reproduced in this volume by his kind permission.

As to the C.V. of Mr. van Straaten, we quote Mr. Heineman's reply to our query:

It was one of those depressing, grey, damp, dreary and rainy days in Amsterdam when it made little difference whether or not you had fallen into a canal. In the gloom I tripped over some steps and fell through a creaky door into a basement bookstore lit by a sombre bulb hanging alone on a cord. I was cursed at in Dutch.

As I got to my feet life changed. There before me was a large table covered by Dutch translations of P.G. Wodehouse, all with covers illustrated by Peter van Straaten, a real master of his craft. Each illustration depicted not only the theme of the book, but also captured the scenes and characters of the story in a few deceivingly simple lines. It was an illustrated digest of Wodehouse, and I bought them all.

The search for the illustrator was not an easy task as van Straaten is somewhat reclusive and lives in a tiny town known but to himself, his family the postmistress and a couple of other natives.

Outside of his hamlet van Straaten's work is widely known in Holland. He does a daily comic strip, political cartoons for the press, book illustrations and scenic drawings. His pen is sharp and his observations keen. He draws his Wodehouse characters as they are visualized by several generations of Wodehouse fans.

Ed.

FINIS